Thriving under Stress

Thriving under Stress

Harnessing Demands in the Workplace

THOMAS W. BRITT, PH.D.

PROFESSOR OF PSYCHOLOGY

CLEMSON UNIVERSITY

STEVE M. JEX, PH.D.

PROFESSOR OF PSYCHOLOGY

BOWLING GREEN STATE UNIVERSITY

Oxford University Press is a department of the University of
Oxford. It furthers the University's objective of excellence in research,
scholarship, and education by publishing worldwide.

Oxford   New York
Auckland   Cape Town   Dar es Salaam   Hong Kong   Karachi
Kuala Lumpur   Madrid   Melbourne   Mexico City   Nairobi
New Delhi   Shanghai   Taipei   Toronto

With offices in
Argentina   Austria   Brazil   Chile   Czech Republic   France   Greece
Guatemala   Hungary   Italy   Japan   Poland   Portugal   Singapore
South Korea   Switzerland   Thailand   Turkey   Ukraine   Vietnam

Published in the United States of America by
Oxford University Press
198 Madison Avenue, New York, NY 10016

Library of Congress Cataloging-in-Publication Data
Britt, Thomas W., 1966–
Thriving under stress : harnessing demands in the workplace / Thomas W. Britt, PhD, Professor of
Social and Organizational Psychology, Clemson University, Steve M. Jex, PhD, Associate Professor
of Psychology, Bowling Green State University.
    pages cm
ISBN 978–0–19–993433–1
1. Stress management.   2. Job stress.   I. Jex, Steve M.   II. Title.
RA785.B758 2015
155.9′042—dc23
    2014033192

9 8 7 6 5 4 3 2 1
Printed in the United States of America
on acid-free paper

*Thomas W. Britt: For Renea, the love of my life, and our children
Alaina, Jordan, Nathan, Nikki, and Noah*

*Steve M. Jex: For my wife, Robin, and our children,
Garrett and Travis*

CONTENTS

ACKNOWLEDGMENTS

Thomas W. Britt

I know that both Steve and I have enjoyed taking the lessons learned from different areas of psychology and trying to communicate these lessons to employees so they might not only adapt to stressful conditions at work, but also thrive under difficult circumstances. I would first like to acknowledge the contributions of Janelle Cheung, a Ph.D. student in the Industrial/Organizational Psychology doctoral program at Clemson University. Janelle helped with many of the Application Exercises that allow employees to better understand and apply the key points of each chapter. I would also like to thank my wife, Renea, for her constant support and encouragement, as well as helping me to make sure the lessons being included in the book were understandable and could help different groups of employees. I would also like to thank my twin sons, Noah and Jordan, for their patience and support during the completion of the book.

Steve M. Jex

I would first like to thank Tom for inviting me to collaborate on this book. As we began to work on it, I came to realize that there is some very useful research on how to thrive under stressful working conditions. Unfortunately, most non-academic readers do not have access to this research, so I hope that our book fills this important void. In terms of getting this book finished, I would like to acknowledge the important contribution of Alison Bayne, a Ph.D. student in the Industrial/Organizational Psychology doctoral program at Bowling Green State University. Alison did some very important work formatting the references cited in the chapters. On a more personal note, I would like to think my wife, Robin, for her constant love, support, and understanding when I was working on this book. After 30 years it's easy to take that for granted, but I truly appreciate everything she does. I would also like to thank my sons, Garrett and Travis Jex, for their support and encouragement during the writing process.

Have you ever been so overwhelmed at work that you wondered how you were going to survive another day? Have you ever felt so stressed and frustrated that you had images of telling everyone off and then leaving for greener pastures? We have all experienced work conditions that tax our ability to cope and survive. Many of us have experienced these demands for long periods of time and may have developed psychological and even physical problems as a result. However, it is also safe to say that there have been times when we have dealt with the stress we were facing and made it through particularly tough times at work, even coming out stronger as a result. Most of us can also recall times when we experienced significant satisfaction and pride in being able to work under difficult conditions, and realized the effect our hard work was having on the organization and other people. You might have even discovered a talent you did not know you had when you worked on a project that was not part of your primary job.

Unfortunately, many approaches to dealing with demands at work view stress as an inherently toxic experience that should be avoided at all costs, and do not recognize how stress might be used to facilitate personal growth, professional development, and higher levels of performance. In addition, researchers and practitioners have shown a preoccupation with burnout as a central outcome of stressful work, without examining other possible responses to tough working conditions. Employees are often viewed as passive recipients of stressful conditions, rather than as active constructors of their work environment who are capable of proactively addressing many of the demands they encounter. We argue that a hyper-concern with the negative effects of stress at work has prevented an understanding of how stress can be harnessed for growth. Furthermore, completely eliminating work demands could have negative effects on employees developing to their full potential.

The ultimate goals of this book are to allow you to examine the way you currently respond to stress at work, to encourage you not to completely eliminate the demands you are facing but to approach those demands in ways that facilitate thriving under stress, and to provide you with strategies for restoring the energy you spend at work so you are in a better position to thrive rather than falter under stress. One theme emphasized throughout this book is that burnout is not the only response to the stressors we face at work, and understanding what it means to thrive under stressful work involves more than stopping the experience of burnout. Although burnout may occasionally occur in response to prolonged and severely stressful work conditions, employees can prevent this outcome, and can do things to increase the likelihood of responding positively to their work demands. In this chapter, we highlight the key concepts covered throughout the book and provide the reader with a description of how the book will unfold.

What does it mean to thrive under stress? Most of us do not want to go to work and watch the clock from 9:00 to 5:00, just waiting for the day to be over so we can go home. Instead, the majority of people want to be personally engaged in their work and have the sense that they are contributing to the mission of the organization and having a positive impact on others. In short, most employees would prefer to thrive at work, as opposed to being so relaxed that they risk falling asleep. Thriving at work is more than the absence of stress. We view thriving as the employee approaching work with vigor and a high level of personal engagement in job performance. Engagement in work involves employees investing energy, as well as a part of themselves, in what they are doing, which leads to feelings of vitality and positive energy toward getting tasks done.[1] Being immersed in meaningful work ultimately allows employees to transform the way they respond to work demands, leading to fewer negative outcomes and more positive outcomes.

Employees who combine high levels of energy with a belief that they can accomplish challenging tasks experience the most positive outcomes at work, both in terms of their performance and in terms of their motivation and well-being. The concept of "flow" refers to being so immersed in a task that you lose self-focus and simply enjoy participating in the activity without worrying about anything else.[2] Although most people associate the experience of flow with such activities as mountain climbing or playing a musical instrument, research shows that the majority of flow experiences occur when people are at work. You may have experienced flow when you were involved in activities in your job where you were doing an important task and felt like you were "firing on all cylinders" in getting the job done. As we will see in Chapter 5, experiencing flow at work is most likely when the employee is involved in a challenging task that taxes his or her ability, and receives feedback about how he or she is doing. We argue that employees who thrive at work are more likely to experience states of flow, and therefore to find work more enjoyable. Better yet, when you experience states of flow, the workday passes faster, creating additional motivation for doing what it takes to thrive at work.

Although you may think that thriving is most likely to occur when stress at work is low, eliminating stress at work will not result in thriving. Sometimes at work, we feel stressed when we are challenged to go beyond our normal levels of performance, or are asked to do a task that is not in line with our prior experience. Although eliminating these kinds of demands might reduce our feelings of stress at the moment, the result would not be an increased feeling that we are thriving at work. Instead, the lack of any challenge or sense that your limits are being tested will likely lead to boredom and the perception of stunted development at work.

If eliminating stress does not result in thriving, what does? Three basic points are emphasized throughout the book:

1. The key to thriving at work is not trying to eliminate demands, but instead recognizing which demands can be viewed as challenges that can be proactively addressed to allow the employee to demonstrate competence and perseverance.
2. Thriving at work is most likely when employees are focused on the meaning of what they are doing for the organization and other people, and having a sense of meaning and purpose at work is most important when employees are facing high levels of job demands.
3. In order to have the necessary energy to thrive under stressful conditions, individuals must adequately recover from work through regularly psychologically and physically detaching from their job and engaging in energy-restoring activities.

The book is divided into three major sections that parallel these goals: understanding the effects of stress at work, strategies for thriving instead of faltering under stress, and how to recover from work demands to restore personal energy. In the remainder of this introduction, we provide a brief overview of each of these major sections, along with a discussion of the Application Exercises in the book that will increase your ability to deal with stress and use it to your advantage. In addition, we discuss how the book contains recommendations for managers to create the conditions necessary for employees to thrive under stressful conditions.

UNDERSTANDING STRESS AT WORK

Although this book is focused on what facilitates employee thriving under stress, in order to accomplish this goal employees must be aware of the different demands in their environment, and must understand the negative consequences that can result from work stress when approached in the wrong way. Many employees who start reading the book may be in the middle of a very stressful situation at work that is affecting them psychologically and perhaps physically, and understanding why these effects are occurring should provide the employee with the motivation to apply the lessons provided in this book for responding better under stress. Most of us have experienced stressors at work dealing with having too much to do and not enough time to do it, unclear guidelines for how to get a job done, and conflicting expectations from supervisors or coworkers. In addition, it is easy for stress at work to spill over into our home life, and for stress occurring in our families to affect us at work. In order to thrive under stressful work demands, employees must be able to identify the demands they are facing, and then approach those demands with the right mindset.

Therefore, the first part of the book (Chapters 1, 2, and 3) addresses the nature of stress at work, with the first chapter in this section identifying the different types of stressors at work and discussing models of how stressful work conditions are related to important employee outcomes. This chapter also discusses resources that reside within the employee and the work environment that might offset the effects of stressors, or might help employees experience some beneficial effects. Chapter 2 addresses the negative ways workplace stress can affect psychological (e.g., anxiety and depression), physical (increased blood pressure and decreased immune system functioning), and behavioral (poor performance, high turnover) outcomes if not approached and dealt with in adaptive ways.

Chapter 3 highlights an important way that stressors at work differ from one another, which is whether they can be seen as a *challenge* or a *hindrance*. Challenge stressors like high workload and having a lot of responsibility can be dealt with by the employee ramping up his or her efforts or recruiting help from others. On the other hand, hindrance stressors, such as not having a sufficient budget to get the job done or organizational politics in the work environment, often cannot be changed despite the employee's own efforts.[5] Therefore, we can cope with challenge stressors by actively doing something about the stressful situation (e.g., working harder for segments of time, asking for help on an a project with a tight deadline), whereas with hindrance stressors, we are better off trying to accept that the demands cannot be changed (e.g., recognizing that certain stressors come with the job and cannot be avoided), and instead focusing on other parts of work that we have control over. In addition, this chapter helps the reader form challenge appraisals, in which the individual views the demand as something that can be mastered through effort and determination, versus threat appraisals, in which the individual views the demand in a way that generates anxiety and a pessimistic interpretation of whether the demand can be addressed.

STRATEGIES FOR THRIVING INSTEAD OF FALTERING UNDER STRESS

The second part of the book (Chapters 4, 5, and 6) emphasizes the conditions that contribute to employees being resilient in the face of difficult work conditions, and ultimately thriving under these conditions. The idea here, which is different from the logic of typical stress management interventions, is that employees can do more than just *tolerate* stress on the job. Chapter 4 identifies characteristics of employees who demonstrate resilience in the face of work demands, and strategies for approaching stress in a healthy manner, such as reinterpreting the implications of demands for performance, remaining mindful regarding the immediate performance situation, and recognizing that stressful conditions can provide an opportunity to grow and demonstrate resilience. In addition, the chapter highlights the importance of developing and effectively utilizing support networks to deal with challenging conditions in the work environment.

Chapter 5 provides the reader with an understanding of what it means to thrive under stress at work, and what employees can do to create the conditions for thriving. An emphasis is placed on understanding the meaning of what employees are doing, both in terms of the impact of their work on the organization and on other people. In addition, thriving at work is more likely when employees reach out to other employees in positive ways and have a sense that they are working on an important and shared mission. Research has shown that employees become motivated and increase their performance levels when they are reminded of the impact of their work on the organization and on other people.[3] For example, a mechanic in an automotive plant can focus on how his or her performance is affecting the safety of vehicles and therefore the safety of people who will be using those vehicles.

Many employees may be doubtful regarding the effectiveness of thinking about the meaning of what they do for encouraging thriving. Certainly, there are some jobs that are so menial and the work so unpleasant that such positive interpretations are impossible, aren't there? In order to address these doubts, our book will devote some attention to recent research on "dirty work," indicating that employees are capable of thriving under stress even in such jobs as sewage workers, trash collectors, and grave diggers.[4] The meaning that employees in these jobs assign to their work (i.e., understanding how what they are doing helps other people) is one of the critical factors that distinguishes those who thrive versus those who do not.

Chapter 6 discusses the newly emerging area of *eustress*, or positive reactions to work demands. Research shows that being exposed to increasing amounts of stress can "inoculate" employees from the negative effects of larger stressors, much like being exposed to small amounts of a virus can inoculate individuals from developing illness.[6] In this chapter we highlight the possibility of positive responses to work demands, and encourage employees to see how the demands they are facing may not only have negative effects, but positive effects as well. Furthermore, in this chapter we discuss employee attributes that make positive responses to stress most likely (e.g., approaching the demands with a sense of optimism and challenge).

THE IMPORTANCE OF RECOVERING FROM WORK

The third section of the book (Chapters 7 and 8) emphasizes that in addition to engaging in particular strategies at work, employees must also be sure to adequately recover from demanding work experiences so as to have the necessary energy to approach demands with a healthy outlook. No one works all the time, and employees need to develop recovery strategies in order to restore energy. Recovery strategies are necessary both during the workday and when the employee leaves work for home. In Chapter 7 we discuss why personal energy is critical for adapting and thriving under stressful conditions. Recent models of energy in psychology emphasize that energy is a limited resource that gets used up if it is not restored.[7] Employees who fail to adequately recover from challenging conditions at work are the most likely to become both burned out, and to lack the necessary resources for harnessing difficult conditions for growth.

Chapter 8 provides specific suggestions for what employees need to do in order to recover from the demands of work and increase their energy reservoirs for the next day. We discuss recent research illustrating that those who psychologically detach from work when it is over (e.g., turn off the computer and e-mail function of iPhone, mentally disengage from work) have more positive moods and more energy for performance at the beginning of the next work day.[8] Disengaging from work has been found to be especially important for people with high levels of commitment to their work, and when the demands encountered on one's job are high. In addition, what employees do in their downtime (e.g., volunteering, exercise) has implications for recovery and the generation of new resources for thriving under various demands at work. We also discuss the beneficial effects of taking extended vacations from work, and how vacations can provide employees with the resources they need to tackle challenging conditions at work.

Chapter 9 addresses what happens when employees find themselves incapable of thriving at work. *Person-job fit* refers to the degree to which an employee is suited for a particular job based on his or her knowledge, skills, abilities, and values.[9] Individuals who find themselves in jobs with poor person-job fit may be unhappy at work despite their best efforts to approach demanding conditions in adaptive ways and to recover from stressful working conditions. In this chapter, we highlight a critical distinction that is also made at other points in the book: the determinants of thriving under stress are not necessarily the same as those that produce negative responses such as burnout. Individuals in a low-demand work environment will likely not experience burnout. However, they will likely experience a failure to thrive, which may lead employees to strongly consider changing their jobs, and perhaps get career counseling regarding more suitable jobs. This chapter will help employees determine if such actions are necessary.

The final chapter of the book, Chapter 10, is an epilogue where the key lessons of the book are reviewed, and readers are encouraged to reflect on how the exercises and points brought up in the book have contributed to their ability to approach stress differently at work. Readers will be encouraged to complete an integrative exercise that will illustrate how they are equipped to respond in positive ways to demands they encounter in their work environment.

APPLICATION EXERCISES AND WHAT THIS MEANS FOR MANAGERS

In order to emphasize the relevance of the material to the employee's own life, each chapter has diagnostic activities and Application Exercises that will facilitate the employee's ability to approach demands in the best way. For example, in the chapter on stressors at work, we provide the tools for employees to identify the stressors in their work environment, and in the chapter on the importance of interpreting demands as challenges we include an assessment of how they are currently approaching these stressors. Exercises encourage employees to consider alternative, more adaptive ways of facing demands at work.

We recognize that a large part of employees being able to thrive under stressful conditions is having managers and organizations that help create the conditions for approaching stress in adaptive ways. Therefore, in each chapter of the book we include sections on *What This Means for Managers*. In these sections, we identify suggestions for what managers can do to reduce the negative effects of stress at work and enhance the positive effects, and other ways they can apply the lessons from the research to facilitate employee thriving at work.

CONCLUDING COMMENTS

We decided to write this book to provide recommendations for thriving under stressful work based on state-of-the-art research conducted in occupational health and organizational psychology. The recommendations we make are based upon the collective weight of the evidence that exists regarding the ways different work demands affect employees, the factors that promote positive responding to stressful work conditions, and how specific recovery strategies can help restore energy so employees can be maximally effective. In areas where less research has been conducted (e.g., positive responses to work demands), we are careful to not make definitive statements that engaging in a particular strategy will result in miraculous effects. We encourage the reader to experiment with different strategies that have been shown to improve responding under stressful conditions among employees in general, and to fully implement those that are most effective for each individual reader.

REFERENCES

1. Spreitzer, G. M., Sutcliffe, K., Dutton, J., Sonenshein, S., & Grant, A. M. (2005). A socially embedded model of thriving at work. *Organization Science, 16,* 537–549.
2. Csikszentmihalyi, M. (1990). *Flow: The Psychology of Optimal Experience.* New York: Harper & Row.
3. Grant, A. M. (2007). Relational job design and the motivation to make a prosocial difference. *Academy of Management Review, 32,* 393–417.
4. Ashforth, B. E., & G. E. Kreiner. 1999. "How can you do it?" Dirty work and the challenge of constructing a positive identity. *Academy of Management Review, 24*(3), 413–434.
5. LePine, J. A., Podsakoff, N. A., & LePine, M. A. (2005). A meta-analytic test of the challenge stressor-hindrance stressor framework: An explanation for inconsistent relationships among stressors and performance. *Academy of Management Journal, 48,* 764–775.
6. Saunders, T., Driskell, J. E., Johnston, J. H., & Salas, E. (1996). The effect of stress inoculation training on anxiety and performance. *Journal of Occupational Health Psychology, 1,* 170–186.

7. Baumeister, R. F., Bratslavsky, E., Muraven, M., & Tice, D. M. (1998). Ego-depletion: Is the active self a limited resource? *Journal of Personality and Social Psychology*, *74*, 1252–1265.

8. Sonnentag, S., Binnewies, C., & Mojza, E. J. (2008). "Did you have a nice evening?" A day-level study on recovery experiences, sleep, and affect. *Journal of Applied Psychology*, *93*, 674–684.

9. Kristof, A. L. (1996). Person–organization fit: An integrative review of its conceptualizations, measurements, and implications. *Personnel Psychology*, *49*, 1–49.

Understanding the Demands of the Workplace

In everyday conversation, the topic of "stress" comes up frequently—undoubtedly *too* frequently. Furthermore, when people talk about stress in everyday conversation, the sources of stress are many and varied: children, health concerns, school demands, taking care of a house, in-laws, lack of money, and the list goes on and on. The focus of this book is on one source of stress: the workplace. Although stress coming from the workplace is clearly just one source of stress among many, it is a very important—we would argue among the most important—source of stress in people's lives.

Why? Since both of the authors have dedicated the majority of their professional careers to studying stress in the workplace, it could certainly be a function of our biased viewpoints. We believe, however, that there are three other reasons that are much more valid. First, compared to any life domain other than family, people spend more time at work than anywhere else. Thus, what happens in the workplace is likely to have a greater impact on people than what happens in other life domains. Second, with the exception of a privileged few, most people typically *have to* work. As a result, we basically have to somehow deal with the negative aspects of the workplace unless we want to starve. Also, as we will see later in this chapter, this fact is somewhat related to a very common theme in the academic workplace stress literature: namely, that a *lack of control* over things such as job duties and work scheduling are common sources of stress for many employees. Finally, *work is important to people.* People spend years preparing for their careers, and many people essentially define themselves in terms of the work that they do. Many people also view work as a place where they develop friendships and other meaningful social relationships.

THE ACADEMIC STUDY OF WORKPLACE STRESS

As stated above, the authors of this book have spent most of their careers engaged in the scientific study of stress in the workplace. Given the prevalence of stress in the workplace, as well as the frequency with which it's talked about in everyday conversation, it might seem a bit odd that some people dedicate their professional lives to studying it. Don't we all know that abusive bosses, inconsiderate coworkers, impossible deadlines, and interruptions from others cause people stress? Yes and no. While we certainly know these things *intuitively*, scientifically studying the impact of these workplace conditions allows us to be more precise in our estimates of the *degree* to which these things cause stress. Scientists put specific quantitative estimates on many phenomena.

The other reason for studying workplace stress scientifically, or anything else for that matter, is that it allows us to develop a greater understanding of *why* it occurs. While it doesn't necessarily take a Ph.D. to figure out that enduring an abusive boss every day is stressful, scientific research has helped us to understand why people find this type of situation to be so stressful.[1] Why is it important to understand *why* things occur? Other than perhaps being able to sound more intelligent than others at a cocktail party, understanding the *why* helps us to prevent problems before they occur.

A second reason that it is useful to study stress scientifically is that it allows us to document *when* certain situations are stressful and when they are not. Consider the following example. We certainly know that heavy workloads and difficult deadlines are *generally* considered stressful to *most* people, but not necessarily all people. There is evidence (discussed in more detail in Chapter 3) that while some people view such situations as threatening or as being a *hindrance*, other people may view the same situations as *challenging*. Furthermore, as one might guess, those who generally view stressful situations as challenges rather than as hindrances tend not to be as negatively affected by those situations. Why is this important to know? If we know that a particular person tends to view such situations as challenges, it would certainly make sense to put such a person in a job that might have the potential for these conditions. Also, what if it were possible to *train* an employee to view these conditions as challenges rather than hindrances?

A final reason for studying stress in the workplace is that the workplace has changed substantially in recent years, and many of those changes have led to increased stress. For example, it is extremely rare for today's employees to remain with one organization for their entire career, due to a lack of job security or, in other cases, employees' desire to pursue more favorable job opportunities. The result of this rather transient workforce is probably weaker social bonds compared to the days when people worked together for long periods of time.

Another major change in the workplace—and one that potentially increases the potential for stress—is the nature of the *psychological contract* between employees and their employer. A psychological contract essentially represents a set of unwritten expectations that parties in a relationship have about each other. In an employment context, employees have expectations about what is reasonable for them to do on behalf of their employing organization, and conversely what their organization should do for them. As stated above, employment security is no longer an expectation for most of today's employees. However, due to advances in technology, many employees today feel that there are few boundaries between their work and non-work lives and that they are expected to be "on call" for their employers. Put differently, many employees today feel that they are expected to give their employers much more than they receive in return. This again creates the potential for higher levels of stress in the workplace.

To summarize, all people know what workplace stress is—a few of us, however, get the added bonus of actually making a career of studying it. Scientifically studying anything helps to provide more precise estimates regarding the extent to which it occurs, provides insight into *why* it occurs, and helps us to understand *when* it occurs. Knowing both the *why* and the *when* are important in organizational efforts to decrease stress and enhance employee well-being.

THEORETICAL MODELS

When scientists/scholars study anything, they typically develop theoretical models of the phenomena they are studying. Why? Really for the same reason that homebuilders have a set of blueprints before they start hammering. Theoretical models make the task of understanding anything more manageable. Perhaps more importantly, theoretical models help researchers to organize and interpret research findings.

In the study of workplace stress there have been numerous theoretical models—in fact too many to mention all of them. It is important, though, that we highlight some of the most important theoretical models that have guided both research and efforts to reduce stress and enhance employee well-being. If we view workplace stress research from a historical perspective, we can really trace the origin of its study back to the University of Michigan's Institute for Social Research (ISR) in the early 1960s. Researchers at ISR, supported by funding from the National Institute for Occupational Safety and Health (NIOSH), embarked on what at that time was the most comprehensive study of workplace stress to date. As a way to guide their investigations, the ISR researchers[2] developed the theoretical model presented in Figure 1.1.

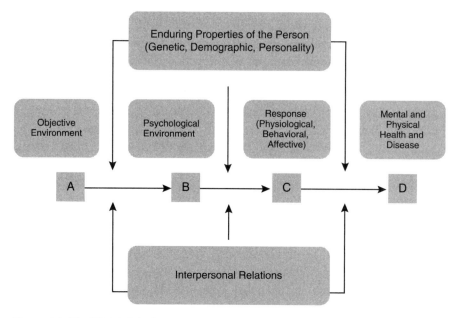

Figure 1.1 The ISR Model of Stress.

As can be seen, the first step in this model is the *objective environment*. This simply represents the situations we may face in any work environment—work-related tasks, a staff meeting, or perhaps a transaction with a customer. The second step in this model, the *psychological environment*, represents how we as individuals experience or appraise these work-related situations. As an example, the prospect of a staff meeting may be experienced very differently, depending on whether one likes or dislikes one's coworkers, or whether one likes or dislikes meetings.

Continuing on, the third step in the model is labeled *response*. This represents the immediate physiological, behavioral, or emotional responses that an individual experiences when the environment is appraised. If a staff meeting is appraised as negative or threatening, one's immediate responses might be physiological arousal in the form of increases in heart and respiration rate, emotional responses of feelings of anger or resentment, and behavioral responses of attempts to leave the situation. The final step in the model, *mental and physical health and disease*, represents the cumulative effect of responding to stressful or threatening situations in the work environment. Essentially, what the ISR researchers proposed is that over time people tend to wear out or break down if they are constantly exposed to stressful situations at work.

Notice that there are two other features of this model that have not yet been mentioned: *enduring properties of the person* (on the top), and *interpersonal relations* (on the bottom). Both of these are meant to illustrate that not every-one perceives and responds to the work environment in the same way. In the case of *enduring properties of the person*, a great deal of research has been done looking at how personality traits of people influence how they perceive and respond to the work environment (more about this will be covered in later chapters). The *interpersonal relations* dimension, quite frankly, has not been utilized in the occupational stress literature in the manner in which the ISR model had intended; rather, researchers have looked at poor interpersonal relations as a stressful aspect of the work environment.[3] However, what the model proposes is that the interpersonal relations we experience within an organization will influence the way we experience and respond to the work environment. As one might suspect, *poor* interpersonal relations within an organization will generally lead to more negative perceptions, and ultimately more negative responses to the work environment.

Perhaps the most well-known of the more recent models of workplace stress is the *demands-control model*, which was developed by Robert Karasek.[4] The basic idea behind this model is actually quite simple: the most stressful jobs are those that are characterized by *high job demands*, coupled with *low job control*. In order words, a lot is demanded of you and you have very little control over how to meet the demands. If we accept this basic premise (and there is some research to support it), then any job can be characterized in terms of demands (high vs. low) and control (high vs. low). If we do this, we arrive at four types of jobs: (1) high strain (high demands, low control), (2) active (high demands, high control), (3) passive (low demands, low control), and (4) low strain (low demand, high con-trol). Common examples of each of these types of jobs can be seen in Table 1-1.

Given the purpose of this model, namely to explain stress in the workplace, the vast majority of research examining it has been conducted on the impact of high strain jobs on people.[5] Although the basic premise of this model has generally been supported, there have been some additional propositions added to it over the years. For example, lack of control in a high demand job is more stressful when one lacks social support from one's coworkers.[6] Furthermore, lack of control is more stressful for those individuals who possess *high self-efficacy*, or who believe that they can successfully accomplish their job

Table 1-1. EXAMPLES OF JOBS REPRESENTING DEMAND-CONTROL COMBINATIONS

Low Demand, High Control *Low Strain Jobs*: architect, natural scientist, lineman

High Demand, High Control *Active Jobs*: engineer, physician, teacher

Low Demand, Low Control *Passive Jobs*: janitor, night watchman

High Demand, Low Control *High Strain Jobs*: nurse, waiter, assembly-line worker tasks. For individuals who possess *low self-efficacy*, or who have doubts about whether they can successfully perform their job duties, having a high level of job control tends to be viewed as stressful.[7] This implies that providing employees with a high degree of job control is not going to help very much if they are poorly trained, or simply lack the skills to do the job.

Also of interest, though not necessarily the focus of a great deal of workplace stress research, is the combination of high demand, high control, which has been labeled *active jobs*. Employees in such jobs have a great deal to do, yet they also have a great deal of control or discretion as to *how* they meet those demands. This is important because it suggests, at least potentially, that the demands we face in the workplace can sometimes be a positive thing, provided employees are able to successfully cope with them. Why, then, can active jobs potentially have a positive impact on people? One explanation put forth by Gabriel De La Rosa and the second author of this book[8] is that high demands and high control tend to facilitate high levels of *job engagement* among employees. We will have more to say about job engagement in future chapters, but suffice it to say that engagement simply represents the level of interest, excitement, and energy with which an employee approaches his or her work. One major purpose of this book is to consider how high demands at work can have positive effects on employees when approached in the right way.

While the demands-control model remains quite popular as a stress model, in recent years it has been modified somewhat by Arnold Bakker, Evangelia Demerouti, and their associates,[9] who developed the *job demands-resources model*. The basic premise of the demands-resources model is essentially the same as that of the demands-control model, but with one major exception. Specifically, Bakker and Demerouti[9] proposed that job control is one of many *resources* that employees can use to meet the demands of their jobs. According to these authors, resources can be external to the employee (e.g., organizational support, participation in decision-making, rewards, etc.) or internal (e.g., an employee's mental approach to his or her job demands).

Although the demands-resources model has not been around as long as the demands-control model, it has generally had stronger levels of research support. The main reason for this is that although job control may be helpful in many instances, there may be some cases where it is not. Researchers who have tested the Demands-Resources model[10] have done a good job of matching the job demands with the corresponding resources on the employee side. The following example illustrates this point. If an employee is having trouble balancing the demands of work and family domains, being able to control how one's job tasks are completed is probably not going to help. On the other hand, what probably *would* help in this situation would be for this employee to have more control over his or her work schedule.

A final theoretical model of workplace stress, which is also relatively recent, is the *effort-reward imbalance model*. The roots of this model, which was proposed by Johannes Siegrist,[11] can actually be found in equity theory, which was put forth by J. Stacy Adams back in 1963.[12] The basic idea of equity theory is that people have an innate desire to be treated fairly; that is, we don't want to be shortchanged or undercompensated in any relationship we enter into. For any readers who have children, equity theory is very apparent when siblings make numerous comparisons (e.g., Christmas gifts, amount of attention, etc.) and complain if they feel their parents play favorites.

According to Siegrist,[11] employees compare the rewards they receive from their work (e.g., compensation, recognition, praise, etc.), relative to the effort they put into it (e.g., physical or psychological). As one might suspect, stressful situations are those in which the rewards one receives from one's work are low, relative to the demands of the work. Given this basic premise, readers can probably think of many occupations that fit this profile: teachers, social workers, day care workers, police officers, and so on.

In addition to proposing this notion of effort-reward (E-R) imbalance, Siegrist[11] proposed the notion of *overcommitment*. Specifically, some individuals tend to be very highly dedicated and committed to their jobs or careers. Given such a high level of commitment, it is unlikely that the rewards such individuals receive could ever be enough to compensate for the effort they put into their work. Thus, overcommitted individuals may feel chronic levels of stress because they will always perceive that their effort is higher than the rewards they receive. Although the E-R imbalance model is relatively recent, and more empirical tests of the model are needed, research has shown that a lack of equity is related to decreased psychological and physical well-being.[13,14]

WORKPLACE STRESSORS

Now that we have described the stress process in a general sense, it is time to get more specific and describe aspects of employees' jobs that they may find stressful. This is an important first step toward understanding how to thrive under difficult work conditions, because understanding the different demands you are exposed to will help you better respond to these stressors in a positive way. Recall the models of the stress process that were described earlier in the chapter. Regardless of the specifics of each of the models, they all start with conditions in the work environment that are often perceived as stressful by employees; these conditions are labeled as *stressors*.

In the occupational stress research literature, the term *stressor* is formally defined as any condition within the work environment that employees might find aversive, and thus have a negative reaction to.[15] Given this definition, there are almost an infinite number of stressors potentially present in the work environment. Researchers, however, have tended to focus on certain stressors that seem to be commonly experienced by employees in most work settings. In order to describe these stressors, it is first useful to group them into five broad categories: (1) *work demand stressors*, (2) *interpersonal stressors*, (3) *role stressors*, (4) *work/non-work boundary stressors*, and (5) *extra-organizational stressors*. Admittedly, these five categories are not necessarily comprehensive—that is, they don't represent *all* stressors—but they do represent the majority of stressors that have been the focus of scientific research. Each of these categories of stressors will be described below.

Work Demand Stressors

It is often the case that people find their jobs stressful because they simply have "too much to do, and not enough time to do it." When you actually consider the work demands that people face in the workplace, however, there are a number of ways we can view them. Perhaps the simplest way of looking at work demands is the number of hours people are required to work per week. Although 40 hours has long been considered the standard workweek, there is considerable variation around that number—some people work less, and some far more. There has also been a long history of research on the effects of work hours,[16] and the weight of the evidence suggests that working long hours over time often does take a toll on people, especially in terms of physical health and well-being.[17] The most dramatic demonstration of this is the phenomenon of *karoshi*, or death from overwork, in Japan.[18]

Although measuring work demands by the number of hours worked has the advantage of objectivity, and in fact work hours *are* an important work demand, work hours capture only a limited aspect of the demands that most people face at work. Given that limitation, many stress researchers have gone to more *perceptual* measures of work demands;[19] such measures are termed *perceptual* because people are asked to report how they perceive their workload. Unlike work hours, perceptual measures capture important issues as the *pace* (e.g., having to work very quickly), the *intensity* (e.g., having periods of a lot of work in a short time frame), and the *difficulty* of the work that people do. Compared to work hours, perceptual measures are related more strongly to adverse reactions such as heath complaints and psychological distress. One of the reasons for this is that in some cases people work long hours, not because they have to, but because they choose to do so. If that is the case, then working long hours is not necessarily stressful. Again, if we go back to the stress models earlier in the chapter, all of them propose that there are differences among people regarding what is perceived as stressful (see Figure 1.1, for example).

Interpersonal Stressors

People typically do not work in isolation; rather, they must interact with others in order to do their jobs. Often these interactions are with other coworkers, but for an increasing number of occupations, interactions are also with clients or customers of the organizations they work for. Although interactions with others can certainly be pleasant, and in fact can be a major source of fulfillment on the job, they can also be quite negative and for many people represent a *major* source of workplace stress. According to Lyne Andersson and Christine Pearson, the most common interpersonal stressor in the work environment is *workplace* incivility,[20] which they defined as low-level deviant behaviors that go against commonly accepted norms of decency and respect that are held in most cultures.

It is generally expected that other people will respect our privacy, refrain from gossiping behind our backs, and not put us down in front of others. Obviously, for anyone who has worked anywhere, we know that people sometimes do these things—that is, people sometimes listen into conversations, they do gossip, and sometimes they do put others down. Although research into the effects of workplace incivility has not been going on for a long period of time, research is pretty clear that employees react negatively to this type of treatment,[21] so it's a major concern for most organizations.

One of the defining characteristics of what is considered uncivil behavior is that of *ambiguous intent to harm*—that is, when somebody acts in an uncivil manner toward another person, it is unclear what that person's motives are. Take, for example, a person who gossips about others. People who gossip certainly could be trying to harm others, but they may be engaging in this behavior for other reasons. It is possible that a person who gossips may be insecure about his or her social status vis-à-vis others at work, or simply might find that gossiping is a way to connect or bond with his or her coworkers.

Unlike incivility, there are some interpersonal stressors in the workplace where the intent to harm is very clear. Two such stressors that have received a good deal of attention from workplace stress researchers are *bullying* and *abusive supervision*. Bullying represents a sustained effort on the part of one or more employees to harass, demean, or otherwise make another employee's life miserable.[22] To understand bullying, readers need only think back to their school days, when there was typically some form of bullying going on—some readers, in fact, may have experienced bullying or perhaps even have bullied others. What is typical of workplace bullying, as well as bullying among children, is that there is typically some *power differential* between the bully and the victim.[23]

Among children and adolescents, this power differential is often based on physical size or peer group status,[24] but in the workplace, power differentials are based on things such as income, status, seniority, and even race or gender.[25] According to Stale Einarson, who has conducted extensive research on the motives behind bullying, there is *clear intent to harm* when someone engages in bullying; this is one of the ways in which bullying differs from incivility. He has also found that people who *engage in* bullying have often been *victims of* bullying themselves. It is also clear from research that employees who experience bullying react much more negatively than do employees who experience incivility. It is not uncommon for victims of sustained bullying to experience physical health problems, significant mental health disorders such as post-traumatic stress disorder (PTSD), and eventually reach a point where they have to leave their jobs.[26]

Abusive supervision, which is a fairly new concept developed by Bennett Tepper, is very much like bullying except that the perpetrator is an employee's immediate supervisor.[1] Readers who have seen the 2009 movie *Horrible Bosses* have at least some sense of the nature of abusive supervision; unfortunately, compared to the movie, there is nothing humorous about this behavior. This interpersonal stressor is often characterized by extreme, arbitrary criticism as well as demeaning comments directed at the employee, often in front of others. Like bullying, there is a clear intent to harm on the part of the abusive supervisor; beyond that, however, there is not a great deal of research on why supervisors engage in abusive behavior. One might speculate that abusive supervisors were victims of abusive supervisors themselves, or perhaps they believe that their abusive behavior somehow helps or motivates their subordinates.

As with bullying, research has shown that employees who are the victims of abusive supervision dislike their jobs and may become anxious and depressed.[1] Recent research has also shown that employees who experience abusive supervision may retaliate or "get back" at their supervisor or their organization.[27] Interestingly, supervisors are capable of being *both* abusive and supportive, and this combination might be particularly detrimental to employees.[28]

Along with work demand stressors, interpersonal stressors are often influenced by the actions (and sometimes *inactions*) of managers. In *What This Means for Managers 1.1* we suggests ways in which managers can reduce the levels of both work demand and interpersonal stressors among their employees. In addition, we discuss the actions that managers should take when they find that employees are being uncivil toward each other, or when even more severe forms of mistreatment occur.

What This Means for Managers 1.1

KNOWING THE DEMANDS FACING YOUR EMPLOYEES

Managers need to be aware of the *demands and interpersonal stressors faced by their employees* and, perhaps most important, how their own actions may contribute to and ultimately reduce these stressors among employees.

Based on the nature of the demands and interpersonal stressors covered in the chapter, specific recommendations for managers include the following:

- Managers need to be aware of the hours employees are working. If employees are working extremely long hours, they simply may have too much work to do for the duration of the workday. It is also possible that an employee may have enough time to do the work, but he or she is not properly trained on how to do it. In either of these cases, a manager can take action to help an employee.
- Managers need to be aware of the interpersonal dynamics within their work group. Sparky Anderson, former manager of the Cincinnati Reds and Detroit Tigers, used to refer to the locker room as his "garden" and made it clear to his players that he would not tolerate any "weeds" in his garden. This type of metaphor may not suit everyone, but the point is still an important one—employees need to know what types of interpersonal behavior will not be tolerated.
- Perhaps the most powerful way that managers can influence interpersonal stressors within their work group is by the way they treat others. If a manager is rude, disrespectful, or abusive to others, he or she will have no credibility when trying to improve the interpersonal climate of a work group.

Role Stressors

All employees occupy roles within an organization. The role may be defined by formal job descriptions that exist within the organization, or informal designations by an employee's supervisors. Role stressors refer to demands created by ambiguity or conflict regarding the roles occupied by a given employee. Researchers have therefore examined both *role ambiguity* and *role conflict*. Role ambiguity represents a situation in which an employee is simply unclear about his or her job responsibilities.[29] The specific parts of one's job for which ambiguity might commonly exist include scheduling job tasks and determining what is and is not acceptable performance.[30]

Role conflict, on the other hand, represents a situation in which fulfilling one set of role responsibilities makes it more difficult to fulfill other aspects. An example might be a teacher who feels that he or she is torn between preparing students for standardized tests and teaching them important information from the curriculum. One thing important to note about role conflict is that the vast majority of research has examined what has been termed *intra-role conflicts*; that is, conflict between role responsibilities associated with the *same* role. Employees may also feel conflict between responsibilities coming from different roles they play in life (termed *inter-role conflict*); this is something we will cover in the next section on work/non-work stressors.

Since research on role stressors began in the early 1960s, considerable evidence exists regarding the effects of both role conflict and role ambiguity. In both cases, employees who experience these stressors tend to exhibit negative psychological, physical, and behavioral reactions.[31,30,32] However, there may be some variation in the extent to which people find this stressor to be aversive, particularly in the case of role ambiguity. For example, some people have a higher tolerance for ambiguity than others,[33] and these individuals may find that role ambiguity provides an opportunity for them to tailor their job responsibilities to their liking.[34] These findings again highlight the important role played by stable properties of the individual in how employees respond to workplace stressors.

Since managers typically play a key part in the transmission of role-related information, they also have the potential to reduce employees' role stressors. In *What This Means for Managers 1.2* we suggest a number of things that managers can do to prevent role ambiguity and role conflict.

Work/Non-work Boundary Stressors

Although work is certainly an important part of most people's lives, it doesn't completely define who we are. People play multiple roles in life (parent, spouse, son/daughter, community member, friend), and each of these roles has a unique set of demands that goes with it. Given the unique sets of demands that go with these multiple roles, the demands of these roles may conflict with the demands of work, in which case people experience some form of *work/non-work boundary stressors*.

By far the most commonly studied work/non-work boundary stressors have beenthe conflicts between the demands of work and the demands of family. The term *work-to-family conflict* represents situations in which the demands of work interfere with the demands of family. For example, an employee may receive a last-minute request from her supervisor to prepare a report for an

What This Means for Managers 1.2

MITIGATING ROLE STRESSORS FOR EMPLOYEES

Since managers are typically a primary source of role-related information for most employees, they can play a key role in preventing these types of stressors. Managers can do some relatively simple things to make sure that role-related information is communicated clearly and that employees' role responsibilities do not conflict or become too burdensome.

Specific suggestions for managers include the following:

- Job descriptions in many organizations are unfortunately out of date and vaguely written. Managers should be familiar with their employees' job descriptions and let someone know if any of them are out of date or simply do not reflect the reality of employees' jobs.
- When communicating role-related information to employees, try to be as clear as possible—don't just assume that employees understand what you mean. It's also a good idea, particularly when assigning complex duties, to ask employees if they understand what you want them to do.
- In addition to communicating directly to employees about role-related information, managers should try to communicate to *others* in the organizations who communicate role-related information to their employees. If your employees report to other people in your organization, communicate with those people to make sure that your employees are not being given conflicting demands or simply being overloaded.

important meeting the next day, which may conflict with her plans to attend her son's soccer game that afternoon.

The direction of these demands can also go in the opposite direction. The term *family-to-work conflict* represents a situation in which the demands of family interfere with the demands of work. Any reader who currently has pre-school children (or has ever had children this age) in day care has probably received a call that his child is running a fever and needs to be picked up. Obviously, in that situation a parent has to drop what he or she is doing at work and pick up the child.

Tammy Allen and a number of her associates have conducted extensive research on both work-to-family and family-to-work conflict and have shown unequivocally that both are viewed as stressful by employees.[35] Other researchers have also found that work demands interfering with family are viewed as more stressful than family demands interfering with work.[36] This could be due to a number of reasons. First, most people place a high value on their family time and therefore find it very stressful when work impinges on it. In addition, people generally have more flexibility when it comes to family demands than to work demands. Therefore, often there is a very low sense of control when it comes to meeting the demands of work as opposed to the demands of family.

In recent years there have been two major developments in the area of work/non-work conflict. First, as was mentioned earlier, there has been a recognition that the demands of work and non-work do not just apply to those who have preschool children. For example, many middle-aged people (whether they are married or not) face the challenges of caring for elderly parents.[37] Many couples are also forced to cope with their college-aged children moving out. Single employees may also experience conflict between work and non-work demands because of friendships or community activities they are involved in.

The other major development in the area of work/non-work conflict is the recognition that the demands of these two domains do not necessarily have to *conflict*. The term *work-family facilitation* has been used[38] to describe a situation in which the demands that one encounters in the work domain help a person to meet the demands in another domain, and vice versa. An example of *work-to-family facilitation* might be a person who is an elementary school teacher finding that his or her teaching skills help with the education of his or her own children. As an example of *family-to-work facilitation*, a manager might find that wanting to spend quality time with one's family results in being more efficient at work.

Although research on work-family facilitation is relatively new, there is some evidence that when people feel that these two life domains complement each other, both physical and mental well-being are enhanced.[39] Obviously, more research is needed on work-family facilitation, but it is promising (and encouraging) that these two aspects of life do not always have to conflict with each other.

As with the other stressors discussed to this point, managers typically play a key role in determining how successful employees are in balancing the demands of work with other areas of their lives. In *What This Means for Managers 1.3* we discuss things that managers can do in order to help employees to balance work and non-work demands. We also suggest potential areas where work and non-work demands may complement each other.

Now that we have covered the major stressors or demands that have been studied in occupational stress research, it is important for readers to assess how relevant these demands are to their own work situations. In order to do this, take a moment to complete Application Exercises 1.1 and 1.2. Application Exercise 1.1 is a checklist of items that represent the demands that we have discussed to this point—this basically allows you to assess which of these

---

What This Means for Managers 1.3

HELPING EMPLOYEES WITH WORK-FAMILY BALANCE

Many organizations these days offer employees "family-friendly" benefits such as day care and flexible schedules, and some have even instituted work-life balance programs. While such programs can often be useful, the real key to helping employees achieve a high level of balance in their lives is the behavior of the managers who directly supervise them. We believe there are a number of things that managers can do in order to help employees balance work with other aspect of their lives. We discuss two of these here, and we will return to these issues in Chapter 8.

- One of the most important ways that managers can help employees to achieve balance is to respect the boundaries between employees' work and non-work lives. There are obviously going to be times in any workplace when a manager might need to contact an employee during the evening, or perhaps may need an employee to work on a weekend. However, these types of intrusions into an employee's personal/family time should be the *exception* rather than the *rule*.
- Another way that managers can help their employees achieve balance is in the way they conduct their own lives. If managers work constantly and consistently allow work to spill over into family and personal time, this sends a powerful message to employees. In contrast, managers who work hard yet value their personal and family time are showing employees that it is possible to be productive, yet also have a life they value outside the workplace.

---

demands are present in your current job. Application Exercise 1.2, on the other hand, requires that you choose the three most important demands in your job and make some judgments about these. We will be asking you to return to the demands you have noted in Application Exercise 1.2 in many of the chapters of this book.

Extra-organizational Stressors

Have you ever worked with someone who seemed to always be depressed, preoccupied, or generally in a bad mood? Have you ever gone to the grocery store and encountered a cashier who was rude and abrupt?

Application Exercise 1.1

SELF-ASSESSMENT OF DEMANDS

In order to respond positively to the demands you face in your work environment, it is first necessary to document the demands that are present in your particular work environment. Therefore, included below are sample items from measures of the demands we discussed in the chapter. While these are not the complete measures, answering them can provide some indication of the levels of demands and resources that you are currently experiencing.

Work Demand Checklist: Listed below are number of statements about your work situation that correspond to some of the demands that were covered in the chapter. Read each statement and check all that apply to your current work situations.

_____1. I often have to work long hours.
_____2. My work hours are longer than other people I know.
_____3. I am often fatigued because I have to work longer than I want to.
_____4. I often have a great deal to do at work.
_____5. I often have to work very hard for short periods of time.
_____6. There is often so much work to be done that I can't do it well.
_____7. My coworkers do not acknowledge me.
_____8. People sometimes avoid me at work.
_____9. I frequently get interrupted in meetings by coworkers.
_____10. My coworkers have very little to do with me.
_____11. My work is often devalued or belittled by others.
_____12. People at work deliberately try to make my life difficult.
_____13. My supervisor is verbally abusive.
_____14. My boss shouts or yells at me for making mistakes.
_____15. My boss yells at me about matters that are unimportant.
_____16. I work with two or more groups who operate quite differently.
_____17. I often receive incompatible requests from two or more people.
_____18. I do things that are accepted by one person and not accepted by others.
_____19. I never know if I've divided my time properly.
_____20. I'm not sure what my job responsibilities are.
_____21. I often don't know what's expected of me.
_____22. The demands of my work interfere with my home and family life.
_____23. Things I want to do at home do not get done because of the demands my job puts on me.
_____24. The demands of my family interfere with work-related activities.

Note: Work Hours = 1–3; Workload = 4–6;[19] Incivility = 7–9;[42] Bullying = 10–12;[44] Abusive Supervision = 13–15;[42] Role Conflict = 16–18;[41] Role Ambiguity = 19–21;[30] Work-Family Conflict = 22–24.[43]

Application Exercise 1.2

MY MOST IMPORTANT WORK DEMANDS

Now that you've completed the brief assessment of the frequency with which you face the demands that were discussed in the chapter, please do the following:

1. List the THREE most important demands that you face in the workplace:

   _____

   _____

   _____

2. For each of these THREE most important demands, indicate the frequency (e.g., every day, once a week, etc.) with which you experience the demand in the course of a normal workday:

   Demand #1:_____

   Demand #2:_____

   Demand #3:_____

3. For each of these THREE most important demands, indicate things that you could do in order to decrease the frequency of the demand from occurring, or to decrease the impact the demand has on you:

   Demand #1:_____

   _____

   Demand #2:_____

   _____

   Demand #3:_____

   _____

We will be returning to these demands in later chapters in the book (including the next three chapters). These chapters will provide you with additional strategies for addressing these demands.

Obviously, one conclusion you could draw in both cases is that these individuals are just negative people and should be avoided; this is fairly easy to do in the case of the grocery store cashier (you can pick another lane), but it might require a bit more effort in the case of the coworker. However, another important factor to consider is that both of these individuals may be going through things that you don't know about—marital problems, financial difficulties, problems with the law, or even substance abuse issues. All of these would fit into the broad category of *extra-organizational stressors*, which represent stressors that exist completely outside the work domain, yet are nevertheless important because their effects can spill over into the workplace.

Perhaps the most well-known research on extra-organizational stressors was conducted over 40 years ago by two psychiatrists, Thomas Holmes and Richard Rahe.[40] These researchers developed the well-known Social Readjustment Rating Scale (SRRS), which asked respondents to indicate which of 43 common life events they experienced over the past year. Holmes and Rahe found that people who had experienced the greatest number of life events, and those with the greatest impact, were more likely to develop physical illnesses. The original SRRS is presented in Table 1-2. Take a minute to check off the events that you have experienced during the past year and tally up your score.

As is evident, some of these events—death of a spouse or child, loss of employment, incarceration—are clearly devastating to people. The more minor events on this scale (e.g., retirement, marriage, vacation) are not typically things we think of as stressful, yet they are still considered to be somewhat stressful because they require some level of change and adjustment. A good example of this is marriage. Although marriage is considered by most

Table 1-2. THE SOCIAL READJUSTMENT RATING SCALE (SRRS)

The Social Readjustment Rating Scale was developed by Holmes and Rahe to assist people in quantifying their level of stress. In this scale, events such as marriage, divorce, and retirement are given a score representing the amount of readjustment (which is often characteristic of stressors) associated with that change. The score is measured in points called *life change units.* The events have been weighted so that more dramatic readjustments are worth more life change units.

To determine your score, check off the events that you have experienced in the past 12 months.

Event	Life Change Units
Death of a spouse	100
Divorce	73
Marital separation	65
Jail term	63
Death of a close family member	63
Personal injury or illness	53
Marriage	50
Fired at work	47
Marital reconciliation	45
Retirement	45
Change in health of family member	44
Pregnancy	40

(continued)

Table 1-2. (Continued)

Event	Life Change Units
Sex difficulties	39
Gain of new family member	39
Business readjustment	39
Change in financial state	38
Death of a close friend	37
Change to a different line of work	36
Change in number of arguments with spouse	35
Mortgage over $70,000*	31
Foreclosure of mortgage or loan	30
Change in responsibilities at work	29
Son or daughter leaving home	29
Trouble with in-laws	29
Outstanding achievement	28
Spouse begins or stops work	26
Begin or end school	26
Change in living conditions	25
Revision of personal habits	24
Trouble with boss	23
Change in work hours or conditions	20
Change in residence	20
Change in school	20
Change in recreation	19
Change in church activities	19
Change in social activities	18
Mortgage or loan less than $70,000*	17
Change in sleeping habits	16
Change in number of family get-togethers	15
Change in eating habits	15
Vacation	14
Christmas	13
Minor violations of the law	11

Total: _____

Here's how you interpret your score. Life change units are points assigned to various experiences. If your score is 300 or higher, you are at a high risk for developing a health problem. If your score is between 150 and 300, you have a 50–50 chance of experiencing a serious health change within two years. If your score is below 150, you have a 1 in 3 chance of serious health change.

*In the original scale the amount was $10,000; $70,000 represents what that would be in 2013 dollars.

Source: Holmes & Rahe (1967).[40]

people to be a happy event, for most people it also requires a good bit of change and adjustment. As powerful as love is, it often cannot prevent the feelings of annoyance when the personal habits of another person clash with our own.

One thing that is important to consider about extra-organizational stressors is that even though they may negatively influence employees, it is quite possible that an employee's supervisor and coworkers will be unaware of what the employee is going through. For example, a person who has a child with a chronic illness may simply not want to talk about it when he or she is at work. An employee who is having serious financial difficulties may feel embarrassed at the prospect of his or her coworkers knowing about it.

The truth is that we often have no idea of the difficulties that fellow employees are facing when they leave the workplace. Yet people are not machines, and employees' reactions to these difficulties will often spill over into the workplace. This is a tough issue for managers to navigate, however, because they typically want to help a subordinate who is having difficulties, but people do have the right to privacy with regard to their lives outside work.

EMPLOYEE RESOURCES

As was shown in the previous section, a large number of potential stressors exist in the work (and non-work) environment that employees may have to contend with. Given the large number of stressors that employees may potentially face in the workplace, how do most people manage to function reasonably well and get their work done? The answer to this question is that people have a number of potential *resources* they can use to neutralize the effects of these stressors. Resources are also sometimes referred to as *protective factors*—that is, things that tend to reduce or neutralize the effects of stressors in the work environment. Notice that we are not saying that these factors *eliminate* stressors; rather, resources simply prevent people from becoming completely overwhelmed by the stressors that they must face on a daily basis. All of the stress models described at the beginning of the chapter recognize this to varying degrees; with some of these, resources come largely from the work environment itself;[4] others are primarily characteristics of the individual.[2]

In Chapter 4 we will discuss in much more detail the use of these resources when we describe characteristics of individuals who tend to be resilient under stressful working conditions. For now, we highlight the most important resources for dealing with workplace stressors. Generally speaking, researchers have investigated two broad categories of resources: (1) personal resources, and (2) environmental resources.

Personal resources are qualities about the individual employee, as well as the employee's life situation, that may make that person more resilient when faced with workplace stressors. These include stable characteristics of an individual, such as his or her personality, personal skills, and abilities that have been shaped by life experiences and the type of family situation in which a person has grown up. There is not much an organization can do to influence an employee's personality or family background. However, as we will show in Chapter 4, there may be a number of personal resources that can in fact be influenced by organizational training and development interventions.

Environmental resources represent characteristics of the work environment that may enhance employee resilience. As with personal resources, there are many aspects of the work environment that could help employees cope more effectively with the stressors they are facing. In the stress literature, however, two aspects of the work environment tend to stand out consistently as resources for employees: (1) social support, and (2) fairness. Social support represents the assistance or help that employees receive when they are faced with stressors in the work environment. As will be discussed in more detail in Chapter 4, there are many potential sources of support available, but the support one receives from his or her direct supervisor is particularly important. Fairness is also important to employees, and as will be discussed in Chapter 4, may be reflected in a variety of ways, such as performance reviews, promotion policies, and compensation decisions. Employees who feel they are treated fairly are typically much more resilient than those who feel they are treated unfairly.

SUMMARY

The purpose of this chapter was to first explain the basic terminology used by workplace stress researchers, and then to acquaint the reader with some of the major theories that have been used to guide their efforts. We then proceeded to describe some of the major stressors that have been examined by workplace stress researchers over the years, and finally we described some of the major resources that may help people to combat the effects of stressors in the workplace. The overall message of this chapter is that there are clearly a number of demands in the workplace, and these demands can certainly have a number of negative effects on employees. Fortunately, however, if people have enough relevant resources, the impact of stressors can be neutralized. We also have emphasized throughout the chapter that managers play a key role in influencing both the stressors that employees experience, as well as some of the organizational resources they have available to combat these stressors. It is also possible that resources can be built up to such a level that employees can actually experience *positive* effects of stressors in the workplace. We begin to explore this intriguing possibility in Chapter 5, but first we will explore the most common reactions to stressors in Chapter 2.

REFERENCES

1. Tepper, B. (2000). Consequences of abusive supervision. *Academy of Management Journal, 43,* 178–190.
2. Katz, D., & Kahn, R. L. (1978). *The social psychology of organizations* (2nd. ed.). New York: John Wiley.
3. Cortina, L. M., Magley, V. J., Williams, J. H., & Langhout, R. D. (2001). Incivility in the workplace: Incidence and impact. *Journal of Occupational Health Psychology, 6,* 64–80.
4. Karasek, R., (1979). Job demands, job decision latitude, and mental strain: Implications for job redesign. *Administrative Science Quarterly, 24,* 285–308.
5. Kain, J., & Jex, S. M. (2010). Karasek's (1979) Job Demands-Control model: A summary of current issues and recommendations for future research. In P. L. Perrewe & D. C. Ganster (Eds.), *Research in Occupational Stress and Well-Being* (Vol. 8, pp. 237–268). Bingley, UK: Emerald Publishing.
6. Johnson, J. V., & Hall, E. M. (1988). Job strain, workplace social support, and cardiovascular disease: A cross-sectional study of a random sample of the Swedish working population. *American Journal of Public Health, 78,* 1336–1342.
7. Schaubroeck, J., & Merritt, D. E. (1997). Divergent effects of job control on coping with work stressors: The key role of self-efficacy. *Academy of Management Journal, 40,* 738–754.
8. De La Rosa, G., & Jex, S. M. (2010). Using the Demands-Control-Support Model to understand manager/supervisor engagement. In S. L. Albrecht (Ed.), *Handbook of Employee Engagement: Perspectives, Research, and Practice.* Northampton, MA: Edward Elgar Publishing.
9. Demerouti, E., Bakker, A. B., Nachreiner, F., & Schaufeli, W. B. (2001). The job demands-resources model of burnout. *Journal of Applied Psychology, 86,* 499–512.
10. Bakker, A. B., Demerouti, E., & Euwema, M. C. (2005). Job resources buffer the impact of job demands on burnout. *Journal of Occupational Health Psychology, 10,* 170–180.
11. Siegrist, J. (1996). Adverse health effects of high-effort/low-reward conditions. *Journal of Occupational Health Psychology, 1,* 27–41.
12. Adams, J. S. (1963). Toward an understanding of inequity. *Journal of Abnormal and Social Psychology, 67,* 422–436.
13. Peter, R., Geisler, H., & Siegrist, J. (1998). Associations of effort-reward at work and reported symptoms in different groups of male and female public transport workers. *Stress Medicine, 14,* 175–182.

14. Siegrist, J., Starke, D., Chandola, T., Godin, I., Marmot, M., Niedhammer, I., & Peter, R. (2004). The measurement of effort-reward imbalance at work: European comparisons. *Social Sciences & Medicine, 58*, 1483–1499.

15. Jex, S. M., & Beehr, T. A. (1991). Emerging theoretical and methodological issues in the study of work-related stress. In K. Rowland & G. Ferris (Eds.), *Research in Personnel and Human Resources Management.* (Vol. 9, pp. 311–365). Greenwich, CT: JAI Press.

16. Buell, P., & Breslow, L. (1960). Mortality from coronary heart disease in California men who work long hours. *Journal of Chronic Diseases, 11*, 615–626.

17. Sparks, K., Cooper, C. L., Fried, Y., & Shirom, A. (1997). The effects of hours on health: A meta-analytic review. *Journal of Occupational and Organizational Psychology, 70*, 391–408.

18. Iwasaki, K., Takahashi, M., & Nakata, A. (2006), Health problems due to long work hours in Japan: Working hours, worker's compensation (*Karoshi*), and preventive measures. *Industrial Health, 44*, 537–544.

19. Spector, P. E., & Jex, S. M. (1998). Development of four self-report measures of job stressors and strain: Interpersonal Conflict at Work Scale, Organizational Constraints Scale, Quantitative Workload Inventory, and Physical Symptoms Inventory. *Journal of Occupational Health Psychology, 3*(4), 356.

20. Andersson, L. M., & Pearson, C. M. (1999). Tit for tat? The spiraling effect of incivility in the workplace. *Academy of Management Review, 24*, 452–471.

21. Bowling, N. A., & Beehr, T. A. (2006). Workplace harassment for the victim's perspective: A theoretical model and meta-analysis. *Journal of Applied Psychology, 91*, 998–1012.

22. Einarsen, S. (1999). The nature and causes of bullying at work. *International Journal of Manpower, 20*, 16–27.

23. Zapf, D. (1999). Organizational, work group related and personal causes of mobbing/bullying at work. *International Journal of Manpower, 20*, 70–84.

24. Juvonen, J., Graham, S., & Schuster, M. A. (2003). Bullying among young adolescents: The strong, the weak, and the troubled. *Pediatrics, 112*, 1231–1237.

25. Einarsen, S. (2000). Harassment and violence at work: A review of the Scandinavian approach. *Aggressive and Violent Behavior, 5*, 379–401.

26. Einarsen, S., & Skogstad, A. (1996). Bullying at work: Epidemiological findings in public and private organizations. *European Journal of Work and Organizational Psychology, 5*, 185–201.

27. Mitchell, M., & Ambrose, M. (2007). Abusive supervision and workplace deviance and the moderating effects of negative reciprocity beliefs. *Journal of Applied Psychology, 92*, 1159–1168.

28. Alexander, K. N. (2011). Abusive supervision as a predictor of deviance and health outcomes: The exacerbating role of narcissism and social support. Unpublished doctoral dissertation, Bowling Green State University, Bowling Green, OH.

29. Kahn, R. L., Wolfe, D. M., Quinn, R. P., Snoeck, J. D., & Rosenthal, R. A. (1964). *Organizational Stress: Studies in Role Conflict and Ambiguity.* New York: John Wiley.

30. Breaugh, J. A., & Colihan, J. P. (1994). Measuring facets of job ambiguity: Construct validity evidence. *Journal of Applied Psychology, 79*, 191–202.

31. Abramis, D. J. (1994). Work role ambiguity, job satisfaction, and job performance: Meta-analysis and review. *Psychological Reports, 75*, 1411–1433.
32. Jackson, S. E., & Schuler, R. S. (1985). A meta-analysis and conceptual critique of research on role ambiguity and role conflict in work settings. *Organizational Behavior and Human Decision Processes, 36*, 16–78.
33. Frone, M. R. (1990). Intolerance of ambiguity as a moderator of the occupational role stress-strain relationship: A meta-analysis. *Journal of Organizational Behavior, 11*, 309–320.
34. Wrzesniewski, A., & Dutton, J. E. (2001). Crafting a job: Revisioning employees as active crafters of their work. *Academy of Management Review, 26*, 179–201.
35. Allen, T. D., Herst, D. E. L., Bruck, C. S., & Sutton, M. (2000). Consequences associated with work-to-family conflict: A review and agenda for future research. *Journal of Occupational Health Psychology, 5*, 278–308.
36. Kossek, E. E., & Ozeki, C. (1998). Work-family conflict, policies, and the job-life satisfactionrelationship: A review and directions for future organizational behavior/human resources research. *Journal of Applied Psychology, 83*, 139–149.
37. Barling, J., MacEwen, K. E., Kelloway, E. K., & Higginbottom, S. E. (1994). Predictors and outcomes of elder-care-based interrole conflict. *Psychology and Aging, 9*, 391–397.
38. Barnett, R. C. (1998). Toward a review and reconceptualization of the work-family literature, *Genetic, Social, & General Psychology Monographs, 124*, 125–182.
39. Grzywacz, J. G. (2000). Work-family spillover and health during midlife: Is managing conflict everything? *American Journal of Health Promotion, 14*, 236–243.
40. Holmes, T. H., & Rahe, R. H. (1967). The Social Readjustment Rating Scale. *Journal of Psychosomatic Research, 11*, 213–218.
41. Rizzo, J. R., House, R. J., & Lirtzman, S. I. (1970). Role conflict and ambiguity in complex organizations. *Administrative Science Quarterly, 15*, 150–163.
42. Burnfield, J. L., Clark, O. L., Devendorf, S., & Jex, S. M. (2004, April). *Understanding workplace incivility: Scale development and validation.* Paper presented at the annual convention of the Society for Industrial and Organizational Psychology. Chicago, IL.
43. Netemeyer, R. G., Boles, R. G., & McMurrian, R. (1996). Development and validation of work-family conflict and family-work conflict scales. *Journal of Applied Psychology, 81*, 400–410.
44. Einarsen, S., Hoel, H., & Notelears, G. (2009). Measuring exposure to bullying and harassment at work: Validity, factor structure, and psychometric properties of the Negative Acts Questionnaire-Revised. *Work & Stress, 23*, 24–44.

2

The Psychological, Physical, and Behavioral Costs of Work Demands

In Chapter 1, we covered the most common stressors that employees in organizations tend to encounter, and briefly addressed the resources that people may use to help them cope with these stressors. Despite the wide variety of resources that people might possess, it is often the case that people experience negative reactions—commonly referred to by researchers as *strains*—particularly when they experience stressors over a sustained period of time. The purpose of this chapter is to describe the most common strains that have been studied by occupational stress researchers, and that are often the focus of workplace stress management interventions. It is important to understand strains because they serve as important signals that the level of stressors we are faced with may be getting too high. Understanding the negative effects of stressors alerts us to better cope with the demands, and ultimately to learn to thrive in the face of them.

STRAINS: AN OVERVIEW

As stated above, the term *strain* is used by workplace stress researchers to refer to adverse reactions that people exhibit when they are chronically exposed to stressors in the workplace. The term *strain* itself is really a metaphor that was borrowed from the field of engineering,[1] which refers to the negative impact on a structure as it is used over time. For example, a bridge will exhibit some structural strain over many years of cars and trucks passing over it. Likewise, when people experience stressors on their jobs day in and day out, they are apt to show some adverse effects in the form of strains.

As with the stressors that were discussed in Chapter 1, there are an almost infinite number of strains or ways that people can respond to stressors in the work environment. Researchers, however, classify strains into three broad categories: (1) psychological, (2) physical, and (3) behavioral. Each of these will be discussed below.

PSYCHOLOGICAL STRAINS

Psychological strains represent the relatively short-term emotions that we typically feel when we are experiencing stressors. Compared to the two other categories that will be discussed, there has been considerably more research examining psychological strains. The reasons for this are twofold. One is simply that psychological strains are much easier to measure compared to physical or behavioral strains; we just need to ask people to report the emotions they are feeling. The other reason is that many researchers view psychological strain as the *mediating mechanism* between stressors and the other two strain categories. What this means is that psychological strains are the most immediate responses to stressors, and these immediate responses have future consequences. As an example, an employee who frequently has arguments with her coworkers might feel a great deal of anger, anxiety, and tension (psychological strains) after these arguments occur. Furthermore, this employee may very well feel these same types of emotions when she begins work each day, and thinks about the prospect of working with these individuals. Ultimately, feeling these negative emotions about work might lead the person to be absent from work frequently or even to look for other employment (behavioral strains).

While the number of psychological strains is potentially quite high, researchers have tended to focus on a relatively small number. Three, in particular, have been studied extensively in occupational stress research: anxiety, depression, and frustration. Anxiety is an emotion that is characterized by feelings of apprehension or nervousness.[2] There is also typically a physical component that goes along with the emotional experience of anxiety; when feeling anxious, a person's heart might race, his or her palms might sweat, and he or she may have trouble sleeping.

Why do occupational stress researchers use *anxiety* as a strain measure? The primary reason is that many stressors in the workplace are characterized by high levels of *uncertainty*. For example, if a person is experiencing role ambiguity (previously discussed in Chapter 1), there is an inherent uncertainty regarding whether or not the job is being done properly. Another example might be having a conflict with a coworker. When a person is having a conflict with another person, there is often a great deal of unpredictability or uncertainty surrounding the interactions one has with that person. Therefore, feelings of anxiety at work are often natural responses to encountering stressors that create uncertainty and a lack of control.

Anxiety can also be helpful because it can trigger coping responses to certain stressors. For example, let's say that a person experiences a great deal of anxiety every time he or she has to give a presentation at work. While certainly unpleasant at the moment, such feelings of anxiety may convince the person to take steps that facilitate coping, and in the long run may facilitate thriving. A person who is highly anxious about public speaking may practice, obtain training, and try to seek out opportunities to engage in this activity. Because of this additional training, the individual may become a highly skilled public speaker and ultimately may come to enjoy it.

Depression, the second most common psychological strain, reflects feelings of sadness, resignation, and negativity. It is important to understand that in occupational stress research what is typically measured is often referred to as *sub-clinical depression*. This is much different from *clinical depression*, which can often be debilitating, and may even require treatment in an inpatient psychiatric facility. Other than severity, the other difference between clinical and sub-clinical depression is the etiology or cause. Although clinically depressed individuals may have events occur in their lives that trigger major depressive episodes (e.g., death of a spouse), the weight of the evidence suggests that the root cause of clinical depression is biochemical.[3] Sub-clinical depression, on the other hand, is much more a reaction to things that occur in the person's life and is of much shorter duration. Most readers can probably think of a time in their lives when something happened (e.g., a bad grade, relationship ending) that made them feel temporarily depressed. However, with the passage of time these feelings of depression most likely faded and things returned to normal.

Why is sub-clinical depression used as a measure of psychological strain in occupational stress research? Probably the best way to explain it is that in general people tend to have the expectation that most aspects of their lives (including work) are going to go smoothly. The more stressors a person experiences at work, the larger the gap between a person's expectations and the reality of his or her situation, at least when it comes to work. This gap tends to precipitate feelings of depression. Think about people you may know, or even yourself, who have a set of goals for how their lives should play out—for example, a person might expect to be married by 25, have two children by the age of 30, be promoted to vice president of their company by the age of 45, and so on. Obviously, if a person's life actually *does* play out this way that's great—he's planned things fine. Let's say, however, that a person does not meet the right person to marry and is still single at the age of 28. This may lead to feelings of sadness, regret, and even self-criticism—all signs of depression. Obviously, there are other ways people can respond when life does not play out the way they want it to, and we'll discuss these in much more detail in later chapters, but often people simply respond by feeling depressed.

Just like anxiety, feelings of depression, provided they are not severe, may also help individuals to realize that a change is necessary in how they respond to their work. Let's say a person is passed over for a big promotion at work and, as a result, is feeling somewhat depressed. Assuming that this person wanted the promotion, it is understandable that he or she is feeling depressed. One potential positive outcome of feeling depressed may be that we re-evaluate our goals or aspirations. When we do this, we may find that some of our goals may be overly rigid, or perhaps unrealistic, and this realization may cause us to change our goals. For example, a person who has not been promoted to company vice president may realize that becoming company vice president is not all it's cracked up to be, and this may lead to a desire to have more balance between work and other aspects of life.

Frustration, which is the third psychological strain, represents the negative emotional state that tends to accompany situations in which our goals are blocked. Emotions synonymous with frustration include annoyance, impatience, and often anger. Most readers have probably had the experience of being stuck in traffic when you were trying to either get to work or to an appointment. Frustration represents the emotional state that you were likely feeling as the minutes ticked by and you realized there was a good chance that you were going to be late for work or your appointment, and there was absolutely nothing you could do about it.

Researchers have used frustration as a psychological strain measure because many stressors, by their very nature, block people's goals. Think about the previous discussion of conflict between work and non-work domains. Whether it's work interfering with family, or vice versa, feelings of frustration are likely to occur because the conflict prevents us from meeting the demands of both roles. Conflict with a coworker works in much the same way. The time that we have to spend thinking about what a coworker might say or do, or actually trying to resolve the conflict with this individual, is time that we can't focus on other things, such as our work. Frustration can also be useful, much in the same way that anxiety and depression can. Feelings of frustration could cause one to work harder, or to find creative ways to cope with the stressors that one is dealing with. Frustration may also be a sign that one should change the goals that one is pursing.

Although psychological strains are internal states, people may often show outward signs that they are experiencing anxiety, depression, or frustration. In *What This Means for Managers 2.1* we discuss some of the signs that managers should look for, which may indicate that employees are struggling with these psychological strains.

What This Means for Managers 2.1

IDENTIFYING EMPLOYEES WITH PSYCHOLOGICAL STRAINS

As stated in the chapter, psychological strains represent internal and often emotion-laden responses that employees may exhibit in response to work stressors. The most typical psychological strains are anxiety, depression, and frustration. Below we describe cues that managers may look for which indicate that an employee is experiencing a particular psychological strain.

Specific cues of dysfunctional psychological reactions to stressors for managers include the following:

- Anxiety is the emotional state we experience when we are worried about things that might happen or are experiencing a great deal of uncertainty at work or in another aspect of our lives. Typical outward signs of anxiety may include an inability to concentrate or maintain focus, a preoccupation with whatever is worrying us, and an inability to relax or sit still.
- Sub-clinical depression is an emotional state that is typically characterized by feelings of sadness and hopelessness. Outward signs of depression may include low energy level, flat affect, and a general lack of desire to socialize with others.
- Frustration represents the emotional state that people experience when their goals or desires are thwarted. Compared to the other two psychological strains discussed in this chapter, the outward signs of frustration are typically more visible—these might include slamming things down on one's desk, repeatedly complaining about things, and even yelling or being verbally aggressive.

PHYSICAL STRAINS

Compared to the other two types of strains, the impact of stressors on physical health is perhaps the most important, due to the cost of healthcare as well as the more far-reaching impact of health problems. The most common way in which occupational stress researchers have investigated the relationship between work-related stressors and health is through *self-report physical symptom inventories*. An example of a widely used physical symptom inventory that was developed by Paul Spector and the second author is presented in Table 2-1. Take a moment to respond to this measure and consider the extent to which you are experiencing the different symptoms. As you can see, the physical

Table 2-1. PHYSICAL SYMPTOM INVENTORY (SPECTOR & JEX, 1998)

Over the past month, how often have you experienced each of the following symptoms?	Not at all	Once or twice	Once or twice per week	Most days	Every day
1. An upset stomach or nausea	1	2	3	4	5
2. Trouble sleeping	1	2	3	4	5
3. Headache	1	2	3	4	5
4. Acid indigestion or heartburn	1	2	3	4	5
5. Eye strain	1	2	3	4	5
6. Diarrhea	1	2	3	4	5
7. Stomach cramps (not menstrual)	1	2	3	4	5
8. Constipation	1	2	3	4	5
9. Ringing in the ears	1	2	3	4	5
10. Loss of appetite	1	2	3	4	5
11. Dizziness	1	2	3	4	5
12. Tiredness or fatigue	1	2	3	4	5

Scoring instructions: In order to obtain your total score, simply add up all of the numbers you circle. Total scores can range from 12, which would be a total absence of physical symptoms, to 60, which would indicate a chronic state of physical symptoms.

Source: Spector & Jex (1998).[4]

symptoms listed are those that we generally associate with stress—and, in fact, research has shown that many of these symptoms are experienced more often by people who perceive high levels of stressors in their jobs.[4] Note, however, that it is also possible to experience many of these symptoms even if one is *not* exposed to high levels of stressors.

Though less common, another method of assessing physical strain is to employ some form of physiological measurement and to see if such measures are related to work-related stressors. The most common physiological measure used in stress research has been blood pressure, which is generally considered to be a major risk factor for cardiovascular disease. Researchers have also investigated a variety of physiological indicators, including serum cholesterol levels, adrenal hormone production, and immune functioning. The basic assumption behind the use of physiological measures is that short-term increases in these indices may have negative consequences in the long run. As an example, let's say that interacting with an abusive boss results in a person's blood pressure temporarily increasing. Although each encounter with this individual might not be harmful, over time the cumulative effects of these encounters may put this person at greater risk for chronic hypertension or even cardiovascular disease. Research in the work stress literature has in fact shown that many stressors are related to physiological measures such as blood pressure,[5] adrenal hormone secretions,[6] immune suppression,[7] and cortisol levels.[8]

A third method of assessing physical strain is to investigate the impact of stressors on documented physical illnesses. In Chapter 1, when the demands-control model was discussed, we mentioned that Robert Karasek used this method to assess the basic premise of his model: namely, that individuals who held jobs characterized by high job demands and low job control would be at greater risk for coronary heart disease (CHD). There have also been other studies over the years investigating the relationship between different stressors and mortality from CHD.[9] Other than CHD, occupational stress researchers have shown that there are relationships between stressors at work and such physical conditions such as digestive disorders, upper respiratory infections, and back injuries.[10]

Another manifestation of physical strain, and one that has received more research attention in recent years, occurs through *presenteeism*.[11] Presenteeism reflects situations in which employees attend work despite the fact that they are ill, or have other physical limitations that prevent them from performing their work tasks up to their full capabilities. Presenteeism is not always a bad thing; for example, there may be times when it is essential that an employee attend work on a particular day, so there is no choice but to come to work ill. Everyone has probably had the experience of having to "suck it up" for a day due to an important meeting or presentation. Presenteeism, however, can be harmful if an employee who comes to work ill performs his or her job poorly, or other negative consequences arise. For example, an employee who has an infectious disease may end up infecting other employees. We have more to say about presenteeism in *What This Means for Managers 2.2*. When considering the impact of work-related stressors on physical strains, it is important to keep in mind that the evidence is *very* mixed; that is, some researchers find that work-related stressors negatively impact physical health, while others find very little relationship. Even if stressors do contribute to physical health problems (and most likely they do), it is important not to lose sight of the other contributing factors. As an illustration, let's take the example of cardiovascular disease—an outcome that has been examined by occupational stress researchers. Although there is evidence that work-related stress does contribute, at least indirectly, to cardiovascular disease,[10] the strength of that contribution is rather small in comparison to other known risk factors (e.g., high fat diet, lack of physical activity, genetic predisposition, etc.). As a result of this, cutting down on one's stress can certainly cut down on one's risk of CHD, but it is probably not going to be of much help if a person eats a very high fat diet, rarely exercises, and has a strong family history of CHD.

What This Means for Managers 2.2

IDENTIFYING EMPLOYEES WITH PHYSICAL STRAINS

As stated in this chapter, physical strains are extremely important due not only to their potential impact on healthcare costs but also for the employees themselves. As a result, managers need to be aware of potential physical and health-related reactions that employees may have toward stressors at work. Below we discuss some of these.

- Probably the most visible sign that an employee is experiencing physical strain is being absent from work. There are obviously many reasons that an employee may be absent, but an employee who is consistently absent from work could be having issues with his or her health.
- Another potential sign that an employee may be experiencing physical strain is a lack of energy and motivation. This can also be a sign of a psychological strain, such as depression, but in many cases it may be an indicator of physical strain.
- A third potential sign of physical strain, which is related to a lack of energy, is *presenteeism*. Recall, this is a term used for employees who physically show up for work, but get very little done because they are ill or have other physical limitations. When people consistently do this, it may be a sign of some underlying physical condition, or perhaps an indication that the demands of work are having an adverse effect. A widely used measure of presenteeism that can easily be adapted to most jobs or work situations is the Stanford Presenteeism Scale.

Source: Koopman, C., Pelletier, K. R., Murray, J. F., Sharda, C. E., Berger, M. L., Turpin, R. S., Hackleman, P., Gibson, P., Holmes, D. M., & Bendel, T. (2002). Stanford Presenteeism Scale: Health status and employee productivity. *Journal of Occupational and Environmental Medicine, 4*, 14–20.

Like the previously discussed psychological strains, physical strains can also be seen as a useful first step toward responding better to difficult work conditions. Assuming that the physical strains we experience are not serious or life-threatening, they can be helpful in that they may motivate us to pay more attention to our physical health. For example, a person who is working long hours and is experiencing a great deal of fatigue may start trying to get more rest, or perhaps exercise in order to increase his stamina. Such a person may also possibly take steps to cut down on the number of hours worked. In later chapters of the book, we highlight how employees can approach demands in more adaptive ways in order to decrease symptoms that may be occurring as a result of stressful work conditions. Recognizing the negative symptoms that can occur from stressful work highlights the importance of taking action to respond to demands in more constructive ways.

As with psychological strains, employees may also shown signs that they are experiencing a variety of forms of physical strains. In *What This Means for Managers 2.2* we discuss some of these signs and recommend potential steps that managers can take to help employees who appear to be showing the physical effects of the demands they are working under.

BEHAVIORAL STRAINS

Just like physical strains, behavioral strains are important because many have very tangible and important consequences for organizations. As with the other two categories of strains, there is a wide variety of potential behavioral strains. Given this variety, it is useful to group them into four categories: (1) productive behaviors, (2) withdrawal behaviors, (3) counterproductive behaviors, and (4) health behaviors. Each of these categories will be discussed below.

Productive Behaviors

Productive behaviors simply represent the things employees do that positively contribute to the goals of an organization.[12] The most common form of productive behavior in organizations is often referred to as *in-role job performance,* which represents the job duties assigned to each member of an organization. For example, as professors the authors of this book are *required* to teach courses, conduct research, and provide service to the university. Another way to think of in-role job performance is that which employees are contractually required to do for their employers.

Although there is not a great deal of research on the relationship between stressors and in-role performance, most findings have shown a negative but very small relationship.[13] In other words, stressors do seem to negatively relate to in-role job performance, but not to a great extent. Why? The main reason is that in-role performance is determined by many factors other than the stressors people are experiencing, for example, ability, experience, personality, and constraints or barriers to performance in the work environment. Because of this, it is possible that some of these factors can compensate for high levels of stressors. It is also the case that most people are rewarded on the basis of their

in-role performance, so they have a vested interest in keeping their in-role performance high even if they are experiencing stressors.

Another form of productive behavior in organizations is referred to as
extra-role job performance, which represents those things that employees
do that contribute positively to the goals of an organization, but that are not
required of employees. The most common form of extra-role job performance
is referred to as organizational citizenship behavior, or OCB.[14] Basically, OCBs
represent behaviors that are not necessarily required by organizations, but
that nevertheless contribute to organizational success. Very common forms
of OCB include helping a fellow employee if he or she has a problem, working
harder to pick up the slack when a fellow employee is ill, or simply exhibiting
courtesy toward others. Research, however, has shown that these things help
organizations to be successful, so they are needed even if organizations can't
require them. Unfortunately, we know that people who are experiencing high
levels of stressors in their jobs are less likely to engage in behaviors reflective
of extra-role performance. In a study conducted by the second author along
with Gary Adams, Daniel Bachrach, and Sarah Sorenson,[15] employees from
two universities who experienced high levels of role stressors (e.g., role ambiguity) also engaged in fewer extra-role behaviors, such as helping others. The
basic rationale for this finding was that these employees had less to lose by
withholding these extra-role behaviors compared to letting their in-role performance slip. In other words, if you don't help others, people may be momen-
tarily upset with you; if you don't do your job, you may end up getting fired.

As with other forms of strain, reductions in productive behaviors can be a
first step toward responding to these demands in more constructive ways. If a
person has suddenly become unproductive, this is a sign that something isn't
right, and a person needs to evaluate the causes. When people do this, they
may find that they simply need to view their job differently, or perhaps change
their routine in some way.

Withdrawal Behaviors

One potential reaction to experiencing high levels of stressors is to engage in a
number of withdrawal behaviors; that is, employees may physically or psychologically withdraw and "check out" from the workplace. By far the most common
form of organizational withdrawal behavior is absenteeism. Although some level
of absenteeism is probably unavoidable due to illnesses or family issues, employees
might sometimes choose to be absent from work because they find the workplace
an unpleasant place to be.[16] Furthermore, absenteeism is expensive to organizations due to lost productivity and potentially the cost of temporary replacements.

Although absenteeism can be thought of as withdrawing by being physically away from work, we know that people can sometimes withdraw when they are *at* work. It's likely that many readers have had days at work where they were daydreaming or engaged in other off-task behaviors (e.g., paying bills online, making travel plans, etc.). There is evidence that off-task behaviors are not necessarily harmful to organizations.[17] In fact, there is some evidence that letting employees have the freedom to do these things on the job can actually have a positive effect. However, if employees spend excessive amounts of time on off-task behaviors, this can have a serious negative effect on the productivity of organizations.

Thus, when it comes to off-task behaviors, organizations are often faced with a dilemma. If they allow employees too much freedom to engage in off-task behaviors, they run the risk of employees abusing this privilege. On the other hand, if they try to monitor employee behavior too closely to make sure there is a minimum amount of off-task behavior, they run the risk of decreasing employees' feelings of autonomy and freedom. High levels of off-task behavior created by dysfunctional responses to stressful work conditions will not only hurt the organization, but will prevent the employee from developing to his or her full potential. That is, although withdrawing helps the employee deal with the immediate consequences of stressful work conditions, the withdrawal comes at a long-term cost of the employee developing in a way that will allow the employee to succeed in his or her job.

Counterproductive Work Behaviors

Counterproductive work behaviors are similar to some of the previously mentioned withdrawal behaviors; in fact, withdrawal behaviors are generally considered forms of counterproductive work behavior. *Counterproductive work behavior* (CWB) is typically defined as behavior that employees voluntarily engage in that is harmful to their employing organization. Some forms of counterproductive work behavior are relatively harmless—for example, wasting a few minutes by talking to a fellow employee. Some forms, however, can be quite damaging to organizations.[18] Examples of these types would be an employee who steals money from his or her employer, or who deliberately sabotages a piece of machinery.

Paul Spector and Suzy Fox[18] proposed that counterproductive work behaviors can be broken down into five general categories: abuse, production deviance, sabotage, theft, and withdrawal. *Abuse* reflects counterproductive behaviors that are directed at other employees, such as sexual harassment and other forms of interpersonal hostility. *Production deviance* occurs when employees deliberately work slower or produce less than they are capable of producing. *Sabotage*, which was mentioned earlier, would occur, for example, if an employee deliberately damaged a computer network with a virus. *Theft* is self-explanatory and simply refers to employees taking things that don't belong to them from the workplace. Finally, *withdrawal* represents a fairly general category of behaviors such as daydreaming, showing up late, or otherwise showing a lack of interest in one's work. Table 2-2 contains a checklist of behaviors representing each of these five categories of CWB.

Research on CWB has shown that employees engage in these behaviors for a variety of reasons,[18] and one of those reasons is work stress. This may be a way to somehow "get back" at the organization for providing a stressful work environment, and it also may simply be a way for employees to displace their negative feelings associated with that stressful work environment. Research

Table 2-2. COUNTERPRODUCTIVE WORK BEHAVIOR CHECKLIST
(FOX & SPECTOR, 2002)

ABUSE

1. Started or continued a damaging or harmful rumor.
2. Been nasty or rude to a client or customer.
3. Insulted someone about his or her job performance.
4. Made fun of someone's personal life.

PRODUCTION DEVIANCE

1. Purposely did your work incorrectly.
2. Purposely worked slower when things needed to get done.
3. Purposely failed to follow directions.

SABOTAGE

1. Purposely wasted your employer's materials/supplies.
2. Purposely damaged a piece of equipment or property.
3. Purposely dirtied or littered your place of work.

THEFT

1. Stolen something belonging to your employer.
2. Tool supplies or tools home without permission.
3. Took money from your employer without permission.
4. Stole something belonging to someone at work.

WITHDRAWAL

1. Came to work late without permission.
2. Stayed home from work and said you were sick when you weren't.
3. Took a longer break than you were allowed to take.
4. Left work earlier than you were allowed to.

Source: Spector et al. (2006).[36]

has also shown that employees may at times engage in CWB simply as a way of coping with boredom.[19] Thus, sometimes people engage in CWB because it breaks the monotony of their work.

In other cases, employees may engage in CWB because other people around them are engaging in CWB. Samuel Bacharach and Peter Bamberger have conducted extensive research on alcohol use in the workplace, and have found that "alcohol-related norms" within work groups can have a powerful effect on individuals' actual drinking behavior.[20] More specifically, employees engage in higher levels of on-the-job drinking when in work groups where it is common for others to drink. Why? Norms tell us what is and what is not acceptable behavior, and because most people want to maintain membership in the groups to which they belong, they typically adjust their behavior to adhere to norms.

Although counterproductive work behaviors can certainly be harmful to an organization and can have negative consequences for an individual, like the other strains we've discussed, they can also have some value in alerting employees that the way they are responding to work stressors is maladaptive and needs changing. Most individuals do not want to think of themselves as the type of person who would deliberately hurt the organization or people in the organization. Therefore, engaging in these behaviors is a wake-up call to employees to approach and cope with their work demands in a more constructive manner.

Health Behaviors

A final type of behavioral strain, and one that is closely tied to physical stressors, is health behaviors. The idea here is that people who are experiencing high levels of stressors in their jobs engage in unhealthy behaviors, or in some cases fail to engage in healthy behaviors, and because of this end up experiencing more health problems. Research has supported this general hypothesis in that work-related stressors have been associated with tobacco and alcohol use, unhealthy eating habits, and a lack of physical exercise.[21]

There are essentially two ways that researchers tend to explain these findings. First, unhealthy behaviors represent a way to cope with work-related stressors. More specifically, drinking alcohol or smoking may temporarily make people feel better if they are experiencing a lot of stressors at work. Second, since many stressors at work exert time demands on people, unhealthy behaviors may emerge simply due to time constraints. A good example of this can be found in an interesting study conducted by Tammy Allen, Kristin Shockley, and Mark Poteet,[22] who found that those employees who perceived higher levels of work interfering with family, and who worked more hours, had fewer family meals and ate at fast food restaurants more frequently. Obviously, not all fast food is unhealthy, but in general it does have higher levels of fat and sugar content, which could ultimately lead to excessive weight gain and increased risk for diabetes, cardiovascular disease, and other health problems.

As with all of the other strains discussed in this chapter, engaging in unhealthy behaviors as a result of work stressors should alert employees that action is needed to better deal with work demands. For example, if a person never has time to exercise and never eats at home, that may be a sign that the demands of one's job have reached an unhealthy level and that something needs to change. Unfortunately, many people do not heed this warning and ultimately don't do anything about their demands until something more drastic happens (e.g., heart attack, obesity, etc.). Like psychological and physical strains, managers may often be able to recognize when behavioral strains are occurring. In *What This Means for Managers 2.3* we discuss some specific behaviors that managers should look for that may indicate that an employee is experiencing excessive work demands. We also discuss ways in which managers might respond to these behavioral strains.

COLLATERAL DAMAGE: CROSSOVER EFFECTS OF STRESSORS

Up to this point we have discussed strains strictly at the individual level; that is, employees experience stressors in the workplace and then react to those stressors in a variety of ways. The reason we have done so is that the vast majority of occupational stress research has examined the stress process in this way. We know, however, that when employees experience strains as a result of the stressors they experience in the workplace, the effects of those strains are not necessarily confined to the workplace. Humans can't always shut off negative feelings when they leave the workplace, so employees often bring these negative feelings home with them. A relatively new and quite interesting line of inquiry within occupational stress research involves *crossover effects*, or the impact of strains experienced by employees on family members or other people in their lives (e.g., friends, neighbors, etc.).

The notion of crossover effects is based on the idea that the boundaries we set up between different aspects of our lives are somewhat *permeable*; that is, what happens in one area of one's life tends to spill over into other areas. For example, if a person is anxious and tense about an upcoming presentation at work the next day, he or she might be irritable at home the night before. Conversely, a person who is worried about his or her financial status at home may take it out on his coworkers by being highly irritable and argumentative.

What This Means for Managers 2.3

BEHAVIOR STRAINS AMONG EMPLOYEES

As stated in the chapter, there are varied behavioral reactions to work demands, including poor performance, withholding of extra-role behaviors, and counterproductive work behaviors. Managers can play a key role in the prevention of these behavioral reactions because they typically monitor employee behavior as part of their managerial role. Below we offer suggestion on how managers should address this important issue.

- With respect to in-role performance, managers should take advantage of opportunities to discuss performance-related issues with employees. Most organizations have annual or semi-annual performance reviews. We believe, however, that performance review should be an ongoing process and two-way dialogue between managers and employees.
- Extra-role behaviors are tricky because by definition they are things that are not *required* by an organization. Nevertheless, if a manager notices that an employee never does anything beyond his or job description, this may be a sign that this employee is overloaded in some way.
- Counterproductive work behaviors are obviously important because they may be very costly to organizations. Thus, managers should be aware of serious forms of CWB and reprimand employees when they engage in them. We also believe, however, that employees sometimes use CWB as a coping mechanism or stress reliever, so it is important to know when to intervene and when not to.

Despite the fact that boundaries are generally permeable for most people, there are differences among people in terms of how they manage the boundaries between different aspects of their lives. For example, some people prefer to keep work separate from other aspects of their lives,[23] while others are more willing to let work spill over into other domains, and vice versa. In studies of couples living together, strains experienced by one member of the couple do predict strain in the other member of the couple; in other words, crossover effects have been supported. Another fairly consistent finding in the crossover literature is that women tend to be more strongly impacted by the strain experienced by men, compared to the other way around. This could be due to gender role expectations (e.g., women are expected to be nurturing and caring), but it has also been argued that one of the reasons for this finding is that many crossover studies include women who do not hold full-time jobs outside the home.[24]

Given that crossover effects have been shown to occur, one might ask *why* they occur. In the crossover literature, researchers have generally offered two plausible mechanisms for crossover effects. The first, which has been called *displacement*, is that people who are experiencing strains due to their work situation tend to lash out at those in other areas of their life (e.g., spouse, children). As a result, those individuals in other areas of their life experience strains as well. Many readers have probably snapped at family members because they were upset about something that happened at work, and it's likely that such episodes evoked symptoms of strain in those family members.

The other mechanism proposed for crossover effects is that of *empathetic concern*. What this means is that when employees experience strain due to stressors in the workplace, those outside the workplace sense this and "feel their pain." Spouses, in particular, are particularly adept at reading the emotions of their partner and sensing when something is not right. Even children, in their own way, feel concern about their parents and feel for them when they are experiencing negative emotions due to the workplace.[25]

In addition to influencing immediate family members, stressors in the workplace may actually have much more far-reaching effects. For example, people who are experiencing health problems due to stressors at work are likely to be frequent users of healthcare services, and therefore might increase healthcare costs for the organizations they work for. Organizations facing higher healthcare costs may then pass those costs on to customers or clients. Similarly, if an employee is frequently absent from work, or is very withdrawn at work, this often results in more work for other employees.

In addition to the effects on customers and fellow employees, one could argue that the communities where employees live are also indirectly influenced by work-related stressors. Employees who are tense and anxious from work may withdraw from their neighbors, and as a result, there may be very little sense of community in neighborhoods. In addition, stressed out employees may be less able or willing to volunteer in their communities to do things such as coaching youth sports teams, volunteering at a nursing home, or working with at-risk teenagers.

Now that we have discussed the most common reactions to work-related stressors, please take a moment to complete Application Exercise 2.1. As you'll see, this exercise requires that you think about the most common reactions that you have had to the most important demands in your current job that you identified in Application Exercise 1.1. In Chapters 3 and 4 we provide recommendations for addressing these demands that should decrease the negative outcomes associated with each demand.

Application Exercise 2.1

REACTIONS TO IMPORTANT DEMANDS

In this chapter we cover the most common negative reactions that people have to the demands or stressors that they face in the work environment. Recall that these reactions often occur at the psychological level, but may also occur at the physical and behavioral levels as well.

In this exercise we would first like you to refer back to Application Exercise 1.2, where you selected the THREE most important demands you face in your work. For each of these demands, we would like you to write down the THREE most common reactions that you have when you encounter these demands.

Demand #1: _____

    Reaction #1: _____

    Reaction #2: _____

    Reaction #3: _____

Demand #2: _____

    Reaction #1: _____

    Reaction #2: _____

    Reaction #3: _____

Demand #3: _____

    Reaction #1: _____

    Reaction #2: _____

    Reaction #3: _____

In the next two chapters we are going to discuss ways in which individuals can reduce the negative effects of workplace demands. Understanding the effects that these demands are currently having will allow you to assess the extent to which you are able to reduce these effects after engaging in the recommendations provided in these chapters.

TO THE EXTREME: LOW BASE RATE
STRAIN RESPONSES

Up to this point, the strain responses that have been discussed are things that are relatively commonplace; that is, many people feel anxious or have relatively minor physical symptoms. In some rare cases, however, employees' responses to work-related stressors are more severe and dramatic in nature. These are things that do not happen with great frequency, but when they do occur, the effects can be devastating. In this section we discuss the two most widely discussed strains of this type: post-traumatic stress disorder (PTSD) and workplace violence.

Post-Traumatic Stress Disorder

By and large, occupational stress researchers have focused on what have been labeled *chronic* stressors. That is, stressors of this type are more or less a constant presence in the employee's work environment. Think back to Chapter 1, where stressors were described, and it is evident that they fit this definition. Role conflict, for example, does not dramatically pop up but rather builds up over time for an employee. The same can be said for the other stressors such as work-family conflict, work overload, interpersonal conflict, and so on.

In some occupations, however, employees may be at a heightened risk for experiencing what has been termed *traumatic stressors*. Traumatic stressors are distinguished from most of the stressors we have discussed earlier on two dimensions: *onset* and *severity*. Traumatic stressors typically have a sudden onset; for example, an emergency room nurse being suddenly attacked by a patient would fit this definition. Traumatic stressors are also more severe in comparison with the typical chronic stressors that are studied in the occupational stress literature. For example, most reasonable people would agree that a police officer witnessing his partner being fatally shot would be a much more severe stressor then being unclear about his role responsibilities.

Post-traumatic stress disorder (PTSD) is a clinically significant (meaning that those who suffer from PTSD typically require treatment from a mental health professional) response that sometimes accompanies exposure to traumatic stressors in the workplace. There is no single defining characteristic of PTSD, but rather it is a cluster of symptoms. In the diagnosis of PTSD, the first criterion is that a person must have had some exposure to a traumatic event or stressor. Much of the research on PTSD has been with military veterans who have been exposed to many of the traumatic conditions associated with being in combat,[26] but PTSD is by no means exclusive to military service. There is evidence, for example, that first responders (police officers, firefighters, ambulance personnel) may also suffer from symptoms of PTSD.[27]

Other than the existence of a traumatic event, the major psychological manifestation of PTSD includes preoccupation with the source of the trauma; in fact, those with PTSD often report having nightmares about the traumatic event, reliving it, or otherwise being preoccupied with it. Furthermore, because of this preoccupation, individuals with PTSD often have trouble holding a job or establishing relationships with others. In addition to these first two criteria, the other two include *avoidance* and *hyper-arousal*. Avoidance occurs when an individual actively attempts to avoid anything that in any way reminds him or her of the trauma, while hyper-arousal occurs when people are easily startled and have difficulty sleeping.

Typically, when people experience a traumatic event or stressor, they experience many of the symptoms of PTSD for a short duration, and then the symptoms gradually go away. In some cases, however, people continue to experience these symptoms for a much longer duration and therefore may experience significant disruptions in their lives; this would be an example of clinically significant PTSD.

Despite the seriousness of PTSD, there are a number of treatments available for this disorder, including psychological debriefing, cognitive-behavior therapy, and medication.[28] Although the success of these treatments varies considerably based on a number of factors, individuals who are treated successfully will typically be able to return to work much faster than those who do not receive treatment. These individuals will also most likely develop coping skills that will allow them to handle the stressors they will likely encounter in the workplace.

Workplace Violence

Despite the level of media coverage they receive, incidents of serious workplace violence and aggression are extremely rare. For example, in a representative sample of US employees,[29] only 7% reported having been the victim of physical aggression at work during the previous 12 months. Furthermore, the most typical source of physical aggression was *not* fellow employees, but rather those outside the organization (e.g., customers, clients, perpetrators of crime, etc.). Despite this relatively low rate of occurrence, physical violence in the workplace does occur, and under some circumstances may be a response to stressors that one is experiencing. Suzy Fox and Paul Spector,[30] for example, proposed that employees who continually experience frustration in the workplace, and at the same time believe there is little they can do about it, may be more likely to exhibit aggressive behaviors. It has also been shown that individuals who view stressors as highly ego-threatening (i.e., a threat to their self-esteem) may exhibit extreme and even violent reactions to demands.[31]

Some post hoc accounts of violent acts in the workplace have posited that perpetrators of such acts are attempting to gain revenge on someone in the organization who they feel has treated them poorly or otherwise wronged them in some way.[32] Again, we emphasize that physical violence and aggression, particularly the employee-to-employee variety, is very rare. Nevertheless, in some extreme circumstances, acts of violence may be a reaction to chronic stressors in an employee's job.

THE BOTTOM LINE: FINANCIAL COSTS OF WORKPLACE STRESS

Up to this point we have focused on individual-level reactions to stressors in the workplace, primarily those of individual employees experiencing stressors, as well as those who might be close to employees (e.g., spouse, children). The primary reason for this focus is quite simple—the vast majority of occupational stress research has centered primarily on individual-level reactions.

Despite this almost exclusive focus on individual-level responses to stressors, the effects of stressors may go well beyond individual reactions and may impact financial indicators within organizations. Most estimates of the costs of workplace stress are typically in the billions of dollars, but the range of estimates varies widely.[11] Regardless of the exact amount, these are certainly numbers that grab people's attention.

Where, exactly, do scholars come up with these numbers? In all honesty, most such estimates are just that—estimates—and there is no way to really prove or disprove their validity. There are, however, some effects of stressors in the workplace that can be translated into a financial metric. Probably the most obvious example of this is organizational healthcare costs, and in fact some research has shown that exposure to stressors is positively related to organizational healthcare costs.[33,34] These costs reflect increased healthcare utilization, increased use of prescription drugs, and most likely decreased productivity.

Many of the behavioral reactions to stressors could have financial ramifications for organizations as well. Even small decrements in job performance that are precipitated by exposure to stressors might have serious financial implications for organizations. This is particularly the case for those who have high levels of responsibility, or who supervise other employees. Absenteeism is another outcome that has been associated with stressors in the workplace and that has a clear financial impact. When an employee is absent, organizations may have to replace that individual with a temporary employee; in some cases, the work that the absent employee was supposed to do simply doesn't get done.

In many countries, most notably in the United States with recent passage of the Affordable Healthcare Act, much more effort has been directed at combating the effects of workplace stressors and improving overall employee health. Many organizations, for example, offer employees exercise facilities and have initiated other programs aimed at smoking cessation and weight loss to improve employee health and ultimately decrease healthcare costs.

Finally, recall in the section on behavioral outcomes we discussed a group of behaviors collectively known as counterproductive work behavior (CWB). CWB represents behaviors that run counter to the goals of an organization and can range from relatively minor things, such as wasting time or paying bills online, to things that are far more serious (e.g., stealing). While it is doubtful that very minor forms of CWB have any adverse financial impact on organizations, the financial impact of more serious forms of CWB may be substantial. Take, for example, employee theft. In the retail sector, it has been estimated that theft now accounts for nearly $16 billion in added costs.[35] This obviously hurts retail organizations, but it ultimately hurts customers of these organizations because these costs are passed on to them in the form of higher prices.

CONCLUSION

The term *strain* has been used for many years by occupational stress researchers to describe reactions that employees often exhibit when they experience stressors. Strains can be classified into three types—psychological, physical, and behavioral—and, more often than not, have been self-reported by employees. As was also pointed out in the chapter, most strain measures can be considered to be *sub-clinical* or at a relatively low severity level. However, in rare cases, for example following exposure to traumatic stressors, reactions might include clinically significant outcomes such as PTSD or even violent behavior.

Although strain is generally viewed as a negative thing, it can also serve a useful purpose, and we believe that it is a first step toward thriving. When people are experiencing strains, this is a sign that the demands of their jobs are reaching a level that is unhealthy. Thus, strains serve as a reminder that something has to change—either a person has to change the way he or she views the job, or in some cases may even need to change jobs altogether.

While the vast majority of occupational stress research has examined the direct effects of stressors on individual employees, we also know that the strain experienced by individual employees can impact others. Research on crossover effects among married couples, for example, has shown that employees may take out their strain on their spouse and others in their family. It is also quite possible, though more research is needed to verify this, that the strains people experience may have effects that go far beyond their immediate family.

Although strains have been examined almost exclusively at the level of the individual employee, it is certainly possible that organizations also experience "strains" in the form of decreased productivity, higher healthcare costs, and ultimately decreased financial performance. Furthermore, the impact of these outcomes often extends well beyond the borders of the organization. In the next chapter we discuss a critical factor that can affect whether work demands have a negative impact on employees, their families, and the organization: the extent to which the employee views the work demands as a challenge versus a threat.

REFERENCES

1. Beehr, T. A., & Franz, T. (1987). The current debate about the meaning of job stress. In J. M. Ivancevich & D. C. Ganster (Eds.), *Job Stress: From Theory to Suggestion* (pp. 5–18). New York: Haworth Press.
2. Spielberger, C. D. (1972). Anxiety as an emotional state: In C.D. Spielberger (Ed.), *Anxiety: Current Trends in Theory and Research* (Vol. 1). New York: Academic Press.
3. Beck, A. T. (2009). *Depression: Causes and Treatment* (2nd ed.). Philadelphia: University of Pennsylvania Press.
4. Spector, P. E., & Jex, S. M. (1998). Development of four self-report measures of job stressors and strain: Interpersonal conflict at work scale, organizational constraints scale, quantitative workload inventory, and physical symptoms inventory. *Journal of Occupational health Psychology, 3,* 356–367.
5. Schaubroeck, J., & Merritt, D. E. (1997). Divergent effects of job control and coping with work stressors: The key role of self-efficacy. *Academy of Management Journal, 40,* 738–754.
6. Ganster, D. C., Fusilier, M. R., & Mayes, B. T. (1986). Role of social support in the experience of stress at work. *Journal of Applied Psychology, 71,* 102–110.
7. Schaubroeck, J., Jones, J. R., & Xie, J. L. (2001). Individual differences in utilizing control to cope with job demands: Effects of susceptibility to infections disease. *Journal of Applied Psychology, 86,* 256–278.
8. Wirtz, P. H., Ehlert, U., Kottwitz, M. U., & Semmer, N. (2013). Occupational role stress is associated with higher cortisol reactivity to acute stress. *Journal of Occupational Health Psychology, 18,* 121–131.
9. Buell, P., & Breslow, L. (1960). Mortality from coronary heart disease in California men who work long hours. *Journal of Chronic Diseases, 11,* 615–626.
10. Ganster, D. C., & Schaubroeck, J. (1991). Work stress and employee health. *Journal of Management, 17,* 235–271.
11. Johns, G. (2010). Presenteeism in the workplace: A review and research agenda. *Journal of Organizational Behavior, 31,* 519–542.

12. Jex, S. M., & Britt, T. D. (2008). *Organizational Psychology: A Scientist-Practitioner Approach* (2nd ed.) New York: John Wiley & Sons.

13. Rosen, C. C., Chang, C. H., Djurdjevic, E., & Eatough, E. (2010). Occupational stressors and job performance: An updated review and recommendations. In P. L. Perrewe & D. C. Ganster (Eds.), *Research in Occupational Stress and Well-Being* (Vol. 8, pp. 1–60). Bingley, UK: Emerald Publishing.

14. Podsakoff, P. M., MacKenzie, S. B., Paine, J. B., & Bachrach, D. G. (2000). Organizational citizenship behaviors: A critical review of the theoretical and empirical literature and suggestions for future research. *Journal of Management, 26*, 513–563.

15. Jex, S. M., Adams, G. A., Bachrach, D. G., & Rosol, S. (2003). The impact of situational constraints, role stressors, and commitment on employee altruism. *Journal of Occupational Health Psychology, 8*, 71–180.

16. Sliter, M. T., Sliter, K. A., & Jex, S. M. (2012). The employee as punching bag: The effect of multiple sources of incivility on withdrawal and performance. *Journal of Organizational Behavior, 33*, 121–139.

17. Krischner, M. M., Penney, L. M., & Hunter, E. M. (2010). Can counterproductive work behaviors be productive? CWB as emotion-focused coping. *Journal of Occupational Health Psychology, 15*, 154–166.

18. Spector, P. E., & Fox, S. (2005). A model of counterproductive work behavior. In S. Fox & P. E. Spector (Eds.), *Counterproductive Workplace Behavior: Investigations of Actors and Targets* (pp. 151–174). Washington, DC: APA.

19. Bruursema, K., Kessler, S. R., & Spector, P. E. (2011). Bored employees misbehaving: The relationship between boredom and counterproductive work behavior. *Work & Stress, 25*, 93–107.

20. Bachrach, S. B., Bamberger, P. A., & Sonnenstuhl, W. J. (2002). Driven to drink: Managerial control, work-related risk factors, and employee problem drinking. *Academy of Management Journal, 45*, 637–658.

21. Hellerstedt, W. L., & Jeffery, R. W. (1997). The association of job strain and health behaviors in men and women. *International Journal of Epidemiology, 26*, 575–583.

22. Allen, T. D., Shockley, K. M., & Poteat, L. F. (2008). Workplace factors associated with family dinner behaviors. *Journal of Vocational Behavior, 73*, 336–342.

23. Ashforth, B. E., Kriener, G. E., & Fugate, M. (2000). All in a day's work: Boundaries and micro role transitions. *Academy of Management Review, 25*, 472–491.

24. Park, Y. (2012). Processes of strain crossover between dual-earner couples. Unpublished doctoral dissertation, Bowling Green State University, Bowling Green, OH.

25. Barling, J., Dupre, K. E., & Hepburn, C. G. (1998). Effects of parents' job insecurity on children's work beliefs and attitudes. *Journal of Applied Psychology, 83*, 112–118.

26. King, D. W., King, L. A., Foy, D. W., Keane, T. M., & Fairbank, J. A. (1999). Posttraumatic stress disorder in a national sample of female and male Vietnam veterans: Risk factors, war zone stressors, and resilience-recovery variables. *Journal of Abnormal Psychology, 108*, 164–170.

27. Andrews, B., Brewin, C. R., Rose, S., & Kirk, M. (2000). Predicting PTSD symptoms in victims of violent crime: The role of shame, anger, and childhood abuse. *Journal of Abnormal Psychology, 109*, 69–73.

28. Foa, E. B., Keane, T. M., & Friedman, M. J. (2000). Guidelines for treatment of PTSD. *Journal of Traumatic Stress, 13*, 539–558.

29. Schat, A. C. H., Frone, M. R., & Kelloway, E. K. (2006). Prevalence of workplace aggression in the U.S. workforce. In E. K. Kelloway, J. Barling, J. J. Hurrell (Eds.), *Handbook of workplace violence* (pp. 47–89). Thousand Oaks, CA: Sage.

30. Fox, S., & Spector, P. E. (1999). A model of work frustration-aggression. *Journal of Organizational Behavior, 20*, 915–931.

31. Baumeister, R. F., Smart, L., & Boden, J. M. (1996). Relation of threatened egotism to violence and aggression: The dark side of high self-esteem. *Psychological Review, 103*(1), 5–33.

32. Wolfe, M. (1994). Dr. Fabrikant's solution. *Saturday Night, 109*(6), 11–13, 16–18, 56–59.

33. Ganster, D. C., Fox, M. L., & Dwyer, D. J. (2001). Explaining employees' health care costs: A prospective examination of stressful job demands, personal control, and physiological reactivity. *Journal of Applied Psychology, 86*, 954–964.

34. Manning, R. R., Jackson, C. N., & Fusilier, M. R. (1996). Occupational stress, social support, and the costs of health care. *Academy of Management Journal, 39*, 738–750.

35. National Retail Security Survey (2003), available at: www.soc.ufl.edu/SRP/final-report_2003.pdf.

36. Spector, P. E., Fox, S., Penney, L. M., Bruursema, K., Goh, A., & Kessler, S. (2006). The dimensionality of counterproductivity: Are all counterproductive behaviors created equal? *Journal of Vocational Behavior, 68*, 446–460.

3

The Importance of Interpreting Work Demands as Challenges Instead of Threats

Why is it that different people who hold the exact same job see the job very differently? For example, some firefighters might view their job as exciting and invigorating, while others may view it as highly stressful and dangerous. Some teachers might experience great fulfillment and satisfaction in being able to help students, while others might view their interactions as a nuisance. In both cases, relatively similar job content can be viewed in almost the exact opposite manner.

What accounts for these differences? The answer to this question is *appraisal*. Appraisal essentially represents our *psychological interpretation* of the things that we experience in the world, including our jobs. Appraisal is very important, if not crucial, in occupational stress research because the vast majority of stressors that are studied are somewhat subjective and thus are open to interpretation. From a purely practical perspective, appraisal is also important. The fact that different people may appraise things differently suggests that people have some *choice* in how they view potential stressors in their work environment. Furthermore, if we have some choice in the way we view the work environment, perhaps it is possible that we can learn to view it in a way that is non-threatening or perhaps even positive.

In this chapter we explore the concept of appraisal in detail, with the ultimate goal of determining how an employee can use this knowledge in order to appraise the work environment—even potentially stressful aspects of it—in a more positive manner that facilitates thriving under work demands. Along these same lines, we revisit a concept that was first introduced in Chapter 1—the distinction between *hindrance* and *challenge* stressors. The chapter concludes with a discussion of three keys to developing challenge appraisals of important work demands.

THE BASICS OF APPRAISAL

As stated above, it's well established in the psychological literature that different people may view the same objective situation in vastly different ways—in other words, *appraisal matters*. What's not so well established or clear-cut, unfortunately, is *why* these differences in appraisal exist. Over the years, however, considerable psychological research has examined the causes of appraisal, so while there is not a definitive answer available, there is certainly enough research and theory to draw some broad conclusions.

By far the most influential stress researcher and theorist who has addressed the issue of appraisal was Richard Lazarus. In the book *Stress and Coping,*[1] Lazarus and his colleague Susan Folkman provide the most detailed and influential description of the appraisal process to date. Lazarus and Folkman first distinguished between two types of cognitive appraisal: (1) primary, and (2) secondary. Each of these will be discussed below.

According to Lazarus and Folkman, *cognitive appraisal* is the process through which people decide whether or not a particular interaction with the environment is relevant to their well-being, and if it is, in what ways. When a *primary* appraisal is made, a person is first evaluating whether or not he or she has anything at stake in the encounter—in other words, is the encounter important at some level? How does a person make this judgment? According to Lazarus and Folkman, the person makes some judgment as to whether there is potential harm with respect to commitments, values, or goals. People also make a judgment as to whether the health or well-being of a loved one is at stake, and potentially whether or not the encounter will impact his or her own self-esteem.

Given this definition of primary appraisal, it is easy to see how a situation at work might be perceived as stressful to one employee, neutral to another, and positive by a third. Let's take the example of an employee's workload. For individuals who place a high importance on their work, and who believe that if they perform poorly it reflects poorly on them as a person, a heavy workload could potentially be viewed as very threatening. If a person believed neither of these things, then a heavy workload would most likely be viewed in a neutral light.

Now consider a person who places a high importance on work, but does not believe that performing poorly reflects on them personally; in fact, this person may view work as a challenge or an opportunity to achieve. For this individual, a heavy workload may create a sense of excitement or may be experienced as almost invigorating. What makes this possible, according to Lazarus and Folkman, is that the appraisals we make about demands are to a large extent under our control, that is, appraisals largely represent *choices* that we make about how to view the situations that we are in. Primary appraisal is also an important concept for managers to understand, since their actions are interpreted through this appraisal process. In *What This Means for Managers 3.1*, we discuss in more detail the important implications of primary appraisal for managers.

The other form of cognitive appraisal described by Lazarus and Folkman[1] is referred to as *secondary* appraisal. Secondary appraisal, as one would expect, occurs after primary appraisal has occurred and represents a person's judgment regarding what can be done about any stressors one has encountered. The secondary appraisal influences an individual's coping, which represents

---

What This Means for Managers 3.1

HELPING EMPLOYEES TO MAKE CHALLENGE APPRAISALS

As we describe in the chapter, most situations in life can be appraised as threatening or non-threatening. Although there may be exceptions, we believe that it is much more advantageous for managers to be viewed as non-threatening by their employees. So how do managers do this? We believe there are three fundamental questions managers need to ask themselves:

- *How do I treat my employees when one of them makes a mistake?* When managers fly off the handle or otherwise overreact when an employee makes a mistake, this serves as a cue to everyone in a work group that a manager is threatening.
- *How do I react when one of my employees gives me some bad news?* Managers who react strongly and negatively when they receive bad news are generally viewed as threatening by their employees. This type of reaction suggests to employees that they should cover up bad news, which can ultimately lead to major problems down the road.
- *How am I perceived by other people?* This can be a tough one. While we all may think of ourselves as having strong interpersonal skills, there are vast differences in people's ability to put others at ease. Doing some self-assessment of your interpersonal skills may reveal areas in need of improvement.

the various strategies that people may use to deal with a stressor when it is present. As discussed in more detail in the next chapter, there are a variety of ways to cope with stressors. For example, one can attempt to change the stressor that one is experiencing, manage the emotions one is feeling while experiencing the stressor, or in some cases simply try to avoid the stressful situation altogether. One thing that's important to recognize about secondary appraisal is that it only takes place if the primary appraisal process determines that a situation is threatening or stressful. If a situation is not perceived as threatening or stressful, according to Lazarus and Folkman, there is really no need for a coping response.

Now that we have described the two major forms of cognitive appraisal proposed by Lazarus and Folkman, it is worth considering for a moment the factors that influence a person's cognitive appraisals. One obvious determinant of both primary and secondary appraisal is the *actual situation* one is facing. Although later in this chapter we will argue (quite forcefully, in fact) that the *perception* of potentially stressful situations is one of the major keys to approaching stressors in a way that can facilitate thriving, there are some situations that are almost universally perceived by people as stressful. For example, the threat of physical violence is likely to be perceived as stressful regardless of one's perceptions. The vast majority of situations in the workplace, however, can be appraised in a variety of ways.

Situations will also inevitably influence secondary appraisal, as well as the choice of coping methods one chooses to use. While some situations lend themselves to constructive forms of coping, such as trying to decrease the stressor that one is experiencing, others may not. A person who is faced with the prospect of losing his or her job because the organization is going out of business is unlikely to be able to do anything about it. In this case, therefore, it would probably not be very useful to try. Rather, in this case a person would probably be much better off trying to accept the situation for what it is and trying to find another job.

In addition to the situations we find ourselves in, cognitive appraisals are also influenced by the people making them. One personal aspect that will certainly influence both primary and secondary appraisal is one's past history. For example, an impending deadline is going to be appraised as threatening or stressful if a person has been unsuccessful meeting deadlines in the past. Conversely, if a person has typically been successful meeting deadlines in the past, an impending deadline will probably not be appraised as threatening, and in fact could very well be seen as challenging or invigorating.

Past history is also likely to influence the process of secondary appraisal as well. For example, if a person has been successful coping with stressors in the past by trying to reduce them directly, this will likely continue in the future.

On the other hand, if a person has found that trying to deal directly with stressors has not worked very well in the past, this form of coping is unlikely to be repeated in the future. Specifically, a person may find that simply avoiding the stressful situation or dealing with the resulting negative emotions is a more effective coping strategy. In addition, a person might find that some relatively dysfunctional behaviors (e.g., substance use) tend to work, at least temporarily, to decrease the symptoms of stressors.

In addition to past history, additional characteristics of an individual may also influence both primary and secondary appraisal. With regard to primary appraisal, it is known that the beliefs we have about ourselves may impact how we perceive different features of the work environment. For example, individuals with low self-esteem may perceive any negative encounters with other employees as psychologically threatening and may ruminate about them for long periods of time. Those with higher self-esteem may perceive such encounters as being relatively benign, or perhaps may view them as challenging.

It is also likely that characteristics of people influence secondary appraisal or coping as well. Although there is a general consensus among coping researchers that coping is not a "trait," or a permanent part of person's behavioral repertoire, people probably have coping preferences based on individual characteristics. As an example, consider the trait of locus of control. Persons with an *internal* locus of control believe that they have some control over events that happen in their lives. Given this belief, individuals with an internal locus of control might have a tendency to take direct action to combat the stressors they may be encountering in the workplace. In contrast, persons with an *external* locus of control believe that things in their life tend to be controlled by external forces (e.g., fate, luck, and powerful people). Given this belief, externals would be less likely to cope by trying to do something about the stressor(s) they are experiencing; rather, externals would cope by doing something about the emotions they are experiencing.

IMPLICATIONS OF APPRAISAL

Now that we have covered the basics of cognitive appraisal, it is important to take a step back and consider the major implications of the cognitive appraisal process. The first major implication is that many things people experience in the workplace could *potentially* be seen as stressors, but they do not necessarily have to be. As we pointed out in the previous section, most things in the work environment can be viewed as threatening, neutral, or positive, depending on the viewpoint of the employee. Therefore, to a large extent, stressors are subjective. Research in occupational stress seems to be consistent with this point, insofar as employees have been shown to react quite differently to similar stressors,[2] and differing levels of stressors are often perceived by people performing nearly identical jobs.[3,4]

Given the subjective nature of the cognitive appraisal process, a logical conclusion that follows is that appraisals can be *modified*. Specifically, if appraisal is an inherently subjective process, people can learn to appraise their work situation in a way that is not only less threatening or stressful, but is in fact positive. Of course we're not suggesting that modifying one's cognitive appraisals is *easy*—if it were, then people would just appraise their work environments differently and stress would disappear—but that modifying appraisals is *possible*.

A second implication of the cognitive appraisal process is that even though most aspects of the work environment can be appraised in multiple ways, there are *some* things in the work environment that are perceived as threatening or stressful by just about everyone. This may seem somewhat contradictory, given what has already been said about the subjective nature of the cognitive appraisal process. However, despite this subjectivity, we believe it is important to understand that some situations cannot and probably should not be modified through appraisal. It's hard, for example, to appraise a physical assault from a coworker as anything but a threat. The same can probably be said for severe abuse from a supervisor or blatant sexual harassment from customers. All of these situations are instances in which a person would certainly be justified not trying to appraise the situation in a less threatening manner; later in the book we discuss how these situations should be addressed.

A third major implication—and this is aimed at secondary appraisal—is that the manner in which we cope with the stressors we are experiencing in the workplace is a *choice*. Despite the fact that coping is influenced by a number of factors, both in the situation and in the person, people ultimately decide the way they cope with stressors. A logical and positive implication of this decision is that people are capable of learning effective ways of coping with stressors. Again, as we pointed out earlier, it is not necessarily easy to learn coping methods that one has typically not used throughout one's life, but it is possible.

In summary, the general conclusion one can draw from what we know about the cognitive appraisal process is that *people have a great deal of control over how they perceive and respond to what they experience in the work environment*. Recognizing that we have this control may itself make people feel better able to cope with their environment; we propose, however, that this control is much more powerful because it gives us the capacity (within limits) to essentially view the work environment the way we want to. Thus, appraisal is an important step on the way to thriving under difficult work demands.

A SPECIAL CASE OF APPRAISAL: CHALLENGE
AND HINDRANCE STRESSORS

Now that we've established the importance of appraising stressors in the work environment, it's time to see how appraisals influence the entire stress process. In occupational stress research, the most concrete development that has come from the concept of appraisal is the recent proposition that stressors can be divided into two types—*challenge* versus *hindrance*.[5] Challenge stressors are those that people tend to appraise as being able to be addressed through increased effort, and these can have a motivating effect on employees. In organizational settings the most common examples of challenge stressors are heavy workloads, impending deadlines, a temporary crisis, or taking over a work unit that is having difficulties. To be sure, these are clearly situations that may be perceived as stressful, yet they may also potentially challenge and engage us. Take the example of impending deadlines. Deadlines often force us to work harder and faster than we normally do, which is often mentally and physically taxing. However, at the same time, there may also be a sense of excitement that goes along with working under a tight deadline and ultimately a feeling of great accomplishment when the deadline is met.

Hindrance stressors, on the other hand, are those that people tend to appraise as obstacles to successful performance that cannot be overcome through increased effort. In organizational settings the most common examples of hindrance stressors are things such as organizational politics, unclear performance expectations, situational constraints or other forms or "red tape," lack of job security, and lack of career progression. Note that compared to the examples of challenge stressors described above, the examples of hindrance stressors all reflect (1) a high level of uncertainty for the employee, (2) relatively low levels of control, and (3) a good deal of frustration.

Table 3-1 contains items from a frequently used measure of challenge and hindrance stressors. Take a moment and think about how you would respond to this measure with reference to your present job. You can see from the measure that the challenge items refer to demands that you could potentially address through extra effort, whereas the hindrance items are more difficult to overcome and therefore are a greater source of frustration. If you find you are endorsing challenge stressors to a greater extent than hindrance stressors, there is a greater potential for you to be energized by the demands. On the other hand, if you find yourself endorsing more hindrance stressors than challenge stressors, there is a greater potential for you to feel frustrated.

Research into the effects of challenge and hindrance stressors has shown some clear differences in the manner in which employees react to these two different types of stressors. Nathan Podsakoff, Jeff Le Pine, and Marcie Le

Table 3-1. MEASURE OF CHALLENGE AND HINDRANCE STRESSORS

In the chapter, a major distinction was made between challenge and hindrance stressors in organizations. Listed below are 6 items that assess challenge stressors and 5 items that assess hindrance stressors. On the scale provided, please indicate how much stress each of these causes you.

1 = Produces no stress at all
2 = Produces only a minimal amount of stress
3 = Produces a moderate amount of stress
4 = Produces a fair amount of stress
5 = Produces a substantial amount of stress

CHALLENGE ITEMS

1. The number of projects and/or assignments I have.
2. The amount of time I spend at work.
3. The volume of work that must be accomplished in the allotted time.
4. Time pressures I experience.
5. The amount of responsibility that I have.
6. The scope of responsibility my position entails.

HINDRANCE ITEMS

1. The degree to which politics rather than performance affects organizational decisions.
2. The inability to clearly understand what is expected of me on the job.
3. The amount of red tape I need to go through to get my job done.
4. The lack of job security that I have.
5. The degree to which my career seems "stalled."

Source: Cavanaugh et al. (2000).[5]

Pine[6] conducted what is probably the most comprehensive study to date comparing the differential effects of challenge and hindrance stressors. These authors summarized the results of 157 studies examining challenge and hindrance stressors and found some clear differences in the way people react to these different types of stressors.

Based on the descriptions of these stressors provided above, it is not surprising that employees tend to react to these demands in almost the opposite manner. For example, the perception of challenge stressors was associated with higher job satisfaction and organizational commitment, and lower levels of turnover intent and withdrawal from work. The pattern of results was nearly the opposite for hindrance stressors—that is, higher endorsement of hindrance stressors was associated with lower satisfaction and commitment, and higher turnover intent and withdrawal.

Despite these clear differences in the impact of challenge and hindrance stressors, it is important to note that there are some similarities in the way in which employees respond to them. Podsakoff and his colleagues,[6] for example, found that both types of stressors were positively related to physical exhaustion; that is, both make people physically tired. These researchers also found that both types of stressors tend to be a bit distracting to people, and thus they tend to detract from learning activities on the job.

Why is it, then, that despite the commonality in this type of reaction, people ultimately react much more negatively to hindrance stressors? Although research has not addressed this issue directly, we might speculate that although people might be tired and a bit distracted when a challenge stressor is experienced, they feel that they will at least have a chance to meet the demands of the stressor at some point. For example, most readers would agree that when one has a lot of work to do, it can be overwhelming and physically exhausting. Despite these negative effects, however, most people feel competent enough to believe that if they work hard enough they will ultimately get their work done. In other words, there is some reason for hope or optimism.

Contrast that example with a person who has worked hard for his or her employer for the past 10 years, yet has repeatedly been passed up for promotions and thus is feeling like his or her career is stalled. This person will also likely feel exhausted and distracted trying to figure out how to break through and finally move up and get his career on track. The key difference in this example, though, is the lack of hope or optimism. If this person has worked hard for the past 10 years and his career is still not going anywhere, what reason would he have to believe that this is going to change anytime soon?

Despite the considerable research that has been done on challenge and hindrance stressors, there are two fundamental questions about this classification of stressors that have not been adequately addressed. First, to what extent does the perception of hindrance versus challenge vary from person to person? As we pointed our earlier, research has shown that challenge stressors tend to be associated with positive outcomes, while hindrance stressors tend to be associated with negative outcomes. This finding, however, begs the question of whether there are fundamental differences between people that influence their perception of hindrance and challenge. We believe the answer to this question is "yes," and that many of the traits that are associated with resilience influence the perception of demands as challenges or threats. More will be said about this later in the chapter.

The second fundamental question about challenge and hindrance stressors that has not been adequately addressed is whether such perceptions can be modified. For example, is it possible to train someone to view most of the demands in her work environment as challenges rather than as hindrances? As we point out in some of the chapters of this book, there are some demands in the workplace that clearly hinder employees, and it is natural that people would label them as such. Being forced to deal with a chronically abusive supervisor, being harassed by rude and profane customers, or perhaps witnessing violence in the workplace are examples of demands that are probably viewed as hindrance stressors, and it is probably a good thing that they are.

Many of the demands that we have discussed in this book, however, are much more ambiguous as to whether they should be viewed as hindrances or challenges. The workload one faces, balancing the demands of work and family, having to work under high levels of job insecurity, and being unclear about one's role responsibilities are but a few examines of demands that could be viewed as both challenges and hindrances. Let's take the example of balancing the demands of work and family. For many people this is perceived as stressful—hence, the term *work-family conflict* that we described earlier. Trying to balance these demands is obviously stressful because it forces us to choose—that is, do we want to be a good employee and get everything done that we need to get done, or do we want to be the best possible parent we can be for our children? Of course, most of us want both! Nevertheless, in many cases we are forced to choose among these demands in ways that make us feel that we are not doing very well in either domain.

Despite these potentially negative aspects of attempting to balance work and family demands, there is also a potentially *positive* side to this dilemma. Anytime we are forced with competing demands, it provides an opportunity for us to clarify what we value and, in essence, to make a statement about who we are. A person who quits a job at a large, fast-paced accounting firm in order to spend more time with his or her family is really making a statement about what he or she values. Essentially what this person is saying is this: *Earning a large salary and having a high-prestige job are less important to me than being able to spend more time with my children.* Conversely, a person who perhaps decides to devote all of his or her time to advancing his or her career, and chooses to remain single is also making a statement: *I love the work that I do, and right now I want to devote most of my time to it.* Note that neither person in these examples is *wrong.* Rather, both are simply making a decision about their priorities in life, and neither would have to do this if there were not initially some conflict.

Another example of appraising a work demand in a more positive light or as a challenge is role ambiguity. As you recall, role ambiguity is a very common stressor that exists when employees are unclear about their job duties, scheduling of their work, and performance standards. Although a great deal of research has documented the negative impact of role ambiguity,[7,8] it is also possible to appraise role ambiguity in a more positive light. For example, if employees are unclear about their job duties, they might use the uncertainty as an opportunity to tailor their job to their own preferences. In fact, as will be discussed in more detail in Chapter 5, Amy Wrzesniewski and Jane Dutton coined the term *job crafting* to refer to this process.[9] Furthermore, uncertainty regarding one's work schedule may also provide some opportunity for an employee to have more control over the schedule, or to facilitate meaningful communication with one's supervisor regarding his or her expectations for the employee.

In order to further illustrate the importance of challenge appraisals, please take a moment and complete Application Exercise 3.1. As you'll see, this requires you to think about ways that you can view the most important demands in your job as challenges. As we'll see later, this is an important key to thriving under these demands.

The distinction between challenge and hindrance stressors is also important for managers to understand because the actions they take, as well as their everyday behavior, can potentially be perceived either way by their employees. In *What This Means for Managers 3.2* we discuss the importance of managers understanding the fine line between challenging their employees and throwing up unnecessary roadblocks to hinder them.

CLEAR AND PRESENT DANGER: DEMANDS THAT CAN ONLY BE THREATENING

OK, so up to this point we have argued that many of the demands discussed in the earlier chapters *could* be appraised in a more positive light. At this point, some readers might be thinking that all they have to do to thrive at work is to simply put on their "rose colored glasses" before they come to work in the morning. While it would be nice if things were that easy and simple, we don't believe they are. In this section we discuss characteristics of demands that probably cannot be perceived in any other way than as threatening (or as hindrance stressors). Later in the book we revisit this issue when we discuss ways to handle these threats.

One type of work-related demand that is most often appraised as being a threat is a physical stressor. Although low to moderate levels of physical activity could potentially have beneficial effects, if a person works at a job that greatly taxes them physically (e.g., excessive hours, heavy lifting, poor ergonomic design), then no amount of positive appraisal is likely to decrease the impact of these environmental demands. For a number of people out there, physical demands are the *main* source of stress at work. Clerical employees, for example, often suffer from repetitive motion injuries in the wrists and fingers and upper extremities, as well as eye and neck strain.[10] People in many other occupations (e.g., nurses, home health aides, package handlers) often face heavy lifting

Application Exercise 3.1

INTERPRETING DEMANDS AS CHALLENGES

As we tried to show in this chapter, many demands in the workplace can be viewed as *either* threats or challenges. Therefore, trying to reappraise a situation that could potentially be viewed as threatening as more of a challenge is a key to thriving.

In order to facilitate this process, refer back to Chapter 1, Application Exercise 1.2. In this exercise, you were asked to choose the THREE most important demands in your current job. What we would like you to do for this exercise is to think of ways that you could start viewing this demand as more of a challenge than a hindrance. As an example, if one of your top demands in the workplace is workload, this can be viewed as more of a challenge by trying to see it as an opportunity to show your skills than as a potential for failure.

If you believe the demands you have identified cannot be interpreted as challenges, there will be specific recommendations in Chapter 4 for coping with demands that cannot be changed.

Demand #1: _____

How can I see this demand as more of a challenge? _____

_____

_____

_____

Demand #2: _____

How can I see this demand as more of a challenge? _____

_____

_____

_____

Demand #3: _____

How can I see this demand as more of a challenge? _____

_____

_____

_____

What This Means for Managers 3.2

INCREASING CHALLENGE WHILE REDUCING HINDRANCE STRESSORS

The distinction we make in the chapter between *Challenge* and *Hindrance* stressors is incredibly important because it suggests that employees may be able to benefit from some stressors, which is really the whole point of this book. We believe that it is also important for managers to understand this fundamental difference, and provide two examples of why.

- Most managers are responsible for assigning work to their employees, and there is nothing wrong with challenging work assignments. Providing work assignments that are nearly impossible is a different matter, though. We believe the key is to give employees assignment that are *difficult*, but at the same time *attainable*.
- Managers should try to reduce the hindrances and barriers that get in the way of employees performing their jobs well. We believe that managers should look out for these obstacles in the work environment and try to remove them when possible. Also, occasionally asking employees, "What can I do to help make you successful?" lets them know that you're trying to remove barriers to their performance.

---

demands that may lead to back injuries—in fact, many workers compensation claims in these occupations are due to back injuries caused by heavy lifting.[11,12]

If the major demands that one faces are physical in nature, we are not suggesting that appraising these physical demands in a more positive light is really going to do anyone much good. In cases such as these, employees need to let someone (e.g., immediate supervisor, occupational health professional) know they are experiencing physical discomfort. Once an organization knows that an individual, or perhaps several individuals, are experiencing physical discomfort, then potentially something can be done about it. For example, employees could be provided with lifting aids, or jobs could be redesigned to make them more ergonomically safe. Obviously, there is no guarantee that an employer will make these types of changes if employees come forward and let the organization know about physical discomfort; it is clear, however, that if employees do not speak up there will be no change.

The other types of work demands that most likely could only be perceived as a threat by employees are physical or interpersonal mistreatment. Physical mistreatment, although fairly rare, does occur in organizations. As discussed in Chapter 1, research on physical mistreatment in organizational settings[13] has shown that people outside the organization in which the incident occurs perpetrate most instances of physical aggression. For example, nurses often have to deal with aggressive patients, and in some cases, even patients' family members. People who work in bars and other entertainment establishments that serve alcohol often have to deal with intoxicated customers who become violent and abusive. Physical aggression perpetrated by fellow employees is actually quite rare, although it certainly does happen.

Despite the power of cognitive appraisal that we have described earlier in this book, it is extremely hard to imagine how being hit, kicked, or bitten by a patient could be viewed by a nurse as anything but a threatening experience. Again, as with physical demands such as lifting or poor ergonomic design, employees experiencing any form of physical mistreatment should immediately let someone in their organization know. Once organizations know about the existence of physical mistreatment, they can put steps into place in order to decrease its prevalence. For example, hospitals might institute training programs designed to help nurses and other patient care employees deal more effectively with aggressive and agitated patients. In some cases, organizations can prevent violence and aggression by adopting "zero tolerance" policies toward customers who exhibit violent and aggressive behavior.

Although it does not result in physical injuries, interpersonal mistreatment in many cases can be just as devastating as physical mistreatment due to the psychological effects it often has on victims. As we described in Chapter 1, interpersonal mistreatment can range from very low-level rudeness and inconsiderate behavior to serious chronic harassment. Although most of the research on interpersonal mistreatment has examined mistreatment perpetrated by fellow employees or supervisors, employees also experience varying degrees of interpersonal mistreatment from those outside the organization as well, for example, from customers or clients.[14]

In an extensive review of the literature on interpersonal mistreatment, Nathan Bowling and Terry Beehr[15] showed that even low-level forms of interpersonal mistreatment can have negative effects on employees. We would add, however, that for low levels of interpersonal mistreatment, cognitive appraisal is a key factor; thus, in some cases it might be possible to brush off or otherwise ignore an isolated instance of rudeness from a fellow employee or customer.

With more intense forms of mistreatment, however, it is highly unlikely that an employee could make anything but a threat appraisal. For example, when a person is continually abused or humiliated in front of others by his or her supervisor, it is difficult to see this treatment as having any possible benefit at all. It is also difficult to see how being the object of gossip, rumors, or degrading humor can be seen as any type of challenge in any sense.

What should a person do when he or she experiences interpersonal mistreatment? With physical demands and physical mistreatment, the obvious answer to that question would be to let someone in the organizational know about it. With interpersonal mistreatment, however, the answer to that question is much more complex and requires much more careful consideration. Let's say, for example, that a person is experiencing interpersonal mistreatment at the hands of his immediate supervisor. Obviously, the person could confront the supervisor about her behavior, and explain how it is making him feel. This could potentially diffuse the situation, but could also be a risky proposition because it could actually make the situation worse.

Another potential option might be to discuss the situation with someone in Human Resources, or in extreme cases to file a harassment case against the supervisor. This could certainly be an effective strategy, especially in an organization that has a strong anti-harassment policy. However, this again carries some level of risk because it may further anger the supervisor, and in many cases those working in Human Resources may have limited authority to actually make the supervisor stop the offending behavior.

Another option available in many organizations is utilization of Employee Assistance Programs (EAPs). Although there is a great deal of variability in the specific components of such a program, most provide employees with access to counseling or other mental health services to help them cope with stressors in their lives or jobs.[16] This can help employees, at least in the short term, cope with an abusive supervisor or a harassing coworker. In the long run, though, EAPs do not get at the root cause of the problem.

Ultimately, in many situations where interpersonal harassment is experienced, the only way a person is going to experience any form of relief is to *leave the situation*. This is obviously a big step, especially for someone who may have dependents or simply may be in a situation where she needs the income from her job. However, in our opinion, there is no reason that a person should put up with consistent interpersonal mistreatment—no human being should have to take it.

DEVELOPING CHALLENGE APPRAISALS

We have established that although some work demands are clearly perceived as threatening, many others can be appraised as either threatening *or* challenging. If that is the case, how can we learn to view more of the demands we encounter at work as challenges? The short answer to this question is simply to just "perceive them as challenges," but unfortunately that doesn't really say much in terms of how one's appraisals can actually change.

Although much recent research has been done regarding the *types of people* who may be more or less likely to view the demands they face as challenges, far less work has been done on *teaching people how to view the demands they face as challenges*. Nevertheless, based on the overall body of research on the positive aspects of stress, we believe there is some concrete guidance for people who in fact do wish to change their appraisals. We believe that there are three keys to developing challenge appraisals: (1) *growth*, (2) *learning*, and (3) *rewards*. Each of these will be described in more detail below.

Growth following stressful events will be discussed in detail in Chapter 6. In the present chapter we address the implications of growth for helping individuals to view demands in less threatening ways. Probably the best way to explain the idea of growth is to use the analogy of weight training. The basic principle underlying weight lifting is actually quite simple—the act of lifting stresses the muscle fiber, and as a result of this stress, the muscle fiber gets larger and stronger. Now to get back to stress in the workplace, in what ways do we "grow" when we face difficult situations at work? That is, how do these demands make us more competent, more compassionate, more confident, or simply just a better person? Let's take an example of common workplace demand—work overload.

One thing that clearly happens when we are overloaded at work is that we gain an appreciation of the work demands of others around us. For example, when we express frustration to others about how much work we have to do, we find out that we're not the only one who experiences this demand. This, in itself, might be comforting. In the long run, however, knowing that other people face work demands like we do may help us grow in a very important way—it may help us more generally develop compassion for others as they face demands emerging from their work or from other areas of their lives. Furthermore, developing more compassion for others may help us in numerous ways, both in and out of the workplace. Experiencing this type of growth may help us become a better spouse, parent, friend, community member, and ultimately become better in our professional lives.

In addition to developing compassion for others, facing and overcoming difficult demands at work help us to grow in another important way—this gives us confidence that we can face and overcome these demands in the future. When people run a marathon for the first time, the biggest source of anxiety is typically whether they can actually last for the full 26.2-mile distance. Why? In most marathon training programs, especially for first-timers, the longest run they typically attempt is less than 26.2 miles. Once a person has successfully completed a marathon, however, she is much more confident because she has gone the distance. This same principle is true in work situations. Once a person has successfully completed a high volume of work in a short period of time, performed successfully while facing a tight deadline, or perhaps success-fully managed to juggle work and family responsibilities, she gains the confi-dence that she can do so in the future. In other words, she has *grown*.

The second key to the development of challenge appraisals mentioned above is *learning*. Again, let's take the example of work overload to illustrate this. As stated above, successfully dealing with heavy workload not only helps us to grow, but it may also help us to learn things that we may not have learned otherwise. For example, in the process of having to cope with work overload, we may learn more efficient or effective methods of performing the work. We may also learn that there are people available to help us that we didn't know about before. Both of these things could help us in the future when we encoun-ter situations where we must deal with a heavy workload. Most important, though, a learning orientation makes it more likely that employees will view their job-related demands as challenges rather than hindrances.

While learning something from your work demands can certainly have some practical benefits in the future, there is an added benefit to learning from the demands that you face—it's enjoyable! As we will discuss in more detail in Chapter 5, research has shown that people who tend to have a "learning orientation" toward their work—in other words, they view demands as oppor-tunities to learn—tend to enjoy their jobs more and tend to experience less job-related strain. There is also evidence that learning new things may also be a way for people to recover from the demands of work.[17] People may learn to cook, to make wine, or to speak a different language simply for the enjoyment of it. This suggests that although we often learn things to accomplish some end state (e.g., to get into a particular career), many people find the process of learning itself to be enjoyable.

The third and final component of developing a challenge appraisal is to find some type of *reward* associated with the demand. In order to illustrate this concept, let's go back to the example of running a marathon. For any readers who have actually run a marathon, you can probably attest to the fact that the *actual experience* of running a marathon is not very pleasant at times. Runners often talk about "hitting the wall" around the twentieth mile, which is undoubtedly not a pleasant experience. Extreme feelings of fatigue, muscle cramping, and general exhaustion are common among runners at this stage. It is also common for runners at this point to basically ask themselves, "What the heck am I doing this for!?"

Given all of the potential unpleasantness associated with running a mara-thon, why do people do it? The answer to that question can be found at the finish line of any marathon. Many people, especially first-time marathon run-ners, are often overcome with emotion when they finally finish their 26.2-mile journey. Some people aspire for many years to do it, and the feelings associated with finally accomplishing their goal can be extremely rewarding. For others, the reward of marathon running is the enhanced level of fitness they enjoy from the training, particularly those who may have struggled from weight issues all of their lives.

Getting back to the work context, what reward do people receive when they successfully overcome demands at work? At the simplest level, when we confront and successfully cope with any type of demand, whether it's in a work or non-work context, we feel some level of mastery over our environment. Stated differently, overcoming demands makes us feel like we aren't just controlled by the circumstances we're in, but that we're able to control things ourselves.

Consider, for example, a newly hired accountant who is faced with her first tax season. As many readers know, this is a time of the year when workload is extremely high for tax accountants, and it's not unusual for them to work 10- or 12-hour days. Let's say our new accountant is assigned the task of completing the tax returns of several clients. Although this assignment may seem a bit overwhelming, successfully completing the tax returns on time will be a major boost to her confidence, and will lead to a feeling of mastery over her work.

In summary, to the extent that we can use the cognitive appraisal process to view the demands that we experience in the workplace as challenges instead of threats, we have a much better chance of thriving under these demands. More specifically, in order to view something as a challenge, there are three fundamental questions one must ask: Is there any way that I am going to experience *growth* as a result of dealing with this demand? Are there things that I will *learn* as a result of dealing with this demand? In what ways will I experience *rewards* if I confront and eventually master the demands that I must face in the work environment? These are also important for managers to understand in order to facilitate challenge appraisals among their employees. In *What This Means for Managers 3.3* we discuss ways that managers can facilitate growth, learning, and rewards among their employees.

What This Means for Managers 3.3

ENHANCING THE BENEFITS OF CHALLENGE

As we discuss in the chapter, three positive things happen when we are challenged—we grow, we learn, and we experience rewards or a sense of accomplishment. Furthermore, managers can have some impact on the extent to which employees experience these benefits.

Specific recommendations are provided for managers below. We reinforce these recommendations in Chapter 5.

- Perhaps the most important way managers can do this is simply to *encourage employees to challenge themselves and take risks.* If employees always stay in their comfort zones and never take on any challenging assignments, they will rarely experiences growth. Of course, taking risks and being challenged sometimes result in failure, so it's important for managers to let employees know that it's OK to fail once in a while.
- Managers should also encourage learning among their employees. When employees face tough, challenging work assignments, managers should encourage employees to think about what they have learned from these experiences.
- Managers should create an environment where employees feel that it's OK to celebrate their success. Managers should try to create an environment where employees are allowed to feel a sense of pride and accomplishment when they accomplish a tough task or achieve a difficult goal.

SUMMARY

Due to the subjective nature of many of the situations we experience in the workplace, cognitive appraisal is a key to both understanding stress in the workplace and, more important, to actually thriving in the face of work demands. In this chapter we reviewed basic psychological theory dealing with the cognitive appraisal process. As was shown, primary appraisal is a key part of the appraisal process because this determines whether any type of demand in the workplace is perceived as a stress. Secondary appraisal is equally, if not more, important because it represents the steps that people take to cope with the stressors they experience.

Building on the notion of cognitive appraisal, we revisited the terms *hindrance* and *challenge* stressor. This distinction, which is based on relatively recent occupational stress research, is important because it suggests that many of the demands that people experience in the workplace can be viewed in a positive light. Furthermore, as we point out in this section, a fair amount of research has shown a clear difference in the way in which people tend to react to hindrance and challenge stressors—hindrance being associated with negative outcomes, and challenge being associated with positive outcomes.

Since many of the demands that we face could be perceived as *either* hindrances or challenges, in the final section of this chapter we discussed what we believe to be the keys to appraising the demands that we face to be challenges. These included three factors: growth, learning, and rewards. In other words, do we grow and learn from confronting and eventually mastering the demands that we face in the workplace, and do we also experience rewards when we do so? We believe that with the exception of some demands that are clearly hindrances, many of the demands that we face in the workplace can be viewed as challenges.

REFERENCES

1. Lazarus, R. S., & Folkman, S. (1984). *Stress, Appraisal, and Coping*. New York: Springer.
2. Jex, S. M., & Beehr, T. A. (1991). Emerging theoretical and methodological issues in the study of work-related stress. In K. Rowland & G. Ferris (Eds.), *Research in Personnel and Human Resources Management* (Vol. 9, pp. 311–365). Greenwich, CT: JAI Press.
3. Spector, P. E., Dwyer, D. J., & Jex, S. M. (1988). Relation of job stressors to affective, health, and performance outcomes: A comparison of multiple data sources. *Journal of Applied Psychology, 73*, 11–19.
4. Spector, P. E., & Jex, S. M. (1991). Relations of job stressors, job characteristics, and job analysis ratings to affective and health outcomes. *Journal of Applied Psychology, 76*, 46–53.
5. Cavanaugh, M. A., Boswell, W. R., Roehling, M. V., & Boudreau, J. W. (2000). An empirical examination of self-reported work stress among U.S. managers. *Journal of Applied Psychology, 85*, 65–74.
6. Podsakoff, N. P., LePine, J. A., & LePine, M. A. (2007). Differential challenge stressor-hindrance stressor relationships with job attitudes, turnover intentions, turnover, and withdrawal behavior: A meta-analysis. *Journal of Applied Psychology, 92*, 438–454.
7. Breaugh, J. A., & Colihan, J. P. (1994). Measuring facets of job ambiguity: Construct validity evidence. *Journal of Applied Psychology, 79*, 191–202.
8. Jackson, S. E., & Schuler, R. S. (1985). A meta-analysis and conceptual critique of research on role conflict and role ambiguity. *Organizational Behavior and Human Decision Processes, 36*, 16–78.
9. Wrzesniewski, A., & Dutton, J. E. (2001). Crafting a job: Revisioning employees as active crafters of their work. *Academy of Management Review, 26*, 179–201.
10. Delp, L., Wang, P. C. (2013). Musculoskeletal disorders among clerical workers in Los Angeles: A labor management approach. *American Journal of Industrial Medicine, 56*, 1072–1081.
11. Arlinghaus, A., Caban-Martinez, A. J., Marino, M., Reme, S. E. (2013). The role of ergonomic and psychosocial workplace factors in the reporting of back injuries among U.S. home health aides. *American Journal of Industrial Medicine, 56*, 1239–1244.

12. Zwerling, C., Sprince, Ryan, J., & Jones, M. P. (1993). Occupational injuries: Comparing the rates of male and female postal workers. *American Journal of Epidemiology, 138*, 46–55.

13. Schat, A. C. H., Frone, M. R., & Kelloway, E. K. (2006). Prevalence of workplace aggression in the U.S. workforce. In E. K. Kelloway, J. Barling, J. J. Hurrell (Eds.), *Handbook of Workplace Violence* (pp. 47–89). Thousand Oaks, CA: Sage.

14. Sliter, M., Jex, S. M., Wolford, K., & McInnerney, J. (2010). How rude! Emotional labor as a mediator between customer incivility and employee outcomes. *Journal of Occupational Health Psychology, 15*, 468–481.

15. Bowling, N. A., & Beehr, T. A. (2006). Workplace harassment for the victim's perspective: A theoretical model and meta-analysis. *Journal of Applied Psychology, 91*, 998–1012.

16. Cooper, C. L., Dewe, P. D., & O'Driscoll, M. P. (2011). Employee assistance programs: Strengths, challenges, and future roles. In J. C. Quick & L. E. Tetrick (Eds.), *Handbook of Occupational Health Psychology* (2nd ed., pp. 337–356). Washington, DC: American Psychological Association.

17. Sonnentag, S., & Fritz, C. (2007). The Recovery Experience Questionnaire: Development and validation of a measure for assessing recuperation and unwinding from work. *Journal of Occupational Health Psychology, 12*, 204–221.

4

What Sets Apart Employees Who Respond Well under Stress?

Probably one of the most interesting, and at same time perplexing, aspects of studying stress in the workplace is the fact that people often vary greatly in the extent to which they respond negatively to stressors. In fact, both authors of this book have devoted a substantial portion of their research careers to examining this issue. The fact that people differ in their responses to stressors, however, has implications that go far beyond academic research. For example, the US Army has long been interested in identifying the characteristics of soldiers who are able to experience combat-related stressors and remain mentally healthy. Police departments and other law enforcement agencies devote considerable resources to identifying those who are able exert good judgment under incredibly dangerous and life-threatening conditions. Finally, colleges and university are interesting in identifying students who might have trouble adjusting to the stressors associated with a demanding and rigorous academic program.

The purpose of this chapter is to review what is known about the concept of *resilience*. Resilience, quite simply, is the ability to experience stressors without being negatively affected by them. Most readers are probably aware of a friend or family member (or perhaps even yourself) whom you would consider highly resilient. Such an individual may experience stressors and other bad breaks in life, yet always seems to bounce back in spite of these things. We may marvel at such individuals, and in some cases even become jealous of them, but the truth is we often don't understand *why* they are resilient. In this chapter our goal is to clarify the "why"; in essence, we will attempt to operationalize, or "unpack," the concept of resilience for the reader. In order to accomplish this goal, we first briefly define what we mean by resilience and examine the major components of this important concept. We then describe each of these components of resilience in depth, and conclude the chapter with a discussion of whether or not resilience can be trained.

This chapter focuses on resilience under stressful working conditions, which is not showing high levels of negative outcomes in the face of stressors. In the next chapter, we move to a discussion of thriving under stressful conditions, which refers to not only the absence of negative outcomes under difficult conditions, but also the presence of positive outcomes. It probably will not come as a surprise that many of the same factors that predict reduced negative outcomes in the face of stress also predict the presence of positive outcomes in the face of stress.

DEFINING RESILIENCE AND UNDERSTANDING WHAT PREDICTS IT

We know it when we see it. Many of us struggle to handle the demands of our jobs, along with the challenges of our personal lives, and yet we often feel like we're not doing well in either domain. On the other hand, we see other people who have more demanding jobs than we have, and just as challenging personal lives, who seem to excel. There are also numerous examples we see in the media of individuals who are able to succeed in life despite growing up in poverty, experiencing abusive home environments, or having to cope with physical disabilities.

While all of these situations are somewhat unique, they are all examples of individuals whom we would consider to be *resilient*. Although there is considerable scientific research examining resilience,[1] there is no standard definition of resilience that is accepted by all members of the scientific community. In the most general sense, we view resilience as the ability to bounce back from adversity—in plain English, what we're really talking about is *stress resistance*. People who are highly resilient are better able to handle stressors than people who are less resilient.

If we just say that resilient individuals handle stress better than individuals who are less resilient, that really doesn't tell us much about what resilience actually is. If we dig a little deeper into the meaning of resilience, we do find some more specific defining characteristics of resilience. Specifically, it has been shown that resilient individuals are able to see work demands as challenges to be overcome, to envision positive outcomes even in the face of work demands, and are confident in their ability to tackle different life tasks. In essence, resilient individuals look at the challenges they face, and the obstacles they must overcome, much differently than individuals who are less resilient.

Considerable research has been conducted to identify the major factors that contribute to resilience. Most researchers agree that resilience is predicted by both stable characteristics of individuals (i.e., "traits"), as well as the circumstances people find themselves in. More specifically, resilience is predicted by the three general dimensions: (1) social support, (2) personality traits, and (3) coping methods. Each of these will be discussed below.

Social Support

There is considerable evidence in the psychological literature that humans are social beings—that is, they often seek the company of other people. Of course, one of the reasons for this is instrumental; that is, we can often accomplish more with other people than we can by ourselves. We also know that people often seek the company of others for another reason, namely, that other people often provide us with emotional support and comfort. Think about the last time you experienced some type of difficulty or crisis in your life. Although it certainly varies from person to person, there is a good chance that you sought out a sympathetic ear, or perhaps some other type of assistance, to help you deal with that crisis.

The research literature on social support in the context of occupational stress is vast, so we will only attempt to summarize some of the basics of this literature. According to Terry Beehr, we can look at social support both in terms of the *source* of the support, and the *type* of support that various sources might provide.[2] For most people social support comes from three major sources, which include coworkers, supervisors, and those outside the organizational context (e.g., friends, family members).

While all three sources of support have been found to be important, there are differences in the impact of each of these sources. For example, supervisors are often in a better position, compared to coworkers, to provide tangible forms of support, such as time off or scheduling flexibility. Coworkers, on the other hand, may be in a unique position to provide emotional support because they are often experiencing the same stressors; in addition, if one's supervisor is causing the stressors that one is experiencing, it is unlikely that a supervisor could be a very useful source of support. In fact, some research has suggested that supervisors who are both abusive and supportive at the same time cause high levels of strain among employees.[3]

Like coworkers, family members are often in a good position to provide emotional forms of support. We also know that the social support provided by family members is unique in other ways. For example, research on post-traumatic stress disorder (PTSD) has shown that individuals who have a supportive family are often able to endure very severe or traumatic stressors without showing many adverse consequences.[4] Thus, the support we receive from family members is very powerful and is a unique contributor to resilience.

Social support is generally classified into two major types: (1) instrumental, and (2) emotional. *Instrumental* support would involve providing a person with tangible help regarding the stressor that he or she is experiencing. For example, if a parent is having trouble balancing work and family demands, an understanding coworker might agree to take on some of that person's work if that person's child becomes ill. This could also be provided by someone outside the workplace; for example, a neighbor might agree to watch someone's children if a crisis comes up at work and that person needs to go to work on short notice.

Emotional support, on the other hand, involves providing emotional resources to someone who is experiencing high levels of stressors. This may come in a number of forms. For example, emotional support may involve things such as empathetic listening, encouragement, or providing advice on how best to deal with a stressor. Note that in contrast to instrumental support, a person who is providing emotional support is not really doing anything to decrease the stressor(s) that the other person is experiencing; rather, emotional support is meant to help the person handle the stressor more effectively from an emotional perspective. Using the previous example of a person experiencing work-family conflict, emotional support might come in the form of encouragement from a coworker, or perhaps empathetic listening from a close friend.

In addition to the general categories of instrumental and emotional support, researchers have identified other more specific forms of support that may also enhance resilience. For example, research has shown that simply being around other people in positive social situations can also be a source of social support.[5] It has also been shown that support may sometimes come in the form of help in appraising one's environment or making sense out of their circumstances (e.g., cognitive support).[6]

In addition to looking at social support in terms of the actual support that is provided from one person to another, we can also look at the *potential* support that a person might have available. The idea here is that simply knowing that support is available may be beneficial whether one uses it or not. If we look at social support in this way, it is useful to consider the *social networks* that people are part of. For example, some people have large social networks, while others have very small social networks. More specifically, some people know a lot of people, while other people know fewer people.

In addition to the sheer size of social networks, we can also look at the strength of the ties that one has in his or her social networks. For example, it is possible to have a relatively large social network, but the strength of the ties within that social network may be weak. Some readers may know people like this—they know a large number of people but are not really close to anyone they know—this would be a *low density* social network. In contrast, it is also possible to have a relatively small social network, but the ties within that social network could be very strong—this would be a *high density* social network. A person with this type of social network would have a small group of very loyal and valued friends. Which type of social network is most strongly associated with resilience? Unfortunately, there has not been a great deal of research addressing this question. However, there is some evidence that it is the *density* of social networks, rather than the sheer size, that tends to be most important to people.

In summary, then, social support—whether it's actual support or simply knowing it's available—is an important contributor to resilience. Furthermore, social support from both coworkers and supervisors has been shown to be a key in helping people overcome many stressors in the workplace. For more traumatic stressors, it appears that the support of family is more important than that of coworkers or supervisors. Given its importance in the workplace, it is important that conditions are created that are conducive to social support. In *What This Means for Managers 4.1* we discuss ways that managers can facilitate a supportive social environment their work groups.

Personality Traits

In the previous section we considered characteristics of a person's environment that contribute to resilience. In this section we consider aspects of individual themselves. The basic idea here is that some people possess certain traits or characteristics that make them more resistant to the effects of stressors than other people. Much research in psychology has investigated personality traits that are associated with resilience, and that is what we review in this section.

Before considering specific personality traits, let's first consider what personality is and some of the major assumptions that psychologists make about personality. While there is not one universally accepted definition of personality, most psychologists would likely agree that personality represents (a) a conglomeration of enduring or stable *traits* that people possess, and (b) characteristic or typical ways that people tend to *act* across situational boundaries. With respect to traits, we might judge a person's personality based on whether he or she is shy versus outgoing, easy to get along with versus disagreeable, and perhaps whether he or she is very dependable versus highly unreliable. These obviously aren't the only traits that we could use to form an opinion about a

---

What This Means for Managers 4.1

PROVIDING SOCIAL SUPPORT TO EMPLOYEES

We can all probably think of many times in our lives when we've received support from others during tough times, and conversely when we have been a source of support for others. Given the importance of social support, we believe that it is important for managers to facilitate social support in their work groups. Below we offer some suggestions for achieving this.

- Probably the most powerful influence on a manager's work group is the manager's own behavior. Simple things like active, interested listening and encouragement can be very powerful. In addition, knowing the organizational resources that employees may be able to use can be a helpful source of instrumental support.
- Managers can encourage their employees to be supportive toward each other. We believe that one important way is to encourage *cooperation* as opposed to *competition* among employees. To the extent that managers can, it is important to emphasize the collective contributions of all employees in their work group and to celebrate their work group's achievements collectively.

It is important for managers to take a stand when they see employees engage in unsupportive behavior toward each other. Simply reminding the unsupportive employee that "we don't do things that way around here" can be more powerful than a formal reprimand.

---

person's personality—psychologists have developed long lists of traits[7]—but they are among the most common.

If we judge personality in terms of behavioral tendencies, we might look at whether a person likes to be with other people or prefers more solitary activities, the career that a person has chosen, or perhaps the person that this individual has married. In all three cases, the behaviors that we are using do not represent the person's personality; rather, we use these behaviors to make *inferences* about a person's personality. As an example, if you knew nothing else about a person other than the fact that he was an accountant, you might make the assumption that he is highly detail-oriented.

Now that we have defined what personality is, let's consider some of the major assumptions that psychologists make about personality. First, although psychologists differ widely on specific personality theories and models they subscribe to, most would agree that personality is formed rather early in life, and is due to the interaction between characteristics of the person and the situations that this person is exposed to. Personality is a *dynamic interaction* between people and situations.

The other major assumption that psychologists make about personality is that it is *relatively* stable over even long periods of time. Studies have shown, for example, that personality traits that people exhibit during adolescence are relatively stable, even during middle age.[8] This does not mean, however, that personality is completely set in stone over the course of a person's life. We know, for example, that although it's not easy, people can change dysfunctional aspects of their personality through interventions such as psychotherapy if they want to.[9] We also know that sometimes things that happen in our lives can facilitate change. For example, a traumatic event in a person's life (e.g., life-threatening illness) may result in a different outlook on life or a change in one's perspective.[10]

Although a vast number of personality traits could potentially be linked to or seen as indicators of psychological resilience, there are four that have been investigated much more extensively than others. These include *hardiness, dispositional optimism, proactive personality*, and *locus of control*. In addition to these individual personality traits, it has recently been proposed that a collection of traits—known as *psychology capital*, or *PsyCap*—influences resilience. Each of these will be described in more detail below.

Hardiness

The personality trait of *hardiness* comes out of the extensive research on resilience conducted by Suzanne Kobasa and Salvatore Maddi. Kobasa and Maddi proposed that highly resilient individuals possess personalities that consist of the three interrelated characteristics of *control, commitment*, and *challenge*; in order to be considered to have a high level of hardiness, one must possess high levels of all three of these sub-traits. The sub-trait of *control* reflects individuals' beliefs regarding whether they have control over things in their lives. As one might guess, high control is indicative of high levels of hardiness. The sub-trait of *commitment* reflects the fact that individuals who are high on hardiness are highly committed to the things that they are doing—that is, things matter to them. Finally, the dimension of *challenge* has to do with the appraisals that are made about stressors. Individuals high on hardiness view stressors as challenges to be overcome, rather than as threats.

Research has shown that individuals who are high on hardiness tend to show less adverse reactions to stressors compared to those who are low on hardiness.[11,12] In fact, Kobasa and Maddi's initial research on hardiness was a study (begun in 1975) in which they followed managers working at the Illinois

Bell Telephone Company over a 12-year period, and showed that those high on hardiness coped with stressors much better than those low on hardiness. More specifically, these researchers found that the three most important predictors of resilience in the face of work demands were hardiness, social support, and physical exercise. Interestingly, research on hardiness has also been conducted in the US military, which suggests that hardiness may serve to buffer the effects of very intense or traumatic stressors as well.[11]

DISPOSITIONAL OPTIMISM

Dispositional optimism is a predictor of resilience studied extensively by psychologists Michael Scheier and Charles Carver. These authors have conducted a large amount of research on optimism as a predictor of physical health and recovery from different surgeries. As one might expect, those who are high on dispositional optimism generally expect positive things to happen to them, and more generally believe that things will work out for the best. Readers may know people like this—people who tend to see the glass "half full" rather than "half empty." It is important to note that having a high level of dispositional optimism does *not* mean that people are completely unrealistic. People who are high on dispositional optimism do recognize when bad things happen in their lives, but when they consider the future they prefer to believe that it will be positive.

Research on dispositional optimism has shown pretty definitively that there are some positive outcomes associated with this trait. For example, optimists tend to report lower levels of psychological distress, tend to be physically healthier, and tend to recover from medical procedures such as surgery more quickly than pessimists. Most relevant to the present discussion, however, it has been shown that optimists tend to show less adverse reactions to stressors compared to pessimists.[16]

The only potential negative associated with dispositional optimism that has been shown in health research is in situations where people are terminally or very seriously ill. Howard Tennen and Glenn Affleck,[17] for example, found that terminally ill patients high on dispositional optimism actually fared worse in terms of psychological adjustment compared to those who were lower on optimism. This obviously does not represent a typical situation that most of us frequently encounter. However, it does suggest that when we know something bad is going to happen and it's out of our control, acceptance might be a better response than being optimistic.

It should also be noted that although there is agreement concerning the benefits, as well as the potential costs, of optimism, not all psychologists agree that optimism is necessarily *dispositional*. Martin Seligman, who is the author of the influential book *Learned Optimism: How to Change Your Mind and Your*

Life, is a proponent of the idea that the tendency to be optimistic is learned and therefore can be trained.[18] This is important because it suggests that people can learn to be more resilient, and to develop ways of looking at their life that can facilitate, rather than inhibit, thriving. We discuss more about training employees to be more resilient at the end of this chapter.

PROACTIVE PERSONALITY

While the concept of *proactivity* is certainly not new,[19] the notion that proactivity could be a stable part of one's personality is. *Proactive personality* is a relatively new personality trait that comes from the work of J. Michael Crant and Thomas Bateman in the field of industrial and organizational psychology. According to these researchers, people exhibit stable differences over time in the degree to which they anticipate problems in the workplace and take care of them before they become major sources of stress.

Initially, research on proactive personality focused on the performance-related implications of this personality trait. A study conducted by Crant,[20] for example, showed that proactive personality was positively related to performance in a sample of real estate salespeople; those higher on proactive personality earned higher sales commissions. For anyone who has held a sales position, this finding probably makes sense because proactivity would likely lead one to seek out sales leads, and to follow up on existing ones.

Although initial research on proactive personality was in the area of job performance, more recent research has examined proactive personality as a resilience factor. For instance, Christopher Cunningham and Gabriel De La Rosa[21] examined whether proactive personality influenced employees' reactions to work-family conflict—a stressor that was discussed in Chapter 1. Recall that work-family conflict occurs when the demands of work interfere with family responsibilities, and vice versa. These researchers found that individuals with high levels of proactive personality reacted less negatively to work-family conflict than those who reported lower levels of proactive personality.

Why would proactive personality have this effect? If one looks at the conflicts that people experience between their work and family lives, many (though certainly not all) can be anticipated ahead of time. For example, if a person's child is playing soccer, it is highly likely that the coach would provide a schedule so that one would know when games would conflict with work. Furthermore, if a person knew ahead of time where potential conflicts might exist, he or she could take steps to ameliorate those conflicts. For example, if his child's game conflicted with an upcoming business meeting, it is possible that the person could get a subordinate to fill in at that meeting rather than missing the game. Conversely, if the meeting could not be missed, it is possible that the person could make sure that another parent provided his child transportation to and from the game. Note that in both cases there are reasonable solutions to the dilemma faced by this employee, but they require some advance planning—something that is more likely for those who are proactive.

While the benefits of proactive personality have been shown in the work-family literature, proactive personality may help people to deal with other stressors as well. As an example of this, recall the role stressors (role conflict androle ambiguity), that were discussed in Chapter 1. Individuals who are highly proactive may take steps to clarify what their role responsibilities are, anticipate potential conflicts between role demands before they occur, and possibly plan ahead to reduce the possibility that they will end up getting buried by their work. In the next chapter we review research indicating that individuals are capable of exhibiting proactive motivation, and that proactively approaching job demands is a contributor to thriving under difficult work conditions.

LOCUS OF CONTROL

The final personality trait that we examine as a predictor of resilience is *locus of control*. This is a trait that was originally defined by Julian Rotter in the late 1960s.[22] According to Rotter, there are stable differences between people in terms of the attributions they make about things that happen to them. Although Rotter originally confined the concept of locus of control to reinforcements (positive events that happen to people), it has been generalized to many other things that happen in people's lives.

People with an *internal* locus of control believe that they control reinforcements and other outcomes in their lives. In a work situation, for example, if a person wanted a pay raise, she would believe that she could take steps to make that happen—perhaps working harder or convincing her supervisor that she is deserving of a higher salary.

In contrast to those with an internal locus of control, Rotter proposed that some people have an *external* locus of control. People with an external control believe that reinforcements and other outcomes in their lives are a result of forces outside their control, such as luck, fate, circumstances, or powerful other people. In the previous example of an employee wanting a pay raise, a person with an external locus of control might *hope* that he would receive a pay raise, but it is unlikely that such an individual would take any steps to make that happen—there really would be no point in doing so.

Research on locus of control in the work domain[23,24,25] has shown pretty definitively that an internal locus of control is associated with more positive mental health outcomes than an external locus of control. Furthermore, having an external locus of control could result in negative reactions to workplace stressors. Phil Storms and Paul Spector,[24] for example, found that employees with an external locus of control had a stronger tendency to respond to frustration by engaging in counterproductive work behavior compared to those with an internal locus of control. More recently, research has shown that employees' locus of control targeted to the workplace has largely the same impact and that this effect generalizes to other stressors in the work environment.[25]

Let us consider for a moment what these results really mean. If a person has an *internal* locus of control, he or she is able to handle frustrating and stressful situations without engaging in counterproductive work behavior; the opposite is true for individuals with an *external* locus of control. Why? Because individuals with an internal locus of control believe they can have an influence on things that happen to them, they may respond to frustrating or stressful work situations in a constructive manner. So, for example, if they are having a conflict with a coworker, they may try talking to that person to resolve the conflict. In contrast, a person with an external locus of control may believe there is nothing in his power to resolve this conflict, and as a result, may engage in some form of counterproductive work behavior—he may spread negative rumors about this person behind his back.

PSYCHOLOGICAL CAPITAL

More recently, Fred Luthans and his colleagues have conducted an impressive program of research on the ability of *psychological capital* to predict a variety of attitudinal and performance outcomes among employees in different contexts. Luthans and his colleagues[13] defined psychological capital as

> an individual's positive psychological state of development that is characterized by: (1) having confidence (self-efficacy) to take on and put in the necessary effort to succeed at challenging tasks; (2) making a positive attribution (optimism) about succeeding now and in the future; (3) persevering toward goals and, when necessary, redirecting paths to goals (hope) in order to succeed; and (4) when beset by problems and adversity, sustaining and bouncing back and even beyond (resilience) to attain success. (p. 3)

Psychological capital, or PsyCap, can be considered a higher order composite trait that subsumes the four lower order traits, each of which has been linked to health and performance in prior research. Table 4–1 contains additional definitions of these important traits, along with items that have been used to assess the four traits by different researchers. Take a moment to respond to the items in Table 4–1 to see where you stand on these important traits. Scores on a measure of PsyCap developed by Luthans and colleagues have been related to a number of important outcomes, including increased job satisfaction, organizational commitment, and job performance, and decreased

Table 4–1. Definitions and Sample Items for the Four Components of Psychological Capital

Hope

Definition: Hope refers to knowing how to achieve goals at work and being able to overcome obstacles when achieving these goals.

Sample Items[34] Respond on the following scale:

1 = Strongly Disagree; 2 = Disagree; 3 = Neutral; 4 = Agree; 5 = Strongly Agree

_____1. I can think of many ways to reach my current goals at work.

_____2. At work, there are lots of ways around any problem that I am facing now.

_____3. If I should find myself in a jam at work, I could think of many ways to get out of it.

Resilience

Definition: Resilience refers to being able to bounce back following adversity and not be negatively affected by life stressors.

Sample Items[35]: Respond on the following scale:

1 = Strongly Disagree; 2 = Disagree; 3 = Neutral; 4 = Agree; 5 = Strongly Agree

_____1. I tend to bounce back quickly after hard times.

_____2. It does not take me long to recover from a stressful event.

_____3. I usually come through difficult times with little trouble.

Optimism

Definition: Optimism refers to the expectations that positive outcomes will happen in the future.

Sample Items[36]: Respond on the following scale:

1 = Strongly Disagree; 2 = Disagree; 3 = Neutral; 4 = Agree; 5 = Strongly Agree

_____1. In uncertain times, I usually expect the best.

_____2. I'm always optimistic about my future.

_____3. Overall, I expect more good things to happen to me than bad.

Self-Efficacy

Definition: Self-efficacy is the belief that individuals are capable of engaging in behaviors to achieve desired outcomes.

Sample Items[37]: Respond on the following scale:

1 = Strongly Disagree; 2 = Disagree; 3 = Neutral; 4 = Agree; 5 = Strongly Agree

_____1. In general, I think that I can obtain outcomes at work that are important to me.

_____2. At work, I believe I can succeed at most any endeavor to which I set my mind.

_____3. I am confident that I can perform effectively on many different tasks at work.

levels of employee stress and behaviors that harm the organization (such as stealing from the organization or verbally abusing coworkers).[11–15] Later in this chapter we discuss training programs that have been developed to enhance an employee's PsyCap.

Coping Methods

Coping represents the things that people do once they have experienced and responded to a stressor.[26] Given the vast number of stressors in the work environment, as well as differences between people, there are an equally vast number of ways that people can potentially cope with stressors in the work environment.[16,27] Over the years, however, occupational stress researchers have described the nature of the coping methods that people tend to use, and perhaps more important, which of these coping methods are more or less successful. Let's look at the issue of describing coping methods first.

As stated above, the number of potential coping methods a person could use is almost endless. In order to deal with this problem, psychologists often create "higher order" classifications of variables in order to make things easier and less complex. Often psychologists create these types of higher order classifications through the use of statistical methods, but that does not always have to be the case. Classifications can also in some cases be developed *rationally*, that is, by looking at coping strategies and determining, based on item content, that they go in the same category.

In the coping arena there are two major higher order classifications of coping methods. These include *problem-focused* versus *emotion-focused* coping, as well as *active* versus *avoidance* coping. Each of these general strategies is described below.

The best way to think about the distinction between problem-focused and emotion-focused coping is that problem-focused coping involves doing something about the stressor, and emotion-focused coping involves doing something about the strain. When one uses problem-focused coping, the emphasis is on eliminating or minimizing the stressor(s) that one is experiencing. As an example, if one is experiencing work overload, a problem-focused coping strategy might be to work extra hours until one's workload is down to a manageable level. It's not that a person is feeling no strain, but the choice that's made in this case is to do something about the stressor.

The other nice thing about problem-focused coping is that managers can take steps to help encourage their employees to engage in this form of coping. In *What This Means for Managers 4.2* we discuss ways that managers can facilitate problem-focused coping among their employees.

Emotion-focused coping is aimed at eliminating or minimizing the strain that one is feeling as a result of dealing with a given stressor. In the previous example of work overload, if a person is feeling anxious and tense in anticipation of having a lot to do the next day, he or she might go for a long run in order to feel calmer. An obvious problem with emotion-focused coping in this case is that it doesn't reduce or eliminate the stressor that has been causing the anxiety and tension in the first place. Another problem with this method of coping, though perhaps less obvious, is that in some cases it may reinforce destructive behaviors. Although exercise is certainly a positive way to cope with the strain that one is feeling, the person in this example could just as easily have achieved the same goal by using illicit drugs or overeating—both of which can have negative effects.

What, then, does research say about the relative effectiveness of problem-focused versus emotion-focused coping? As one might guess, research has shown that *in general* problem-focused coping tends to be the most effective,[28]

What This Means for Managers 4.2

HELPING EMPLOYEES USE PROBLEM-FOCUSED COPING

Although there are some exceptions, most research has shown that people who are experiencing stressors tend to fare much better when they use active, problem-focused coping methods. Given the importance of these coping methods, it is important for managers to encourage their employees to adopt them. Below we offer some suggestions in this regard.

- One of the most powerful things a manager can do is to model positive coping behavior. Therefore, managers who confront stressors actively, and look for solutions to the stressors facing them, are likely going to encourage these behaviors among their employees.
- Many times employees don't directly cope with stressors because they're afraid to. Therefore, we believe that it is important for managers to encourage employees to be open about the stressors they are experiencing.
- Problem-focused coping can often be difficult if employees don't know the organizational resources they have available to solve problems. Managers should make sure they are knowledgeable about such organizational resources so that they can pass this information on to their employees, and ultimately facilitate problem-focused coping efforts.

and based on the previous examples it is fairly easy to see why. When one uses problem-focused coping, it is possible that the stressor will be eliminated or minimized, which is typically not the case when one uses emotion-focused coping.

Is there any situation in which problem-focused coping would not be more beneficial than emotion-focused coping? Research has shown that indeed there may be some situations in which this is the case. Specifically, in situations where a stressor is largely *uncontrollable*, problem-focused coping may not be beneficial or may even be harmful. In the health literature, for example, people who have serious illnesses that cannot be treated are better off accepting their diagnosis rather than trying to do something about it.[17]

How would this finding apply to the workplace? One could argue, for example, that there are distinct differences in the controllability of stressors. Generally speaking, people typically have less control over interpersonal stressors than they do over demand-related stressors. Furthermore, even within those two general categories, there are likely to be vast differences among employees in the extent to which it is possible for them to exert control. A corporate executive has a great deal more power than a first-line supervisor, and thus has a great deal more control over his or her workload and interactions with others at work.

Coping researchers have recognized the importance of job control and have examined how it influences the most effective coping strategies. Research conducted by Angelique de Rijk, Pascale LeBlanc, Wilmar Shaufali, and Jan de Jonge,[29] for example, showed that problem-focused coping buffered the relationship between stressors and strains only when employees perceived a high level of control over the stressors they were experiencing. This really supports the previous point, and more generally suggests that even though problem-focused coping can be very useful, it certainly does have its limits.

At this point we have primarily discussed problem-focused coping, but what about emotion-focused coping? Given the previous discussion on the limitations of problem-focused coping, a reasonable question to ask is whether there are any situations in which emotion-focused coping is superior? Actually, there is evidence on this issue.

Terry Beehr, Leanor Johnson, and Ronie Nieva[30] conducted an investigation of coping among a sample of police officers in both a large metropolitan police department and a much smaller more rural police department. This study is noteworthy in a couple of respects. First, these researchers not only surveyed police officers themselves but also surveyed their spouses. Second, they examined outcomes that were specific to police officers and other occupations where there is the potential for experiencing trauma; these included divorce potential and thoughts of suicide.

What did this study find? First, across the range of strains that these researchers investigated, emotion-focused coping was associated with *lower* levels of strain. Recall that this runs contrary to much of the research in the occupational stress literature on coping. In this particular population, it is possible that there would not be much that one could gain from engaging in problem-focused coping efforts—these police officers in all likelihood can do little to decrease crime in the cities where they work.

Another interesting finding that emerged from this study was that the coping of spouses was important. For example, police officers who had spouses who used religion as a means of coping tended to experience lower levels of strain compared to those whose spouses did not use this form of coping. This suggests that coping is contagious, in a sense, and that it is not just an individual phenomenon.

The other major distinction that is made in the coping literature is between *active* versus *avoidance* coping. Active coping represents an active effort on the part of a person to do something about either the stressor one is experiencing or the strain one is feeling. Thus a person who is engaged in active coping may very well focus on the stressor that he or she is experiencing and may somehow try to reduce or eliminate it. However, one could also actively cope by focusing on the strain one is experiencing as well. For example, a person who actively exercises may be engaging in active coping in that this person is making a conscious effort to decrease his or feelings of anxiety or tension experienced as a result of experiencing stressors.

In contrast to active coping, avoidance coping is focused on taking one's attention away from the stressor one is experiencing and/or the strain one is feeling as a result of it. The most common way that people engage in avoidance coping is by simply trying not to think of or talk about stressors or strains. In some instances, though, it may be possible to engage in actual avoidance of the stressor that one is experiencing. For example, if a person is having a conflict with a coworker, one way to cope with this situation might be to plan his day so that he is not required to interact with this individual. This obviously is not an optimal solution to this person's problem, but in the short term it might suffice.

As one might guess, research has shown that in general active coping is much more effective than avoidance coping in terms of reducing strain.[28] When a person uses active coping, she has a much better chance to reduce the effects of the stressors she is feeling, if not reducing the actual stressors themselves. In addition, the use of active coping makes people feel that they are at least doing *something* about the stressful situation they are in, which in itself may provide some degree of comfort.

Avoidance coping, on the other hand, is dysfunctional in a number of ways. When we avoid any problem, it typically doesn't go away, and in many cases, it gets worse. For example, when people are in debt and are having trouble paying their bills, avoiding creditors may make them feel better temporarily, but it will ultimately make the situation worse. In the context of workplace stress, when we choose to avoid the stressors and strains we are experiencing, they certainly won't go away, and often they get worse.

The other problem with avoidance coping is that it may lead to some very maladaptive and even destructive behaviors. One could argue, for example, that problem drinking, drug use, and even addictive gambling may represent ways that people try to avoid thinking about the stressors in their personal and working lives. While these sorts of behaviors may provide temporary relief from stress-related symptoms, they may also have serious negative consequences for a person's health and family life.

Given all of the negatives associated with avoidance coping, readers might be wondering whether there are *any* situations in which this form of coping might be effective. That's an interesting question, but unfortunately one that has not received a great deal of research attention. On the surface, one might be tempted to speculate that avoidance is never an effective way to deal with anything in one's life. However, if one thinks back to some of the interpersonal stressors described in Chapter 1, avoidance may sometimes help people cope. For example, if a person works for an abusive supervisor, it might be possible to arrange one's schedule so that she doesn't have to interact with that person a great deal. In fact, it has been shown that the negative effects of an abusive supervisor are stronger the more one has to interact with one's supervisor.[3] It is also possible that if one does not get along with a coworker, perhaps due to serious personality conflict, it might be possible to simply avoid situations where one has to work closely with this person.

Obviously, avoidance is never likely to be an optimal or long-term solution to any work-related stressor. Furthermore, there may be some cases where avoidance simply cannot be used or where it isn't feasible. However, in some unique situations where a stressor is largely unchangeable, avoidance may be used at least temporarily until more effective long-term solutions can be found.

Now that we have discussed these four different forms of coping, it is important for readers to apply them to their own work situations. Table 4-2 contains sample items for each of the four coping methods that were discussed—this provides a little better feel for what each method of coping would specifically entail. After looking over these items, take a moment to complete Application Exercise 4.1. This requires you to list possible coping responses, and based on the nature of the demand, to determine which of these would be most effective.

Table 4-2. A Coping Strategy Checklist

One of the most comprehensive measures of coping available to researchers today is the COPE, which was developed by Michael Scheier and George Carver. This measure has been used in numerous studies that have investigated how people adapt to a variety of work and non-work demands.

Although the COPE contains items that represent 15 different forms of coping, there are four scales that correspond very closely to the forms of coping that were discussed in the chapter: problem-focused coping, emotion-focused coping, active coping, avoidance coping. Items representing each of these are listed below. Each of these items represents a possible response when one is faced with a demand at work.

Problem-Focused Coping

1. I make a plan of action.
2. I try to come up with a plan of action.
3. I think about how I might best handle the problem.
4. I think hard about what steps to take.

Emotion-Focused Coping

1. I get upset and let my emotions out.
2. I get upset and am really aware of it.
3. I let my feelings out.
4. I feel a lot of emotional distress and find myself expressing those feelings a lot.

Active Coping

1. I concentrate my efforts on doing something about it.
2. I take additional action to try to get rid of the problem.
3. I take direct action to get around the problem.
4. I do what has to be done, one step at a time.

Avoidance Coping

1. I say to myself "this isn't real."
2. I refuse to believe that it has happened.
3. I pretend that it hasn't really happened.
4. I act as though it hasn't even happened.

Source: Carver, Scheier, & Weintraub (1989).[34]

CAN RESILIENCE BE TRAINED?

At this point, readers hopefully have a clearer picture of what is meant by resilience, as well as the major predictors of this important attribute. Given all of this information, a logical question readers might now be asking is, "Can this information be used to train people to be more resilient, and therefore deal more effectively with stressors?" Given the vast number of stressors that people experience in their daily lives, many of which are uncontrollable, it would certainly be useful if we could train people to be more resilient.

Unfortunately, there has not been a great deal of research addressing the trainability of resilience, although there have been some notable exceptions. Salvatore Maddi and his colleagues have developed a training program designed to increase individuals' level of hardiness, with the ultimate goal of enhancing resilience. At the core of the training program is an emphasis on "transformational" or hardy coping, which the authors described as the following: "one can decrease the stressfulness of circumstances through cognitively and emotionally exploring one's appraisals of them so as to reach broader perspective and deeper understanding and using the information gained in this way to develop and carry out decisive, problem-solving action plans."[12] In other words, individuals exposed to stressful conditions can change how they are affected by these conditions by understanding the meaningful context in which these demands are occurring. An individual's ability to engage in transformational coping is presumably a function of his or her hardiness levels. Remember in Chapter 3 that we highlighted the importance of developing more adaptive appraisals of the stressors one experiences.

The program focuses on the development of transformational or hardy coping through first having employees describe the stressful conditions they are facing, and then learning skills for addressing these conditions. The three skills highlighted for development are *situational reconstruction* (being able to place a stressful situation into a broader context to better understand the situation), *focusing* (being aware of information from the body to gain emotional insight), and *compensatory self-improvement* (being able to accept situations that cannot be changed and focusing on improvement in areas that can be changed). These skills are reinforced in three stages: employees develop action plans for altering the stressful circumstances they are facing; they receive feedback following their implementation of the plans; and they plan how they will use these skills in future situations.

The training program has evolved over the years into a multi-component program referred to as HardiTraining.[31] The training is conducted in a group format, and is structured according to five major areas: hardy coping, hardy social support, hardy relaxation, hardy eating, and hardy physical training. *Hardy coping* has already been described. *Hardy support* involves employees examining how they interact with important others, and learning how to resolve conflicts and to give and receive social support. The final three areas are collapsed under "self-care," where employees learn how to control their arousal so it is at an optimal level for performance. Employees also learn the importance of relaxation techniques, proper nutrition, and exercise for maintaining arousal at a level that will enable them to effectively cope with stressful work demands. Research suggests that the HardiTraining program is effective at increasing levels of hardiness and reducing the negative outcomes of workplace demands.

Application Exercise 4.1

COPING WITH YOUR PRIMARY WORK DEMANDS

As discussed in this chapter, the most effective means of coping with work-related demands tend to be *problem-focused* or *active* coping methods. However, there are instances where *emotion-focused* or *avoidance* coping strategies can also be effective. These methods of coping tend to be more effective when employees lack control over the demands they are facing. For example, if one of your work demands was conflict among coworkers, although you may try a problem-focused coping strategy of confronting the coworkers causing the conflict, a better option may be to avoid the coworkers (as much as possible) who are causing the conflict.

Think back to the top three demands you generated in Application Exercise 1.1 in Chapter 1. For each of those three demands, we want you to consider a problem-focused or active way you could cope with the demand, and an emotion-focused or avoidance way of coping. After generating these coping strategies, think about which ones will be the most effective at dealing with the demands you are facing, and try them out.

Demand #1: _____

Problem-Focused/Active Coping Strategy: _____

_____

Emotion-Focused/Avoidance Coping Strategy: _____

_____

Demand #2: _____

Problem-Focused/Active Coping Strategy: _____

_____

Emotion-Focused/Avoidance Coping Strategy: _____

_____

Demand #3: _____

Problem-Focused/Active Coping Strategy: _____

_____

Emotion-Focused/Avoidance Coping Strategy: _____

_____

_____

There has also been an effort to develop training interventions to enhance the previously discussed trait of psychological capital (PsyCap). Specifically, Fred Luthans and his colleagues have argued that the components of PsyCap are "state-like" enough to be altered through training programs, and have developed training programs to alter PsyCap. Luthans and colleagues[32] developed an online training program to increase the four components of PsyCap (optimism, self-efficacy, resilience, and hope). The program consisted of two 45-minute online sessions separated by one week.

In the first session, the online facilitator provided information on the capacities of resilience and self-efficacy, and illustrated how the two positive states were relevant to job performance in general and the employee's specific job. The online presentation included video files of popular movie clips to show examples of the two positive states. Individuals were then encouraged to consider work situations where they were "stuck" or "in a bind" regarding their ability to be resilient or efficacious, and were directed to think about what factors in those situations they could control and what actions they could take to deal with the situation. Individuals then engaged in written "self-reflection exercises" in which they thought about their past thoughts, behaviors, and emotions in different work situations, and how what they learned in the session could facilitate their performance in future situations.

In the second online session, employees learned about the importance of hope and optimism. An emphasis was placed on the importance of the employee's personal values and goals, and how to set realistic but challenging goals. The facilitator emphasized the importance of setting goals that are both challenging and personally valuable, and provided examples of these types of goals (these examples were not provided in the article reviewed). Employees were instructed to write down challenging and valuable goals, and then to chose one goal to focus on for the remainder of the training session. The chosen goal was then broken into sub-goals to increase perceptions that the challenging goal was in fact attainable. The employees also focused on the positive outcomes that would result from attaining the goal, the multiple ways they would achieve the goal, and how to overcome obstacles to obtaining the goal. All of these activities were designed to increase hope, optimism, and self-efficacy.

In addition, Luthans and colleagues[33] also developed an in-person, group-based PsyCap intervention modeled after the online program. The authors also go into more detail about the skills targeted for each of the four positive states being developed. The skills designed to increase hope include recognizing the multiple paths that can be used to achieve a given goal, and thinking ahead about how to handle obstacles that may arise. The skills designed to increase realistic optimism include increasing one's confidence in being able to achieve meaningful goals, and envisioning the positive outcomes that result from goal attainment. The skills designed to increase self-efficacy include the individual thinking about prior successes, witnessing how other individuals in the group have succeeded in overcoming their obstacles, and experiencing support from others in the group regarding the employee's ability to attain the goal. Finally, the skills for increasing resilience include making the employees aware of the resources they have to accomplish desired goals (personal and social), and getting them to realize how their initial thoughts of confidence or anxiety about attaining valued goals can affect their resilience in the face of obstacles.

The obvious difference between the online and in-person PsyCap training programs is the added influence of other group members on how the employee approaches the various exercises designed to increase the four positive states. Fellow group members provide feedback on ways the employee can achieve goals and overcome obstacles, as well as allowing the employee to see how others plan to achieve goals and overcome obstacles. In addition, Luthans and colleagues[32] indicate that in the in-person training, the first stage is devoted to exercises to increase each dimension of PsyCap, and the second stage is devoted to exercises that illustrate how the four dimensions of PsyCap are all integrated.

Although the authors do not describe the specific integration exercises that are employed, it is relatively apparent how the four positive states are interrelated to one another. For example, increased hope, self-efficacy, and optimism likely increase the employee's perceived resilience to bounce back from adversity when attempting to obtain challenging and valuable goals, and generating multiple paths to achieve goals (hope) will generate higher levels of self-efficacy and optimism that goal attainment is likely.

Luthans and his colleagues have shown that PsyCap training is capable of producing an increase in the four positive attributes of resilience, self-efficacy, hope, and optimism, and can also increase the employee's level of performance.[32,33]

SUMMARY

The purpose of this chapter was to describe the various individual components of the broader construct of *resilience*. As described in the beginning of the chapter, resilience is simply the ability to not show negative outcomes in the face of workplace demands. Although there is no definitive profile of the resilient person, research has shown that a number of variables tend to predict resilience, and these can be broken down into three general areas: (1) social support, (2) personality, and (3) coping.

Generally speaking, highly resilient people have high levels of social support in their lives—this may come from family, but in many cases comes from friends and coworkers. In terms of personality, highly resilient people generally tend to be high on the personality dimensions of hardiness, dispositional optimism, proactive personality, and internal locus of control. Finally, it has been shown that high resilience can also be distinguished on the basis of one's choice of coping behavior. Coping that is active and this is focused on decreasing the stressors is generally associated with higher levels of resilience compared to avoidance and a focus only on decreasing strain. It should be remembered, though, that there is sometimes a role for avoidance and emotion-focused coping; the key is to recognize when they are and when they are not appropriate.

Although there is not a great deal of research on training people to be more resilient, there is some evidence that some components of resilience may be amenable to training interventions. In general, there is evidence that people may be able to be trained to *appraise* the environment in more adaptive ways and to perhaps understand how to attract social support from others. It is less likely, however, that more fundamental aspects of one's personality that are associated with resilience can be changed through interventions.

REFERENCES

1. Jex, S. M., Kain, J., & Park, Y. (2013). Situational factors and resilience: Social support, organizational Issues. In R. R. Sinclair & T. W. Britt (Eds.), *Building Psychological Resilience in Military Personnel: Theory and Practice*. Washington, DC: American Psychological Association.
2. Beehr, T. A. (1995). *Psychological Stress in the Workplace*. London: Routledge.
3. Alexander, K. N. (2012). Abusive supervision as a predictor of deviance and health outcomes: The exacerbating role of narcissism and social support. Unpublished doctoral dissertation, Bowling Green State University, Bowling Green, OH.
4. Johnson, H., & Thompson, A. (2008). The development and maintenance of post-traumatic stress disorder (PTSD) in civilian adult survivors of war trauma and torture: A review. *Clinical Psychology Review, 28*, 36–47.
5. Sherbourne, C. D., & Stewart, A. L. (1991). The MOS social support survey. *Social Science and Medicine, 32*, 705–714.
6. Caplan, G. (1974). *Support Systems and Community Mental Health*. New York: Behavioral Publications.
7. Murray, H. A. (1938). *Explorations in Personality*. New York: Oxford University Press.
8. Staw, B. M., Bell, N. E., & Clausen, J. A. (1986). The dispositional approach to job attitudes: A lifetime longitudinal test. *Administrative Science Quarterly, 31*, 56–77.

9. Smith, M. L., & Glass, G. V. (1977). Meta-analysis of psychotherapy outcome studies. *American Psychologist, 32*, 752–760.

10. Tedeschi, R. G., & Calhoun, L. G. (1996). The Posttraumatic Growth Inventory: Measuring the positive legacy of trauma. *Journal of Traumatic Stress, 9*, 455–471.

11. Bartone, P. T. (1999). Hardiness protects against war-related stress in army reserve forces. *Consulting Psychology Journal, 51*, 72–82.

12. Maddi, S. R. (2002). The story of hardiness: Twenty years of theorizing, research, and practice. *Consulting Psychology Journal, 54*, 175–185.

13. Luthans, F., Youssef, C. M., & Avolio, B. J. (2007). *Psychological Capital: Developing the Human Competitive Edge*. Oxford: Oxford University Press.

14. Avey, J. B., Luthans, F., & Jensen, S. M. (2009). Psychological capital: A positive resource for combating employee stress and turnover. *Human Resource Management, 48*(5), 677–693.

15. Avey, J. B., Luthans, F., & Youssef, C. M. (2010). The additive value of positive psychological capital in predicting work attitudes and behaviors. *Journal of Management, 36*(2), 430–452.

16. Scheier, M. F., & Carver, G. S. (1985). Optimism, coping, and health: Assessment and implications of generalized outcome expectancies. *Health Psychology, 4*, 219–247.

17. Tennen, H., & Affleck, H. (1987). The costs and benefits of optimistic explanations and dispositional optimism. *Journal of Personality, 55*, 377–392.

18. Seligman, M. E. (1991). *Learned Optimism: How to Change Your Mind and Your Life*. New York: Knopf.

19. Fay, D., & Frese, M. (2001). The concept of personal initiative (PI): An overview of validity studies. *Human Performance, 14*, 97–124.

20. Crant, J. M. (1995). The proactive personality scale and objective job performance among real estate agents. *Journal of Applied Psychology, 80*, 532–537.

21. Cunningham, C. L. J., & De La Rose, G. M. (2008). The interactive effects of proactive personality and work-family interference on well-being. *Journal of Occupational Health Psychology, 13*, 271–282.

22. Rotter, J. B. (1966). Generalized expectancies for internal versus external control of reinforcement. *Psychological Monographs: General and Applied, 80* (1, Whole No. 609).

23. Spector, P. E. (1982). Behavior in organizations as a function of an employee's locus of control. *Psychological Bulletin, 91*, 482–497.

24. Storms, P. L., & Spector, P. E. (1987). Relationships of organizational frustration and reported behavioral reactions: The moderating effect of locus of control. *Journal of Occupational Psychology, 60*, 227–234.

25. Sprung, J. M., & Jex, S. M. (2012). Work locus of control as a moderator of the relationship between work stressors and counterproductive work behaviors. *International Journal of Stress Management, 19*, 272–291.

26. Latack, J. C., & Havlovic, S. J. (1992). Coping with job stress: A conceptual evaluation framework for coping measures. *Journal of Organizational Behavior, 13*, 479–508.

27. Lazarus, R. S., & Folkman, S. (1984). *Stress, Appraisal, and Coping.* New York: Springer.

28. Keoske, G. F., Kirk, G. F., & Keoske, R. D. (1993). Coping with job stress: Which strategies work best? *Journal of Occupational and Organizational Psychology, 66,* 319–335.

29. De Rijk, A. E., Le Blanc, P. M., Schaufeli, W. B., & de Jonge, J. (1998). Active coping and need for control as moderators of the job demand-control model: Effects on burnout. *Journal of Occupational and Organizational Psychology, 71,* 1–18.

30. Beehr, T. A., Johnson, E. B., & Nieva, R. (1995). Occupational stress: Coping of police and their spouses. *Journal of Organizational Behavior, 16,* 3–25.

31. Khoshaba, D. M., & Maddi, S. R. (2001). *HardiTraining.* Irvine, CA: Hardiness Institute.

32. Luthans, F., Avey, J. B., & Patera, J. L. (2008). Experimental analysis of a Web-based intervention to develop positive psychological capital. *Academy of Management Learning and Education, 7,* 209–221.

33. Luthans, F., Avey, J. B., Avolio, B. J., & Peterson, S. J. (2010). The development and resulting performance impact of positive psychological capital. *Human Resource Development Quarterly, 21,* 41–67.

34. Carver, C. S., Scheier, M. F., & Weintraub, J. K. (1989). Assessing coping strategies: A theoretically based approach. *Journal of Personality and Social Psychology, 56,* 267–283.

35. Snyder, C. R., Harris, C., & Anderson, J. R. (1991). The will and the ways: Development and validation of an individual-differences measure of hope. *Journal of Personality and Social Psychology, 60,* 570–585.

36. Smith, B. W., Dalen, J., Wiggins, K., Tooley, E., Christopher, P., & Bernard, J. (2008). The brief resilience scale: Assessing the ability to bounce back. International *Journal of Behavioral Medicine, 15,* 194–200.

37. Scheier, M. F., & Carver, C. S. (1985). Optimism, coping and health: Assessment and implications of generalized outcome expectancies. *Health Psychology, 4,* 219–247.

38. Chen, G., Gully, S. M., & Eden, D. (2001). Validation of a new general self-efficacy scale. *Organizational Research Methods, 4,* 62–83.

5

Beyond Coping

Thriving under Work Demands

INTRODUCTION

One theme running throughout the book is that the consequences of dealing with stressors at work are not always negative, and that the complete lack of stress may not be a desirable state for the employee. In the previous chapters, we have focused on what enables employees to reduce the negative effects that can result from stress at work. In this chapter, we move to a discussion of how employees may be able to thrive under demanding work conditions. In addition, we emphasize how proactively approaching the tasks you do at work and the demands and opportunities that are available to you may create the conditions for being engaged and thriving under difficult circumstances.

An important point to note in this chapter is that what allows employees to thrive under stressful work is not simply the opposite of what prevents negative outcomes in the face of stress. As mentioned in the Introduction to the book, researchers have spent much more time focusing on the negative outcomes of a demanding work environment than on the ways in which employees may be able to harness demands in order to thrive and develop. You will notice that the number of citations to research related to thriving and other positive responses to stress in the next two chapters are dramatically fewer than the number in the chapters addressing the negative effects of stress. The disparity in research attention devoted to the negative and to adaptive responses to demanding work conditions was one of the primary motivators for us to write this book.

This chapter also provides a detailed account of those factors in the work environment that contribute to an employee thriving. One important factor is employees understanding the importance of what they are doing, and how one's job benefits the organization and others. Being able to see how your work benefits others provides the motivation necessary to excel under stressful conditions, and provides a sense of meaning when you are at work. Reminding oneself of this contribution will contribute to enhanced motivation during stressful conditions, and will help provide a different lens for viewing the demands that you face.

A second important factor in thriving at work is doing what you can to create conditions at work that allow you to use your skills, abilities, and interests in the most effective way. Too often employees are treated as passive recipients of their work environments, and recent research has shown that employees may have the ability to construct their work environment (and certainly how they respond to their work environment) to a greater extent than previously thought. Although there are certainly occasions when the demands facing employees are beyond their control, we will discuss how, even in low-control jobs, employees may be able to "craft" their jobs in small ways to create greater meaning and to change how they view their demands.

A final important factor in thriving at work involves recognizing the importance of other people in your work environment. Employees are most likely to thrive at work when they interact with coworkers in a supportive, productive way, helping one another to achieve higher levels of performance. Relatedness, or interacting with others in a meaningful way, is a primary human need,[1] and employees who thrive ultimately satisfy this need in part through their work relationships.

In this chapter, we first address the experience of thriving at work and why thriving matters for employees' well-being and performance. We then discuss the different predictors of thriving at work, and what employees and managers can do to create the conditions necessary for thriving. We conclude the chapter with a discussion of why thriving at work is especially important when employees are experiencing high levels of work demands, and how job demands may actually contribute to the experience of thriving.

THE EXPERIENCE OF THRIVING AT WORK

So far, we have emphasized how we want employees to not only tolerate the demands they face at work, but also to channel these demands so that they can even thrive under difficult conditions. Recall our definition of thriving in Chapter 1: the employee approaches work with vigor and a high level of personal engagement in job performance. Most of us have an intuitive sense of what thriving means, but providing a precise description of the experience is a bit more difficult. Researchers themselves have had a tough time pinning down what it means to thrive at work, coming up with many variables that all appear to address the experience of thriving. These experiences include being personally engaged on the job, being highly involved in work, experiencing feelings of vitality and vigor at work, feeling immersed in tasks at work so that one experiences a sense of "flow," and the perception of growing or flourishing at work.

Although small differences exist between the meanings of these different experiences, we would argue that all of them capture a sense of what it feels like to thrive at work. Employees who thrive at work are personally engaged in what they are doing, care about the results of their job performance, believe they are growing and developing, and have feelings of vitality and vigor when doing their work. In Table 5-1, we include a sampling of items that researchers have used to assess whether employees are showing thriving-related experiences at work. Think about how you might respond to these types of items regarding how you typically feel at work. Clearly, higher scores on these types of items are associated with a greater degree of thriving at work, whereas lower scores indicate a failure to experience thriving.

Before we go into detail about the experience and outcomes of thriving at work, we want you to complete Application Exercise 5.1: This exercise encourages you to recall a time in the recent past when you really enjoyed your job and had a sense that you were thriving at work. We suspect that no matter

Table 5-1. SAMPLE ITEMS USED BY RESEARCHERS TO ASSESS THE EXPERIENCES ASSOCIATED WITH THRIVING AT WORK

The following items are typically measured on scales where employees are asked to indicate how often they feel the experiences at work. Responses are usually made on a 5-point scale anchored by 1 = "never" to 5 = "all of the time."

SAMPLE ITEMS ASSESSING PERSONAL ENGAGEMENT IN WORK[33,34]

1. My job inspires me.
2. I am immersed in my work.
3. I get carried away when I am working.
4. I invest a large part of myself into my job performance

SAMPLE ITEMS ASSESSING VIGOR AND VITALITY AT WORK[3,35]

1. I feel energetic.
2. I feel I can think rapidly.
3. I feel able to show warmth to others.
4. I feel alive and vital.
5. I am looking forward to each new day.

SAMPLE ITEMS ASSESSING GROWING AND DEVELOPING AT WORK[35]

1. I find myself learning often.
2. I continue to learn more as time goes by.
3. I see myself continually improving.
4. I am developing a lot as a person.

Application Exercise 5.1

THRIVING AT WORK

Common experiences of thriving at work include feeling energized, having a sense that you are developing as an employee, approaching work tasks with a sense of enthusiasm and vitality, and feeling like you are personally engaged in what you are doing. Think back to the most recent time at work when you felt you had these types of thriving-related experiences.

Part A. First, describe what you were doing at that time and how what you were doing made you feel like you were thriving:

_____

_____

_____

_____

_____

_____

Part B. Second, what factors in your work environment contributed to you feeling like you were thriving at this particular time? Was it the nature of the work you were doing, the particular mood you were in, the influence of the people around you, or some combination of these factors?

_____

_____

_____

_____

_____

_____

Throughout this chapter, we are going to be discussing those factors that contribute to employees thriving in their jobs. You should see these factors operating in your own experiencing of thriving at work. Furthermore, you can sustain an experience of thriving for longer by practicing the strategies highlighted in this chapter.

what your particular job, the experiences you had of thriving likely involved feelings of vigor, a sense that you were highly engaged in the tasks at hand, and perhaps the belief that what you were doing was clearly in line with your interests and abilities. In short, you probably experienced many of the feelings presented in Table 5-1. We will return to the section of the Application Exercise on what contributed to your experience of thriving a little later in the chapter.

WHY THRIVING MATTERS FOR WELL-BEING AND PERFORMANCE

In addition to thriving-related experiences being enjoyable in their own right, they also contribute to bottom line indicators of performance desired by the organization. We now take a look at these feelings and experiences in more detail, and illustrate how they are important for employee well-being and performance. We first address the experience of vitality and vigor at work, followed by the sense that you are developing to your full potential at work, and conclude with the importance of personal engagement in your job performance.

A number of psychologists have highlighted the importance of experiencing vitality for psychological and physical health, referring to the concept with terms such as *vitality, vigor, positive energy*, and *morale* to describe the experience of being energized at work. Richard Ryan and Christina Frederick originally defined subjective vitality as "one's conscious experience of possessing energy and aliveness" (p. 530), and provided evidence that a high level of subjective vitality was associated with a host of positive outcomes.[2] Arie Shirom has also highlighted the importance of vigor at work, which he argues is a type of "positive energy" that combines feelings of enthusiasm and positivity.[3] Shirom argued that vigor at work is composed of three key dimensions: physical strength (feeling physically capable and strong), emotional energy (being able to give emotionally to others at work), and cognitive liveliness (feeling a sense of mental energy to be creative and generate novel ideas at work). We have all encountered fellow employees who seem to have a great attitude and an endless supply of energy for taking on the task at hand. Perhaps you have even felt this way at work, when you felt enthusiastic about what you were doing and had plenty of energy for getting the job done. Not surprisingly, a large amount of research supports the benefits of vitality-related experiences for employee well-being and performance.[2,3]

One of the major reasons that vitality is related to higher levels of well-being and performance at work is because having high levels of energy provides employees with the resources they need to get things done and to get them done well. The more energy you have, the more tasks you can accomplish during a given period of time (we go into additional detail on the importance of energy in Chapter 7). A second reason that vitality is associated with beneficial outcomes for employees is that the experience of aliveness and energy is a type of positive emotion, and positive emotions have been shown to give employees the mindset necessary to find multiple solutions for work-related problems.[4] Most of us can recall a time when we were trying to solve a tough problem at work, and how difficult it was when our energy levels were low. In contrast, when our feelings of vitality are high, our entire view of the problem can change, leading to a greater likelihood of finding creative solutions to the problem.

In addition to the experience of vitality, Gretchen Spreitzer and her colleagues emphasize that a sense of learning and development is necessary in order for the experience of thriving to occur.[5] We can all probably recall times when we felt we were "stuck in a rut" at work, and had the sense that we were not going anywhere. Employees want to believe that they are developing the skills they need to progress in their jobs, whether this progression involves getting better at the key tasks they perform, or developing new skills that will result in being promoted either within or outside the organization. Doing the same tasks over and over without a sense of increased proficiency or development may not be stressful, but it certainly will not result in an experience of thriving at work. On the other hand, employees who get feedback that their performance is improving and have the sense that they are learning new skills that will contribute to their future development will experience the perception that they are learning, which will contribute to a sense of thriving.

Research has also supported the motivational and performance benefits of employees believing that they are learning and developing. Carol Dweck conducted groundbreaking research on the importance of how individuals approached learning in their environments, and found that individuals who approached new tasks as an opportunity to learn and develop new skills adapted best to experiences of both success and failure.[6] The concept of an employee's "goal orientation" has been adapted to the workplace. Employees who have more of a learning or mastery orientation to work (where they are focused on viewing challenging work conditions as opportunities to learn new skills or ways of handling work tasks) do a better job at creating challenging work experiences and perform better.[7] These employees view challenging work experiences as opportunities to develop new skills, and are not especially bothered by failure. Instead, these employees use failure as feedback to better prepare for future experiences.

In contrast, employees who have a *performance* orientation to work are concerned more narrowly with how their performance is evaluated by themselves and others. These individuals are worried more about demonstrating their competence than with learning new skills and exploring new strategies at work that may not succeed. Although having a performance orientation to work can be associated with higher levels of performance, employees with this orientation tend not to respond well to failure or setbacks at work, viewing such experiences as assaults on their competence rather than opportunities to succeed.

The final experience that we examine as an indicator of thriving at work is a sense of personal engagement with job performance. "Employee engagement" has become a buzzword in recent years, with many researchers and practitioners coming up with their own definitions and assessments of engagement. However, certain core features of job engagement that are common to most of these definitions include employees investing themselves in their job, which results in expending physical, emotional, and mental resources to performing well at work.[8] An extreme form of job engagement is "flow." As discussed in the Introduction to the book, flow occurs when employees become so absorbed in work they have little attention left over for thinking about anything else.[9] When experiencing flow at work, employees may notice that time passes quickly and there is enjoyment in the work activities themselves, in addition to the rewards that might result from doing well. The concept of flow also highlights that job engagement may fluctuate within the same employee over time, and therefore it is important to understand not only why some employees report higher levels of job engagement than others, but also what causes an employee's level of engagement to vary over time.[10]

Supporting the value of job engagement for important employee outcomes, researchers have found that employees who experience higher levels of job engagement show higher levels of effort, persistence, and performance. In addition, the average job engagement of the employees in a company is predictive of the company's bottom line in terms of customer satisfaction, productivity, profitability, and reduced employee turnover.[11] Job engagement has also been linked to higher levels of well-being and lower levels of physical health symptoms among employees in multiple studies.[12,13] Finally, job engagement can be especially helpful for employees when stressors at work are at a high level, illustrating the importance of engagement in allowing individuals to thrive under difficult work conditions.[12]

WHAT CONTRIBUTES TO THRIVING IN THE WORKPLACE?

Given the importance of thriving at work for well-being and performance, researchers have been active in better understanding aspects of the employee and factors in the work environment that contribute to an employee thriving in the workplace. Before addressing these factors, take a look at your responses to

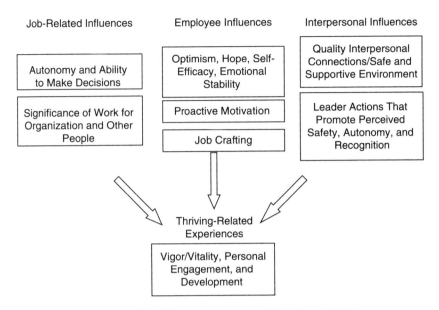

Figure 5.1 An Overall Model of the Determinants of Thriving at Work.

Part B of Application Exercise 5.1 you completed earlier. This exercise encouraged you to think about the factors that were present in your work environment (and in yourself) the last time you felt like you were thriving at work. These factors should come up as we discuss the determinants of thriving in the workplace.

A number of different models have been developed to highlight those factors residing in the work environment and within the employee that are predictive of thriving-related experiences.[3,5,27,30] We combined these different models into an overall model of the determinants of thriving in Figure 5.1. In the following paragraphs, we describe the components of this model. As we discuss this model, it is important to distinguish those factors that are under some control by the employee from those factors that leaders within the organization have a responsibility to help strengthen.

Job-Related Influences on Thriving at Work

We first start with the job-related influences on an employee's ability to thrive at work, and highlight two primary factors: employees perceiving that they have autonomy over their job performance, and understanding the impact their work has for the organization and other people. Employees are much more likely to thrive at work when they have a sense that they control how they do their job, rather than being micromanaged by supervisors. A large amount of research has been conducted on the benefits of individuals engaging in activities based on autonomous motivation, where the source of the behavior stems from the person rather than the environment.[14] In contrast, controlled motivation occurs when individuals perform tasks as a result of external pressure, in which case the motivation for the activity is "pulled" by someone else, rather than coming from the individual. Studies have shown that persistence on tasks and ultimately task performance is greater when individuals are approaching the task in an autonomous manner.[14]

Gretchen Spreitzer and her colleagues argue that when employees feel a sense of autonomy and control over their work environment, they are more likely to engage in "agentic" work behaviors (e.g., trying out new ways of doing their job, re-prioritizing their activities based upon a better plan), which basically means that people feel in control over what they are doing, and also feel the freedom to branch out and explore new ways to do their job better.[15] The authors argue that the perception of autonomy allows employees to concentrate on what they are doing at work without having to worry about being micromanaged or having their attention waiver because of frequent interruptions. In addition, the freedom that comes from autonomy allows employees to explore new ways of doing things and feeling safe that if these new strategies do not work out, there will not be immediate punishments or derogation by leaders.

Employees who perform these types of agentic behaviors should experience increased thriving that will have positive implications for their own health and development. Paul Spector has noted how the perception of control over one's job has positive effects on the employee's physical health and well-being.[16] Furthermore, the rewarding experience of thriving will reinforce engaging in the agentic behaviors in the first place, creating a cycle that will increase thriving over time.[15] Of course, if the work environment changes (employees are given less choice in how they do their work, fail to get necessary information, or feel they cannot trust key leaders), employees may lose task focus, become risk-averse in exploring novel strategies, or lose sight of how their work relates to others. The drop in these agentic behaviors should be associated with a decrease in the experience of thriving.

In addition to the importance of autonomy, another major job-related influence on thriving is the significance of one's job in contributing to the mission of the organization as well as to people outside the organization. Employees are more likely to thrive when they believe in the importance of what they are doing. The importance of one's work in an organization has been defined in multiple ways, including the employee feeling like what he or she is doing is making a contribution to the organization's objectives, is benefiting fellow employees or even one's own development, and that one's work is having an impact on beneficiaries (such as teachers having an impact on the development of students).[17]

Adam Grant and his colleagues have conducted a number of studies examining the different ways in which job importance can influence employee motivation and performance, with the underlying point being that involvement in work that benefits other people contributes to the meaning that employees assign to their job. When employees experience a sense of meaning at work, they are more likely to thrive under difficult working conditions.

Consider a study conducted by Grant and his colleagues examining the effects of reminding employees of the impact they are having on beneficiaries of their work.[18] As one might imagine, being a call center employee whose job is to cold call university alumni to raise money for scholarships can be a stressful job, filled with rejection. Callers who try to raise funds are frequently met with flat-out refusals and at times outright hostility. The authors decided to remind callers of the beneficiaries of their efforts: students who received scholarships allowing them to attend college. Grant and his colleagues randomly assigned one group of callers to interact with a scholarship recipient who told them about what the scholarship had done for him, a second group of callers received a letter from a scholarship recipient, and a third group did their job as usual.

These researchers found that the callers who met face-to-face with the beneficiary increased the amount of time they spent on the phone with prospective donors by 142% compared to before the study began, and raised 171% more money! In contrast, those callers who received the letter from the scholarship recipient or did their work "as usual" did not increase their time on the phone or the amount of money raised. These results showed clearly that making employees aware of the important effects their work was having increased both motivation and performance under what can be stressful working conditions. We believe that the employees in Grant's study who saw the impact their work was having on beneficiaries experienced greater meaning in the work they were doing, which increased both motivation and performance.

Grant has discussed how realizing the impact of one's job on others can sustain motivation, well-being, and performance in such stressful occupations as firefighters and inner-city attorneys.[17] A few years ago, the first author of the book and a colleague conducted a study with intelligence professionals working for the US government.[19] Although these individuals encountered numerous stressors in their attempt to sift through large quantities of information to detect potential threats to the United States, the employees also viewed their work as highly significant and meaningful, given the implications of their efforts for protecting national security. We found that endorsement of these positive work experiences was associated with less of a perceived impact of work-related stressors on performance. Although employees in these types of jobs endure numerous (and dangerous) occupational stressors, the positive impact they are having on members of the community and the community itself provides them with the meaning needed in order to work under these difficult conditions.

Many readers may be involved in jobs where the significance of what they are doing is not clear, either in terms of the impact their work has on the organization or on individuals outside the organization. A common critique of "positive" approaches to stressful work is that only individuals involved in highly engaging and stimulating occupations can really focus on the importance of what they are doing when dealing with various stressors. However, Blake Ashforth and his colleagues have highlighted the importance of focusing on task significance even in what has been termed "dirty work," defined as occupations that are "tainted" or stigmatized by society.[20]

These authors examined how managers dealt with stressors related to stigmatization in occupations such as animal control officers, morticians, probation officers, and exotic entertainers. One of the most recommended strategies by managers for dealing with the negative consequences of the stigma associated with these occupations was to counteract the negative views assigned to the job by highlighting the positive value (and therefore meaning) associated with the job. For example, animal control officers could focus on protecting the public or preventing unnecessary suffering by stray animals, morticians could highlight the importance of providing families of the deceased with a dignified burial, probation officers can highlight the importance of their work for law and order, and exotic entertainers may focus on the quality of their performance from a dancing perspective. Although research has not been conducted examining whether employees in these occupations who try to focus on the significance of what they are doing function better in their work, we expect that such employees would assign greater meaning to their work, and would therefore be more likely to thrive rather than falter under stressful conditions.

Having discussed the different ways that employees can focus on the importance and significance of what they are doing, we would like you to consider the significance and positive impact of your own work. In order to do that, please complete Application Exercise 5.2, which is designed to facilitate a reflection of how your work positively influences your organization and other people, both immediately and further down the road. One of the ways you can experience greater vitality and personal engagement in your own job is to remind yourself of the impact you are having.

Application Exercise 5.2

THE SIGNIFICANCE AND IMPACT OF YOUR JOB

In order to thrive at work, employees need to understand the significance of what they are doing for themselves, the organization, and other people. Take a minute and describe why your job is important for each of these three areas.

A. Describe why your job is important to you. Possibilities may include providing money for you and/or your family to live, the ability to do something you are good at, or allowing you to develop new skills for a future job.

_____

_____

_____

_____

B. Think about how your job contributes to the overall mission of your organization. Describe how what you do matters for the organization.

_____

_____

_____

_____

C. Think about how your job benefits other people. These other people may be coworkers, immediate customers, or people who may use a product you are involved in developing. Describe the different ways what you do at work may benefit others.

_____

_____

_____

_____

In addition to employees doing what they can to approach their work with a sense of autonomy and to consider the significance of their job when working, managers within the organization also play a critical role in providing employees with control over how they do their work and recognizing employees for the significant contributions they make to the organization. The importance of managers creating the job-related influences on thriving is highlighted in *What This Means for Managers 5.1.*

What This Means for Managers 5.1

HELPING EMPLOYEES THRIVE

Managers who are able to create the conditions necessary for employees to thrive at work will not only aid employees responding positively under stress, but also create units that perform better. Managers possess the authority to facilitate the key factors involved in thriving at work, including giving employees autonomy over their work and helping employees see the impact they are having on their organization and the broader community. A key leadership skill is the ability to instill in the employee a belief in the importance and magnitude of what he or she is doing. These characteristics of effective leadership are critical to helping employees being able to thrive at work.

Specific suggestions for managers include:

- Experiment with giving your employees more freedom in how they carry out their primary job tasks. If they get their job done, it should not matter exactly how they do it. Try not to micromanage how they do their work. For example, if you currently require your employees to report their progress to you daily, consider having them report to you less frequently, but be sure they know you expect them to get more done between meetings.
- This may sound obvious, but let employees know when they have done a good job. Prior studies have shown that employees respond well to simple praise, even without bonuses. Don't assume that employees will think that no feedback means they are doing their job well. Just telling employees "good job" from time to time can sustain their motivation.
- Consider creative ways you can highlight the positive impact that employees are having on the organization and people outside the organization. One effective way would be to bring in a beneficiary of the employees' efforts to give a testimonial regarding how their work has been helpful. Another way would be to make sure each employee understands his or her contribution to the key successes of the organization.

Employee Influences on Thriving-Related Experiences

In addition to the work environment and the nature of the individual's job, another set of predictors of thriving-related experiences involves characteristics of the employee. As seen in the middle column of Figure 5.1, it probably does not come as a surprise that many of the factors that allow employees to respond better to stressful work conditions also contribute to an employee's ability to thrive at work. As discussed in Chapter 4, researchers have argued that an employee's psychological capital can be assessed by examining the employee's levels of optimism, hope, self-efficacy, and emotional stability.[21] Employees who score higher on these dimensions are more likely to report thriving-related experiences at work, including feelings of vigor and vitality. Importantly, we also discussed in Chapter 4 that these positive attributes are not set in stone, but can be developed in employees. We would argue that organizations should be motivated to enhance psychological capital in their employees, both to help employees better deal with stress, and to help create employees who are more likely to thrive at work.

A second quality of employees critical for thriving is proactive motivation at work. Sharon Parker and her colleagues have defined proactive motivation as "taking control to make things happen rather than watching things happen" (p. 828).[22] These authors point out that proactive motivation leads individuals to set goals for changing either the work environment or themselves in order to better adapt to changing circumstances within an organization. Much of the time, employees experience strain at work when working conditions change in an unexpected way, such as when workload increases or decreases, or when expectations for an employee become uncertain. Parker and colleagues argue that proactive employees do not wait for stressful working conditions to overwhelm them, but instead set goals that will allow them to deal with the changing conditions and demonstrate willpower in achieving those goals, despite a chaotic environment.

Consider an employee faced with a situation where the guidelines for how to complete a project are unclear or outdated. Instead of reflecting on how ambiguous everything is, an employee demonstrating proactive motivation will show initiative in setting a goal for developing new guidelines, and then making sure that the project follows these new guidelines in order to be completed on time. As another example, employees are frequently asked to do things they are not trained to do. Although this experience can be stressful, employees who set goals for completing the training necessary for the new responsibilities and who motivate themselves to perform well in the new area will obviously handle the new responsibilities better than employees who resent the new tasks and fail to generate any plan for completing the tasks in an effective way. They may also grow and develop as a result of possessing the new skills.

Of course, coming up with a proactive mindset in the face of stressful working conditions is not an easy feat. If it was, the world would be filled with employees taking initiative to thrive under difficult working conditions, and this is clearly not the case. Parker and her colleagues developed a model highlighting the key components of proactive motivation and a discussion of those factors that facilitate employees approaching work with such a mindset.[22] First, employees who demonstrate proactive motivation can be characterized by two primary factors: possessing "proactive motivational states" and showing a "proactive goal generation and striving." Regarding the first factor, proactive motivational states are characterized by employees believing they are able to change future working conditions or oneself, having good reasons for engaging in the proactive behavior, and experiencing positive motivational states (i.e., vigor, vitality) that provide employees with the energy to carry out their goals. Regarding proactive goal generation and striving, it is important for employees to clearly imagine how work conditions, or their responses to work conditions, can be different in the future, and to develop a clear plan for bringing about the desired changes. In addition, employees need to use the energy provided by the proactive motivational states to keep on track in terms of meeting the goals that have been set (i.e., goal striving).

Consider an employee who determines that there are unsafe working conditions on a shop floor, and senses that his or her supervisor is not particularly committed to safety in the workplace (especially at the expense of higher production output). If that employee is going to proactively attempt to improve the safety of the work environment, he or she is going to need to determine specific goals for a safer climate, as well as a plan for addressing obstacles that he or she may encounter in trying to create a safer work environment. Given the challenges inherent in changing the work environment, this employee must have confidence in being able to demonstrate the importance of safety for the organization's achievement of its objectives, must be motivated to change the work environment because of the importance of the goal, and must experience the vitality necessary to address obstacles that may arise in changing the safety environment of the organization.

We would argue that employees who find they are frequently experiencing proactive motivation are likely to also be thriving at work, as proactive motivation is experienced as possessing positive motivational states such as vitality and self-efficacy, while simultaneously being oriented toward changing the future work environment, and by definition learning and developing within one's job. In addition, Parker and colleagues' model of proactive motivation highlights the role of job-related stressors in the experience of proactive motivation.[22] These authors argue that employees should be more likely to demonstrate proactive motivation when they encounter stressors at work, because the experience of stress represents a discrepancy between a current state of the employee and the desired state of not being stressed out. Individuals who are experiencing unpredictable workloads or unclear performance guidelines should be motivated to proactively decrease those demands to move closer to the desired states of planning for differential workloads and clarifying work expectations. This point highlights an argument made frequently in this book, that some degree of stress at work is necessary to generate positive growth and development. Of course, if employees do not have supportive managers or work environments, the desire to proactively change the work environment may be present, but the ability to affect change will be more difficult.

Job Crafting

Another proactive way that employees can contribute to their own potential to thrive under difficult work conditions is by changing their jobs in ways that allow them to better appreciate the significance of what they are doing, and to create a job that is more consistent with their skills, abilities, and interests. As noted in Chapter 3 of this book, Amy Wrzesniewski and Jane Dutton are two psychologists who developed the concept of *job crafting* to describe how employees can redesign their jobs, and the way they think about their jobs, to increase the potential to thrive at work.[23] According to these authors, job crafting can occur by employees changing the types or frequency of the tasks they perform at work, the relationships they experience at work, or the way they think about their work.

In terms of changing the nature of the tasks you do at work, you may be a human resources manager and you may decide that because of your interest in the success of the company, you want to be more involved with the company's recruitment of top talent. You could then approach your supervisor about increasing the amount of time you spend on recruiting activities, while spending less time on other aspects of your job that you could potentially delegate to others.

In terms of changing the relationships you have at work, you might make a conscious effort to reach out to employees in other sections of your company to learn what they do in order to do your job more effectively. As we will see in the next section of this chapter, forming quality relationships with others will not only allow you to perform your job better, but will also help contribute to a positive interpersonal climate that has been associated with higher levels of thriving-related experiences.

In terms of changing the way you think about your job, the importance of viewing the work you do in adaptive ways has been emphasized throughout the book. We have discussed the importance of how you appraise the demands you encounter, how to view demands as challenges rather than threats, and how to approach your job tasks with a proactive mindset.

Researchers who developed the concept of job crafting encourage employees to diagram their job and to think about where they are spending their time, and whether this time allocation is consistent with their primary interests and abilities.[24] We will briefly describe the job crafting process here. The complete job crafting exercise is available at www.jobcrafting.org. The exercise first encourages you to describe the current tasks you do at work as a series of boxes, and to base the size of the box on how much time you spend on the tasks. For example, if you were an owner of a small business, you would likely have boxes for dealing with the budget for the business, customer relations, employee relations, product development, and so on. In addition, these boxes would be of different sizes, depending on the amount of time you generally spend on the different tasks.

After diagramming your job in this manner, the authors encourage you to consider your motives, strengths, and passions that are utilized at work. For example, you may have *motives* to see your company succeed, to develop junior employees, and to have a positive work climate in your business. You may consider your *strengths* to be developing a strong product, being fiscally accountable, and anticipating the demands of the consumer. Your *passions* may be being creative in product design and effectively marketing your product.

Having identified your motives, strengths, and passions, consider how the time you spend on various tasks and activities at work allows you to further develop those attributes that will heighten your personal engagement at work. In doing this exercise, you could draw an arrow to which tasks allow you to fulfill each of your motives, demonstrate each of your strengths, and engage in each of your passions. Once you have this basic diagram, you can begin to think about how you might restructure your job tasks in order to spend more time on those activities that matter more to your motives, strengths, and passions. You can also think about how you can incorporate building relationships with others into your tasks and activities, and change the way you think about the nature of your tasks.

Although most employees are not in a position to completely change the way they do their work, the developers of the job crafting exercise believe that most employees have some leeway in how they do their jobs. Therefore, and as noted at different points in this book, most employees should be capable of approaching their job in a way that puts them in a better position to respond to the demands they face. We recommend experimenting with some small changes to the way your job is conducted, and monitoring how these changes affect your motivation and performance. For example, you may reallocate a slightly greater increase in time to job tasks you care more about, and see how that influences your effort and performance. The reinforcement that comes from making small changes will make it easier to make additional changes. In addition, the changes may be perceived positively by managers, who wind up encouraging the new directions you are taking. Of course, it is also possible that the changes you make to your job do not have the effects you desired, in which case you may have to go back to the drawing board in considering how to craft your job.

The important lesson of job crafting within the context of thriving under stressful work is that employees need to take advantage of the opportunities they have to proactively design the way they conduct and perceive their work in order to help create thriving-related experiences that will maximize performance and well-being when dealing with difficult situations. Maria Timms and her colleagues have recently extended the concept of job crafting to addressing demands and resources that employees have in the work environment. These authors argue that employees can proactively seek out demands that challenge them to develop and perform better, while at the same time taking steps to minimize their exposure to job demands that harm performance.[25] These authors found that employees who indicated trying to create challenging work demands reported higher levels of engagement in their work one month later. Therefore, creating challenging work demands can result in increased engagement at work, which is a thriving-related experience linked to performance, well-being, and job satisfaction.

We addressed the importance of challenge versus hindrance/threat appraisals in Chapter 3. Proactive motivation and job crafting are concepts that reinforce the importance of employees not being passive victims of demands in the workplace, but as active agents in how they respond and adapt to different stressors. We feel it is important to point out that we are not suggesting that employees bear responsibility for exposure to stressful conditions at work. Instead, we are suggesting that a focus on employee burnout as an outcome measure has resulted in insufficient attention being directed toward the ways in which employees creatively and effectively address the demands that exist in the workplace, and how they may use demands in proactive ways to further their own development. In the next section, we highlight the important role of interpersonal connections at work in allowing employees to approach work demands in proactive and adaptive ways.

Highlighting the Role of Interpersonal Connections in Thriving at Work

In addition to job-related and employee-related influences on thriving-related experiences, a number of researchers have also highlighted the importance of quality social connections as predictors of thriving. As seen in Figure 5.1, we argue that both quality connections between coworkers and the actions of leaders are critical determinants of thriving-related experiences at work. A number of authors have emphasized the importance of building a climate of trust, respect, and support among employees in order to lay the foundations for employees to proactively accomplish their goals and the goals of the organization.[3,15,22,26] The importance of building close-knit relationships between employees may be especially important in occupations characterized as "dirty work," as one strategy for dealing with the stigmatizing nature of the different jobs was for employees to form social buffers with other employees. Such a strategy provides employees with a social network at work that protects them from the negative opinions of the broader community.[20]

One of the reasons interpersonal connections at work are predictive of increased thriving under stressful work conditions is that human beings have a basic need to belong to social groups, and to feel they have a number of positive relationships with others.[1,14] Within the workplace, William Kahn has also discussed the importance of the social context of the work environment in determining whether employees will be highly engaged in their work.[27] According to Kahn, employees are most likely to be personally engaged in their work when they feel a sense of safety in the work environment. This sense of safety comes about through the employee trusting coworkers and through leader behaviors that are consistent and supportive.

The importance of a work environment characterized by trust, support, and respect leads to a discussion of the importance of leadership in establishing such a climate. In Figure 5.1 we highlight the importance of leadership in establishing supportive climates that are characterized by a sense of psychological safety, where employees are recognized for the contributions they are making to the organization. Kahn has also highlighted the importance of leadership in creating a sense of psychological safety, and other researchers have also discussed the importance of perceived safety for employees engaging in innovative behaviors at work.[28,29] Most organizations want employees to think of innovative ways of improving the organization, but unless a climate is created where mistakes can be made, employees are unlikely to move beyond the status quo in how they do their work.

Markus Bar and Michael Frese conducted a study examining the climates that existed within an organization for employees taking initiative and feeling psychologically safe if they made a mistake.[30] These authors found that companies characterized by climates for initiative and psychological safety performed better, in terms of return on investment and meeting goals, than companies characterized by employees who lacked initiative and did not feel it was safe to make a mistake. Additional research has shown that leaders who make it clear that every employee's contribution is valued end up with units higher on psychological safety, which then predicts important organizational outcomes.[31]

The importance of quality social connections between coworkers in allow-ing employees to thrive at work has implications both for managers and employees themselves. As seen in *What This Means for Managers 5.2*, manag-ers can do a lot to create the type of quality interpersonal work environment that encourages employee thriving versus faltering under stressful conditions. However, as we discussed earlier, you as an individual employee can also influ-ence the quality of your social relationships at work by investing energy and effort in helping coworkers accomplish tasks and becoming aware of what your coworkers are doing. Understanding how your work fits with the work of

---

What This Means for Managers 5.2

CREATIVE A THRIVING-SUPPORTIVE INTERPERSONAL CLIMATE

Managers are in a unique position to affect the interpersonal climate in which employees do their work. Given that interpersonal relationships at work may not be the top priority for leaders within an organization, leaders often do not consider it within their role to worry about the climate that exists among coworkers. However, research has shown that leaders set the tone for a respect-ful, civil, and supportive climate within the organization, and this climate has a direct impact on the organization's ability to function well when faced with high demands. In addition, leaders who create the expectation that it is OK to make mistakes within the organization when employees are trying to improve upon the procedures of the organization will help develop employees who are more likely to be innovative and creative.

Specific suggestions for managers include:

- Emphasize the importance of all unit members working together collectively to accomplish the mission of the organization. This can be done verbally in meetings, and also highlighting how meeting the objectives of the organization will require different personnel working together.
- Treat employees with respect and dignity. If employees see their leaders acting respectful and trusting, they will be more likely to emulate that behavior when interacting with each other.
- Consider ways to build quality connections among members of the organization. Examples may include occasional get-togethers with employees of the organization outside the workplace, and meetings with representatives from different departments within an organization to encourage a better sense of shared vision within the organization.

others will not only improve your individual performance, but will also facilitate you making the interpersonal connections you need to facilitate higher levels of performance under stress.

Thriving at Work under Stressful Conditions

Thriving at work has largely been examined without reference to how stressful working conditions are for employees. However, recall that proactive motivation is more likely when work becomes more stressful, and employees need to take action in order to change the amount of demands they face or the way they perceive and approach those demands. We argue that thriving-related experiences may be especially critical when work conditions become stressful. A number of researchers have discovered that the experience of positive motivational states relevant to thriving (vitality, learning, and engagement) can serve as buffers against the negative effects of stressful work conditions.[12] For example, consider soldiers dealing with the aftermath of being exposed to high levels of combat. In a recent study conducted on soldiers who had been on a combat deployment, soldiers who reported high levels of morale (a motivational state comparable to vitality) were less likely to show symptoms of post-traumatic stress disorder (PTSD) under high levels of combat exposure. In contrast, soldiers reporting low levels of morale were much more likely to show symptoms of PTSD as combat exposure increased.[32]

One reason for these findings is that positive motivational states such as morale and vitality provide individuals with the energy and attitude they need to cope with highly stressful events at work. As work becomes more hectic, deadlines tighten, and the number of hours spent at work increases, it becomes more important to sustain thriving-related experiences in order to change the way those demands are experienced and addressed. Furthermore, coming up with new solutions for addressing the demands encountered at work allows the employee to develop new skills that will facilitate success in the work environment.

CONCLUSION

The present chapter has highlighted what it means to thrive at work, and has discussed those job-related, employee, and interpersonal influences on the development of thriving-related experiences. Throughout the chapter, we have emphasized that employees are not passive recipients of their work environments, but are capable of actively addressing the demands the encounter and how they perceive those demands. In addition, we emphasized the role of leaders and fellow employees in helping to create the conditions necessary for employees to thrive at work. In the next chapter we continue our discussion of how responses to stressors at work are not always negative, and what distinguishes employees who are able to positively respond to work demands.

REFERENCES

1. Baumeister, R. F., & Leary, M. R. (1995). The need to belong: Desire for interpersonal attachments as a fundamental human motivation. *Psychological Bulletin, 117*, 497–529.
2. Ryan, R. M., & Frederick, C. (1997). On energy, personality, and health: Subjective vitality as a dynamic reflection of well-being. *Journal of Personality, 65*, 529–565.
3. Shirom, A. (2010). Feeling energetic at work: On vigor's antecedents. In A. B. Bakker & M. P. Leiter (Eds.) *Work Engagement: Recent Developments in Theory and Research.* New York: Psychology Press.
4. Frederickson, B. (2001). The role of positive emotions in positive psychology: The broaden and build theory of positive emotions. *American Psychologist, 56*, 218–226.
5. Spreitzer, G., Sutcliffe, K., Dutton, J., Sonenshein, S., & Grant, A.M. (2005). A socially embedded model of thriving at work. *Organization Science, 16*, 537–549.
6. Dweck, C. S. (1986). Motivational processes affecting learning. *American Psychologist, 41*, 1040–1048.
7. Aryee, S., & Chu, C. W. L. (2012). Antecedents and outcomes of challenging job experiences: A social cognitive perspective. *Human Performance, 25*, 215–234.
8. Christian, M. S., Garza, A. S., & Slaughter, J. E. (2011). Work engagement: A quantitative review and test of its relations with task and contextual performance. *Personnel Psychology, 64*, 89–136.
9. Csikszentmihalyi, M. (1990). *Flow: The Psychology of Optimal Experience.* New York: Harper & Row.
10. Sonnentag, S. (2003). Recovery, work engagement, and proactive behavior: A new look at the interface between nonwork and work. *Journal of Applied Psychology, 88*, 518–528.
11. Harter, J. K., Schmidt, F. L., & Keyes, C. L. M. (2003). Well-being in the workplace and its relationship to business outcomes: A review of the Gallup studies. In C. Keyes & J. Haidt (Eds.), *Flourishing: Positive Psychology and the Life Well-Lived* (pp. 205–224). Washington, DC, US: American Psychological Association.
12. Bakker, A. B., & Demerouti, E. (2007). The job demands–resources model: State of the art. *Journal of Managerial Psychology, 22*, 309–328.
13. May, D. R., Gilson, R. L., & Harter, L. (2004). The psychological conditions of meaningfulness, safety, and availability and the engagement of the human spirit at work. *Journal of Organizational and Occupational Psychology, 77*, 11–37.
14. Ryan, R. M., & Deci, E. L. (2000). Self-determination theory and the facilitation of intrinsic motivation, social development, and well-being. *American Psychologist, 55*, 68–78.

15. Spreitzer, G., Porath, C. L., & Gibson, C. B. (2012). Toward human sustainability: How to enable more thriving at work. *Organizational Dynamics, 41,* 155–162.

16. Spector, P. E. (2009). The role of job control in employee health and well-being. In C. L. Cooper, J. Quick, M. J. Schabracq (Eds.), *International Handbook of Work and Health Psychology* (3rd ed., pp. 173–195). Malden, MA: Wiley-Blackwell.

17. Grant, A. M. (2007). Relational job design and the motivation to make a prosocial difference. *Academy of Management Review, 32,* 393–417.

18. Grant, A. M., Campbell, E. M., Chen, G., Cottone, K., Lapedis, D., & Lee, K. (2007). Impact and the art of motivation maintenance: The effects of contact with beneficiaries on persistence behavior. *Organizational Behavior and Human Decision Processes, 103,* 53–67.

19. Britt, T. W., & Bradley, P. S. (2009, November). Positive work experiences as predictors of how much workplace stressors impact performance. Poster presented at the 8th International Conference for Work, Stress, & Health, San Juan, Puerto Rico.

20. Ashforth, B. E., Kreiner, G. E., Clark, M. A., Fugate, M. (2007). Normalizing dirty work: Managerial tactics for countering occupational taint. *Academy of Management Journal, 50,* 149–174.

21. Luthans, F., Avey, J. B., Avolio, B. J., & Peterson, S. J. (2010). The development and resulting performance impact of positive psychological capital. *Human Resource Development Quarterly, 21,* 41–67.

22. Parker, S. K., Bindl, U. K., & Strauss, K. (2010). Making things happen: A model of proactive motivation. *Journal of Management, 36,* 927–956.

23. Wrzesniewski, A., & Dutton, J. E. (2001). Crafting a job: Revisioning employees as active crafters of their work. *Academy of Management Review, 26*(2), 179–201.

24. Wrzesniewski, A., Berg, J. M., & Dutton, J. E. (2010). Turn the job you have into the job you want. *Harvard Business Review,* June, 114–117.

25. Tims, M., Bakker, A. B., & Derks, D. (2013). The impact of job crafting on job demands, job resources, and well-being. *Journal of Occupational Health Psychology, 18,* 230–240.

26. Spreitzer, G., Sutcliffe, K., Dutton, J. E., Sonenshein, S., & Grant, A. M. (2005). A socially embedded model of thriving at work. *Organization Science, 16,* 537–549.

27. Kahn, W. A. (1990). Psychological conditions of personal engagement and disengagement at work. *Academy of Management Journal, 33,* 692–724.

28. Edmondson, A. (1999). Psychological safety and learning behavior in work teams. *Administrative Science Quarterly, 44,* 350–83.

29. Kark, R., & Carmeli, A. (2009). Alive and creating: The mediating role of vitality and aliveness in the relationship between psychological safety and creative work involvement. *Journal of Organizational Behavior, 30,* 785–804.

30. Baer, M., & Frese, M. (2003). Innovation is not enough: Climates for initiative and psychological safety, process innovations, and firm performance. *Journal of Organizational Behavior, 24,* 45–68.

31. Nembhard, I. M., & Edmondson, A. C. (2006). Making it safe: The effects of leader inclusiveness and professional status on psychological safety and improvement efforts in health care teams. *Journal of Organizational Behavior, 27,* 941–966.

32. Britt, T. W., Adler, A. B., Bliese, P. D., & Moore, D. (2013). Morale as a moderator of the combat exposure-PTSD symptom relationship. *Journal of Traumatic Stress*, *26*, 94–101.

33. Schaufeli, W. B., Salanova, M., Gonzalez-Roma, V., & Bakker, A. B. (2002). The measurement of engagement and burnout: A two sample confirmatory factor analytic approach. *Journal of Happiness Studies*, *3*, 71–92.

34. Britt, T. W. (2003). Aspects of identity predict engagement in work under adverse conditions. *Self and Identity*, *2*, 31–45.

35. Porath, C., Spreitzer, G., Gibson, C., & Garnett, F. G. (2012). Thriving at work: Toward its measurement, construct validation, and theoretical refinement. *Journal of Organizational Behavior*, *33*, 250–275.

6

Positive Effects of Stress at Work

Although most of the research and self-help books on the topic of work stress have emphasized the negative consequences of stress, growing attention has been devoted to the positive effects that can result from being placed under demanding conditions. All of us can likely remember times when it felt good to be challenged, and to perform well despite encountering obstacles along the way. Although you probably would have never intentionally created obstacles to heighten your satisfaction with your performance, the fact that you were able to complete a project under demanding conditions added to the pride you felt in your work. The present chapter builds on the theme that began in Chapter 5, focusing on how exposure to work demands can result not only in negative outcomes, but positive outcomes as well.

Hans Selye coined the term *eustress* (literally "good stress") to refer to these positive consequences of dealing with demands,[1] and Richard Lazarus discussed the positive outcomes of stress a few years later.[2] Although authors have noted that individuals placed under various demands sometimes experience positive consequences, researchers are only beginning to understand the factors that make these positive outcomes more likely. In this chapter, we discuss Selye's concept of *eustress*, and provide an overview of a model of the positive effects that can result from stressors at work. We identify positive thoughts and emotions that may come from being exposed to stress, and discuss those factors that increase the likelihood of these positive responses (e.g., optimism, hardiness).

This chapter also describes work on Stress Inoculation and Exposure Training, a technique borrowed from clinical psychology that illustrates how exposure to increasing amounts of stress can allow employees to develop the skills they need to more effectively deal with real-world stress in their jobs. Evidence suggests that this training is effective at reducing anxiety and improving performance in different contexts (e.g., among teachers and nurses, when making career decisions).[3] This approach is founded on the idea that exposure to stress has positive effects when combined with skills training that will facilitate employees' ability to view demands as challenges in stressful job environments.

Finally, we discuss recent work on how employees may derive benefits from being exposed to high levels of stressors as a result of realizing that they are more resilient than they thought. A large amount of research has been conducted in non-work settings detailing how individuals may experience benefits as a result of going through extremely stressful trials in their lives. Although it is important not to de-emphasize the negative effects of stressful events, researchers have documented different benefits that can also occur as a result of severe stressors, such as increased personal strength, ability to relate better to others, spiritual changes, and appreciation for life.[4,5]

POSITIVE RESPONSES TO WORK STRESS

Most of us can remember a time when we were working under difficult conditions, whether those conditions were a tight deadline, insufficient resources to get the job done, or unclear guidelines for what was expected of us. Although these types of conditions have the potential to produce negative responses such as frustration and anxiety, most of us also have experiences where we got the job done despite the demands that were present. In addition, we would probably admit that on certain occasions being pushed to do a job under difficult conditions led us to develop new skills and increased confidence in performing our jobs. In these cases, the stressors we experienced at work actually served to increase our skills and performance. In the words of Jim Loehr and Tony Schwartz, "Stress is not the enemy in our lives. Paradoxically, it is the key to growth" (p. 13).[6] These authors point out that, just as muscles need to be pushed in order to grow, employees need to experience increased challenges if they are going to grow and develop.

Despite the intuitive appeal of this idea, the majority of research in occupational health psychology has focused on the negative effects of stressors at work. Researchers are only beginning to systematically examine how exposure to stressful conditions can actually produce growth in employees. Therefore, this chapter is shorter than others in the book. In addition, we admit that the experience of positive outcomes resulting from exposure to work demands is more unpredictable than the experience of negative outcomes, and employees should not fault themselves if positive outcomes do not occur. In order to help you think of some of the positive responses that may come from dealing with stressful work events, please take a minute to complete Application Exercise 6.1.

Application Exercise 6.1

Considering the Positive Effects of Work Demands

Most of the time when you think of the effects of experiencing demands at work, only negative effects come to mind. However, as discussed in this chapter, it is also possible for employees to experience positive effects from making it through a tough situation at work, and figuring out a way to deal with a difficult situation. We would like you to think back to a time at work when you were under a lot of stress, but were ultimately able to get through the difficult conditions.

Part A. Describe the stressful occasion at work, including when the particular stressor began and ended.

_____

_____

_____

Part B. Think about some positive outcomes that might have resulted from being exposed to these difficult conditions. For example, if you had to do your job with fewer resources than you would have liked, perhaps getting through the stressful experience illustrated how you could get by with less. If you were stressed by not knowing how to do your job, perhaps you learned how to clarify the expectations others have of you.

Try to think about **two** positive responses that may have occurred.

    1. _____

    2. _____

Part C. Consider the demands you indicated experiencing at work in Application Exercise 1.1. Try to think of one positive outcome that could result from addressing each of those demands.

Demand #1: _____

Possible positive response: _____

Demand #2: _____

Possible positive response: _____

Demand #3: _____

Possible positive response: _____

In their holistic model of stress, Debra Nelson and Bret Simmons described how stressors at work can result in both positive (eustress) and negative (distress) outcomes.[7] Their model is presented in Figure 6.1. These authors argue that work stressors are inherently neutral, and how employees appraise work stressors is the main determinant of whether the stressor will produce positive or negative responses. Although we disagree with the idea that all work stressors are neutral (a supervisor hurling abusive comments at an employee will likely be appraised almost universally as negative), we have seen how the appraisal of work stressors can have an important effect on the outcomes these stressors have on employees. In Chapter 3, we addressed the importance of appraisal in reducing the negative effects of work stressors. We now highlight some of the positive outcomes associated with appraising work demands in particular ways.

As seen in Figure 6.1, Nelson and Simmons argue that most researchers have focused on negative responses to stress, including frustration, anger, anxiety, and burnout. However, the authors argue that positive responses to stress are also possible, and these include such psychological states as hope, positive affect, vigor, and meaningfulness. Hope refers to the belief that important goals can be obtained, as well as a plan for achieving desired goals. Positive affect is the experience of positive emotions at work, including feeling happy, joyous, and content. Vigor is a special type of positive affect that combines an enthusiastic attitude with energy. Meaningfulness refers to the sense that what you are doing matters and fits into a broader context. Many of these outcomes were identified as thriving-related experiences in the last chapter. The model identified in Figure 6.1 illustrates that these experiences can come from work demands when interpreted in the right way.

All of these positive responses are pleasurable and provide individuals with the energy they need for performing well under stressful work conditions. As mentioned earlier, these responses to workplace stressors are most likely to occur when an individual appraises stressors in adaptive ways. However, what determines whether individuals make adaptive appraisals of their work demands? Nelson and Simmons argue that a number of employee personality traits are associated with appraising work demands in ways that result in positive outcomes. Many of these traits were identified in Chapter 4 when discussing characteristics of people who experience fewer negative outcomes when reporting high levels of stressful work.

As seen in Figure 6.1, just as employees try to cope with the negative effects of stress at work, Nelson and Simmons argue that a parallel process occurs in terms of savoring the positive effects of stress. Research in the broader area of psychology has highlighted the benefits of savoring positive life experiences, and how gratitude for the good things in life can promote happiness.

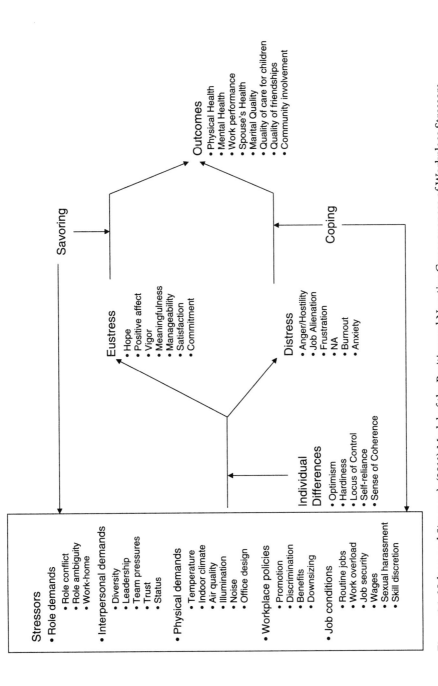

Figure 6.1 Nelson and Simmon's (2011) Model of the Positive and Negative Consequences of Workplace Stressors. NA = Negative Affect.

A number of studies have found that individuals who do such activities as writing letters expressing their gratitude to others and counting the blessings they have in life experience an increase in their happiness levels.[8] Apparently engaging in these activities increases positive emotions, thoughts, and behaviors, which then results in increased well-being.[8]

Similarly, employees who reflect on their experience of positive motivational states, such as optimism, commitment, and the meaningfulness of their work, will presumably experience higher levels of beneficial outcomes associated with these states. Just as we need to devote attention to reducing the negative effects associated with stressful work, we also need to remember to be grateful for the positive effects of exposure to work demands that we may also encounter. The final component of Nelson and Simmons's model highlights how the positive and negative responses to stress come together to influence outcomes important to the employee, such as physical health, mental health, quality of relationships, and community involvement.

A good example of a job demand that has the potential for both negative and positive outcomes is emotional labor. Judith Hochschild coined the term *emotional labor* to refer to conditions in which employees have to deny the true emotion they feel on a given occasion, and instead produce an emotion desired by the organization.[9] Although emotional labor may be more likely in some jobs than others (think customer service representatives who must repeatedly deliver "service with a smile" even when feeling the opposite emotion), most employees experience this demand from time to time. For example, we can all likely remember a time when we were not particularly happy because of something that happened to us at work or home, but we put on a happy face when getting through a meeting or presentation. Having to suppress a natural emotion while producing an unnatural emotion actually requires two different acts of self-control, and this may quickly deplete an employee's energy level.

Researchers have found that employees can deal with the demands of emotional labor by engaging in either *surface* acting or *deep* acting.[10] Surface acting is a more superficial process, in which employees try to put on a happy face without really feeling happy. In contrast, deep acting involves employees actually trying to feel the emotion in question by changing their appraisal of a situation or recalling a happy memory. Research has shown that surface acting is not particularly effective in creating a positive emotional display in customers' eyes, and usually creates more strain for the employee. In contrast, deep acting results in higher ratings of employees by customers (and greater tips for the employee), and does not appear to result in strain for the employee.[10,11] These findings indicate that employees who engage in deep acting in order to deal with the work demand of emotional labor may put themselves in a position to experience positive outcomes. These outcomes might be both higher levels of performance and greater well-being, given that creating positive emotions should result in higher levels of positive affect as a result.

Recently, organizational psychologists have conducted additional work on how stress at work can be related to increased performance under certain conditions. Larry Hunter and Sherry Thatcher studied bank employees, and examined how the stress they felt at work was related to their performance in terms of the number of financial products the employees sold over the course of 12 months.[12] Felt stress at work was assessed through indicators such as "There are lots of times when my job drives me right up the wall" and "My job gets to me more than it should." Endorsement of these items clearly means that employees were experiencing stress working for the bank. The authors also assessed the amount of experience that employees had on the job and how committed they were to the organization.

Highlighting the importance of how characteristics of the employee affect the extent to which stress at work can have positive consequences, the authors found that felt stress at work was related to a greater number of financial products being sold only for employees who had greater job experience or who were high on commitment to the organization. In contrast, felt stress at work was related to decreased performance when employees had not been working for the company for a long period, or were not particularly committed to the organization. These results indicate that employees need to have the necessary experience and motivation to channel felt stress into better performance.

A similar finding was obtained among researchers studying a different sample of employees working at the Office of Motor Vehicles in Louisiana.[13] These researchers assessed the extent to which work stressors that challenged employees (e.g., the time pressure experienced, the number of projects that needed to be completed; see Chapter 3) predicted the ratings employees received of their annual performance by their supervisor. The authors also assessed the extent to which employees felt they were supported by their organization, in terms of whether the organization valued their contribution and would help them when needed.

The results of this study showed that higher levels of work stressors that challenged the employees were related to higher performance evaluations by supervisors, supporting the argument that employees may respond to demanding conditions at work with higher levels of performance. However, an even more important finding was that higher levels of challenging work demands were related to higher levels of performance only among employees who felt supported by their organization. When employees did not feel supported by their organization, challenging work demands were unrelated to performance evaluations.

Taken together, the results from these two studies provide important insights into understanding when the experience of stress at work results in higher levels of performance. First, employees need to have the necessary experience in order to be able to respond well to demanding conditions. Second, employees need to feel a sense of commitment to the organization. Third, employees need to feel supported by the organization when they are working under stressful conditions. These results highlight the importance of the employee's manager in creating the conditions necessary for employees to respond positively to stressful work conditions. In *What This Means for Managers 6.1*, we discuss how managers need to be sensitive to equipping employees with the proper mindset in order to see benefits of stress at work. Managers need to ensure

---

What This Means for Managers 6.1

ENHANCING POSITIVE RESPONSES TO STRESSORS

We feel it is important to emphasize that just because stressors can result in increased performance, this does not provide managers with a license to increase the stress levels of employees without properly equipping them to handle the stressful conditions. Although stressors can be linked to higher levels of performance under certain conditions, it is still the case that higher levels of workplace stressors usually result in higher levels of mental health symptoms, which will ultimately interfere with performance. In addition, studies show that higher levels of demands are linked to higher levels of performance primarily for employees who are experienced, perceive support from the organization, and who are committed to the organization.

- Knowing that job experience is linked to the ability to perform well under stress, ensure that employees have sufficient time on the job in order to develop the skills needed to perform under demanding conditions.
- Given that employees respond better to higher levels of stress when they are committed to the organization, recognize that policies and actions that benefit the employee are likely to increase the employee's commitment to the organization, resulting in better performance under stressful conditions.
- Supervisors who care about their employees' well-being will create employees who feel more supported by the organization, which will provide the employees with the mindset necessary to perform better under stressful conditions.

---

that employees have the proper experience to function under stressful working conditions, support employees in performing well under such conditions, and help employees develop a commitment to the organization that places their performing under stressful conditions in a more meaningful context. In the next section of the chapter, we also discuss the importance of training employees in ways that allow them to develop the skills they need in order to handle the increasing demands they may encounter in a job.

STRESS INOCULATION AND EXPOSURE TRAINING

One reason that trying to eliminate all the demands you encounter at work would not be a good idea is that being exposed to some stress can increase your ability to handle greater levels of stress in the future. The concept of exposure to stress increasing one's resilience in the face of future stress was inspired by the same logic as that of getting vaccinations in order to prevent more severe illnesses. Vaccinations work by providing the individual with a small dose of the given illness so that the body can generate the antibodies that will be effective at fighting off a larger dose of the illness at a later point in time. In the same way, we can be "inoculated" against high levels of stress by being provided with experience dealing with lower levels of stressors, so that we develop the mindset and coping strategies necessary for responding well under stress. If we never have any experience dealing with adversity at work, we will become quickly overwhelmed when faced with high levels of demands.

Donald Meichenbaum was one of the first clinical psychologists to examine Stress Inoculation Training (SIT) as a method for helping his clients to demonstrate higher levels of well-being and performance in the face of life stressors. Applied to the workplace, SIT consists of three stages.[3] The first stage involves helping employees to understand the nature of the demands they face, and the responses these demands can provoke. Chapter 1 of this book identified the different demands employees typically face, and Chapter 2 highlighted the negative consequences of these demands if they are not dealt with in an appropriate way. In order to have a positive response to work stressors, it is necessary to understand the particular demands in your work environment, and the effects these particular demands may have on you if not addressed. For example, if you are working as a manager of a company that is responsible for the creation of a product, you may encounter demands related to tight deadlines, high work overload, and responsibility for the actions of subordinates. Knowing how these demands affect you when not dealt with in an optimal way provides information on how to prevent these effects from occurring, and motivation for approaching the demands in a way that facilitates performance under the difficult conditions.

Once the stressors and the responses to these stressors are known, the second stage of SIT involves helping employees learn skills for dealing with the demands and influencing their responses to these demands. These skills include such procedures as relaxation training, focusing attention on controllable aspects of their job, cognitive restructuring (thinking about the demands you face in a different way), and overlearning key job tasks so that they become more automatic under high demands. A summary of strategies for responding well to stressful work conditions is provided in Table 6-1.

Table 6-1. SUMMARY OF STRESS TRAINING SKILLS

Stress Training Skill	Description
Cognitive control techniques	Given narrowing of attention under stress, individuals are trained to focus on task-oriented cognitions and ignore non-task-oriented cognitions (i.e., emotions, distractors)
Physiological control techniques	Individuals learn techniques to control physiological responses to stress, including relaxation techniques and biofeedback.
Modeling	The trainee models the behavior of another individual. S/he is able to watch someone else engaging in the stressful task with success, which will give him/her the ability to copy the behaviors.
Overlearning	The individual learns tasks beyond basic proficiency, to a point where the tasks can be performed automatically.
Attentional training	This training focuses on enhancing a trainee's ability to focus attention. Research has found that individuals who get training on maintaining attentional focus stay more focused and overcome distractions easier.
Training time-sharing skills	Stressful situations may require individuals to manage multiple tasks simultaneously. Performance can be enhanced in this dimension in situations where the different tasks encountered in the real world are the same as those encountered in training.
Enhancing flexibility	When individuals get stressed they become more rigid in their decision-making. Flexibility can be enhanced by having the trainees practice a wide variety of tasks during training. The tasks should be of varying contexts, come from different perspectives, and utilize different skills.

Source: Driskell et al. (2001).[21]

In addition to identifying which coping strategies work best for dealing with the identified stressors, employees must also rehearse these strategies so that they will become readily activated during actual stressful conditions in the work environment. To continue the example of a manager responsible for the production of a given item, the manager may determine that refocusing attention and deep breathing are especially effective ways to address the demands associated with high workload and tight deadlines, whereas the strategy of modeling the behavior of others is especially effective when dealing with subordinates who are not performing according to expectations. One common theme throughout this book is that employees will differ in the strategies that best allow them to thrive under stressful work conditions. Therefore, employees need to find the strategies that are most effective for them in dealing with the demands they face, and then practice using these strategies to perform better under stressful conditions.

In the third phase of SIT, employees apply the coping skills they have learned in conditions that approximate the actual work environment. The third phase of SIT can take place in training settings that attempt to recreate the types of stressors workers will encounter on the job. It is also possible to have employees role-play various stressful situations (e.g., facing a tight deadline, handling multiple tasks at once, dealing with unsupportive coworkers), and then practice the use of coping strategies designed to mitigate the negative effects of a given stressor (e.g., practice relaxation or refocusing of attention when feelings of anxiety due to time pressure are detected).

A team of researchers compiled the results of 37 studies that had evaluated the effectiveness of SIT in reducing stress and improving performance in a variety of situations, including teachers dealing with students, patients going through dental procedures, and students who were experiencing test anxiety.[3] The authors examined the effects of SIT on anxiety surrounding the ability to perform well in a given domain, the individual's overall state anxiety, and actual performance, and found that SIT had the biggest effect on performance anxiety, followed by state anxiety and performance. Somewhat surprisingly, these authors found that SIT had stronger effects when the individual conducting the training did not have a doctoral degree than when the individual had a doctoral degree. These results indicate that the effectiveness of SIT does not depend on having a doctoral-level psychologist conducting the training.

Most companies have training programs designed to improve employee performance by developing skills desired by the company. SIT could be included within such a training program, with employees practicing the use of particular stress management strategies when exposed to realistic demands in the training setting. The importance of managers incorporating SIT training into the work environment is included in *What This Means for Managers*

What This Means for Managers 6.2

USING STRESS EXPOSURE TO INCREASE STRESS RESISTANCE

Managers need to be aware of how training programs such as SIT may facilitate adaptive outcomes in stressful work environments. An important lesson of SIT is that employees tend to do better dealing with high-stress work conditions when they are gradually exposed to increased demands at work. In this way, they gain experience building up coping strategies that will allow them to master the more difficult conditions, and generate confidence that they will be able handle more challenging responsibilities.

Specific suggestions for managers include:

- Provide employees with information regarding the coping strategies that have been particularly effective in allowing other employees to deal with the demands they encounter on the job.
- Create a mentoring program in your organization in which more experienced employees are paired with more junior employees in order to promote the use of different strategies to address the unique demands associated with the occupation.
- Consider including an SIT program within your organization in order to provide employees with experience dealing with increasing levels of demands on the job. Taking the time to develop employees who are able to better deal with higher levels of job demands will be superior to overwhelming them with high levels of job demands right off the bat, which will harm performance and decrease employee well-being.

6.2. However, all employees can apply the principles of SIT themselves within the context of their particular work situations. As a result of the Application Exercises in Chapters 1 and 2, you should already have identified the particular demands in your work environment, and be aware of the negative consequences that can result from work demands when not addressed in the correct way. If possible, try to slowly increase the demands encountered on your job, for example, by increasing the pace of your work or the extent to which you interact with others when accomplishing tasks. As you do this, be sure to use particular strategies identified in Table 6-2 that you find effective when performing under higher levels of workload or interactions with others. Being able to perform well under higher levels of work demands will reinforce the continued use of these strategies and allow you to better experience the benefits of more stressful work conditions.

BENEFITS FROM STRESSFUL EVENTS

Having addressed the positive effects of stress on different outcomes, we now examine whether employees may derive benefits from being exposed to highly stressful, even traumatic, events in the workplace. We have all heard the expression that "what doesn't kill you makes you stronger," and psychologists have been busy conducting research on whether this ancient expression has any truth to it. Most of this work has been in non-work settings, but researchers are also beginning to examine how employees may grow from highly stressful events at work.

A large amount of research has been conducted in non-work settings detailing how individuals may experience benefits as a result of going through extremely stressful trials in their lives. For example, victims of national disasters, crime, or certain illnesses often report experiencing benefits in the months and years following the events. Richard Tedeschi and Laurence Calhoun coined the term *post-traumatic growth* (PTG) to refer to the experiencing of changing for the better following exposure to stressful or traumatic events.[5] These authors also developed the Post-traumatic Growth Inventory (PTGI) to assess these positive changes following stress. These authors argued that most individuals have been through a highly stressful event in their lives that would have the capacity to change how they viewed the world, and therefore the measure is relevant to most people. However, these authors also note that positive responses to crises frequently co-occur with mental health symptoms such as anxiety, depression, and a decreased sense of well-being. Therefore, acknowledging the benefits that may have occurred in response to the crisis does not mean ignoring the negative effects that may have also occurred.

A brief version of the PTGI is provided in Table 6-2. Take a minute and think about how you might respond to this measure if you have experienced a recent highly stressful event in your life. In terms of the different domains addressed in this measure, items 1 and 2 assess *appreciation of life*, items 2 and 6 assess *new possibilities*, items 7 and 9 assess *personal strength*, items 4 and 8 assess *spiritual change*, and items 5 and 10 assess *relating to others*. Many studies have found that individuals report positive changes in these domains following highly stressful life events, and that the amount of positive change reported is related to the perceived severity of the event. In addition, a number of studies have shown that PTG following stressful events is related to higher levels of well-being, although again researchers emphasize that PTG may also coincide with increased mental health symptoms (e.g., depression and anxiety).

We should point out that there is some controversy over research in PTG. One issue involves whether individuals are capable of accurately making judgments of how much they have changed following highly stressful events.[14]

Table 6-2. POST-TRAUMATIC GROWTH INVENTORY (SHORT FORM)

The following items refer to possible outcomes of a major crisis in your life. Before completing the items, please briefly describe a recent personal crisis you have experienced:

_____

_____

_____

Please respond to the following items using the scale below:
0 = I did not experience this change as a result of my crisis.
1 = I experienced this change to a very small degree as a result of my crisis.
2 = I experienced this change to a small degree as a result of my crisis.
3 = I experienced this change to a moderate degree as a result of my crisis.
4 = I experienced this change to a great degree as a result of my crisis.
5 = I experienced this change to a very great degree as a result of my crisis.

_____ 1. I changed my priorities about what is important in my life.
_____ 2. I have a greater appreciation for the value of my own life.
_____ 3. I am able to do better things with my life.
_____ 4. I have a better understanding of spiritual matters.
_____ 5. I have a greater sense of closeness with others.
_____ 6. I established a new path for my life.
_____ 7. I know better that I can handle difficulties.
_____ 8. I have stronger religious faith.
_____ 9. I discovered that I'm stronger than I thought I was.
_____ 10. I learned a great deal about how wonderful people are.

Source: Adapted from Cann et al. (2010).[22]

A second issue is whether perceptions of change represent genuine growth or merely a temporary coping strategy for dealing with a traumatic event.[15] Nevertheless, the general idea that positive responses to even traumatic events are possible has received a large amount of support.

When applying the study of benefit finding to employees, benefit finding is *the perception of positive consequences from the experience of stressful events at work*. Importantly, finding benefits from stressful events at work may operate differently from finding benefits in non-work contexts. Consider employees in highly stressful jobs, such as police officers, firefighters, military personnel, and first responders. Employees engaged in these types of jobs know that experiencing high-intensity stressors is likely, and they train to be prepared for these dangerous conditions. For example, soldiers know there is a strong likelihood that they will be exposed to traumatic events during a combat operation, and therefore the experience of a traumatic event during deployment is not totally unexpected. Similarly, police officers and firefighters know that highly stressful events may occur when they are performing their jobs. In stark contrast, an individual exposed to an unexpected stressor such as a natural disaster, crime, or serious medical condition has little time to prepare for the event.[16]

In addition to stressful events being more expected in high-risk occupations, personnel working in these occupations train to be able to deal with multiple traumatic events, including situations that may involve sustained levels of threat (e.g., a military combat deployment, a prolonged hostage negotiation at a bank, or a drug bust). Most occupations involving routine exposure to highly stressful events also incorporate a variant of SIT described earlier in the chapter, which prepares them (as much as possible) for the experience of these events on the job.

Given that stressful and even traumatic events may be expected in certain occupations, the possibility exists that the experience of such events may be associated not only with mental health symptoms, but also with the perception of benefits resulting from being able to perform one's job under stressful conditions. Furthermore, the perceived benefits of going through the stressful events may then act to reduce mental health symptoms and improve functioning under stress. An overall model describing these relationships is provided in Figure 6.2. This model illustrates how exposure to high levels of work demands produces a direct effect on increased mental health symptoms, but also an indirect effect on reducing mental health symptoms through the increased benefits that may result from exposure.

Studies examining military personnel who have participated in different types of operations indicate that soldiers report benefits both during and following different deployments, and that the reports of benefits are greater when the soldier is engaged in meaningful work during the deployment.[17,18] Furthermore, evidence shows that reporting more benefits is associated with better adjustment following different types of stressful deployments.[19] The reasons for this relationship are still being investigated. It could be that those individuals who perceive benefits from being deployed are engaging in a bit of rationalization, basically arguing, "I can't have gone through that experience for nothing. Something good has to come from it." On the other hand, it could be that soldiers really grew from being able to perform in demanding conditions, and developed coping mechanisms that would allow them to handle stress better in their future work environments.

This dynamic of working in stressful conditions being positive for employees was also highlighted in a study of psychiatric nurses, who were working in the chaotic environment of an emergency room where psychiatric patients

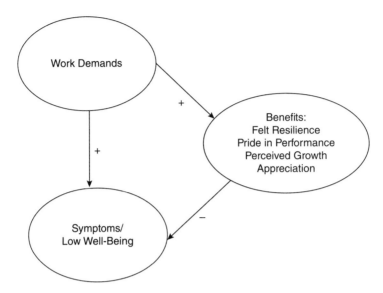

Figure 6.2 How Work Demands May Be Related to Increased Symptoms and Indirectly to Reduced Symptoms Through Perceived Benefits.

were presenting with severe symptoms.[20] The researchers found that nurses reported different benefits from working in the stressful environment, including a description of the ability to perform in an emergency room setting as a "proving ground" that identifies employees who are ready for increased levels of responsibility under difficult conditions. Many employees also observed that managing the chaos evident in the work environment was the very essence of what their job entailed, and therefore the exposure to the stressful environment gave them the opportunity to demonstrate that they could effectively cope with their demands.

The possibility of finding benefits from highly stressful work highlights the point made earlier in the chapter that employees need to consider the possible positive consequences of doing their jobs under difficult conditions. However, researchers are just beginning to examine how employees in high stress jobs may derive benefits from their work, and therefore we are cautious about recommending that all employees try to find the good in all the bad things that happen to them in their jobs. In addition, the studies that have been conducted on benefit finding in stressful jobs have only focused on a few occupations. It remains unclear whether employees in all occupations have the capacity to find benefits in all the different stressors that may be encountered in one's job.

For example, it is hard to imagine finding benefits in being belittled by your supervisor or being the victim of rude and insensitive comments by coworkers. It may be easier to think about benefits you may have experienced from working under highly challenging tasks or being responsible for an important project that created stress because of the impact that failure would have had. In addition, the benefits associated with successfully performing a task under stressful conditions may be apparent shortly after the stressful experience, whereas benefits associated with exposure to work stressors such as abusive supervision or sexual harassment may not be apparent until a later point in time, if at all. For example, an employee who has an abusive supervisor may later appreciate a new supervisor who is fair and supportive. Likewise, employees subjected to a toxic work environment may develop coping strategies that allow them to better deal with conflict in the future. In these cases of clearly toxic workplace stressors, the potential positive responses that may occur in the future are small in comparison to the negative effects that occur during the experience.

However, there is nothing wrong with realizing that doing your job under difficult conditions has contributed to your growth and ability to work under increasingly stressful conditions. At this point, it might be worth reconsidering your responses to Application Exercise 6.1, and again thinking about possible positive outcomes that may have resulted from demands you have encountered at work. It is important to note that stressors at work do not always result in benefits to the employees who are exposed to the demands. However, employee health and performance may be improved through recognizing the benefits that may be occurring, and focusing on these benefits when considering both the negative and positive outcomes of stress.

CONCLUSION

In the present chapter we have emphasized that exposure to workplace stressors not only has negative consequences for employees, but under certain conditions may also result in positive effects. We have been careful to note that discussing the positive outcomes that may result from stressful work does not discount the negative effects these stressors may have, but that being aware of the benefits of stress can help employees place different stressors in their proper context. In addition, knowing both the positive and negative effects that can occur from stress at work allows employees to engage in strategies to increase the probability of positive consequences occurring, while decreasing the negative effects of stress. The major lesson from SIT is, when possible, to gradually increase exposure to stressful conditions in order to acquire the coping strategies necessary to deal with the increased stress. The major lesson from the studies examining perceived benefits following stressful events is that sometimes even high levels of stress can produce benefits, and that being aware of these benefits may help put the experience of stress in a more meaningful context.

REFERENCES

1. Selye, H. (1956). *The Stress of Life*. New York: McGraw-Hill.
2. Lazarus, R. S. (1966). *Psychological Stress and the Coping Process*. New York: Springer.
3. Saunders, T., Driskell, J. E., Johnston, J. H., & Salas, E. (1996). The effect of stress inoculation training on anxiety and performance. *Journal of Occupational Health Psychology, 1*, 170–186.
4. Calhoun, L., & Tedeschi, R. (2006). The foundations of posttraumatic growth: An expanded framework. In L. Calhoun & R. Tedeschi (Eds.), *Handbook of Posttraumatic Growth: Research and Practice* (pp. 1–23). New York: Routledge.
5. Tedeschi, R. G., & Calhoun, L. G. (1996). The posttraumatic growth inventory: Measuring the positive legacy of trauma. *Journal of Traumatic Stress, 9*, 455–471.
6. Loehr, J., & Schwartz, T. (2005). *The Power of Full Engagement: Managing Energy, Not Time, Is the Key to High Performance and Personal Renewal*. New York: The Free Press.
7. Nelson, D. L., & Simmons, B. L. (2011). Savoring eustress while coping with distress: The holistic model of stress. In L. E. Tetrick and J. C. Quick (Eds.), *Handbook of Occupational Health Psychology* (2nd ed., pp. 55–74). Washington, DC: American Psychological Association.
8. Lyubomirsky, S., & Layous, K. (2013). How do simple positive activities increase well-being? *Current Directions in Psychological Science, 22*, 57–62.
9. Hochschild, A. R. (1983). *The Managed Heart: Commercialization of Human Feeling*. Berkeley: University of California Press.
10. Grandey, A. A. (2003). When the show must go on: Surface and deep acting as predictors of emotional exhaustion and service delivery. *Academy of Management Journal, 46*(1), 86–96.
11. Chi, N., Grandey, A. A., Diamond, J. A., & Krimmel, K. R. (2011). Want a tip? Service performance as a function of emotion regulation and extraversion. *Journal of Applied Psychology, 96*, 1337–1346.
12. Hunter, L.W., & Thatcher, S. M. B. (2007). Feeling the heat: Effects of stress, commitment, and job experience on performance. *Academy of Management Journal, 50*, 953–968.
13. Wallace, J. C., Edwards, B. D., Arnold, T., Frazier, M. L., & Finch, D. M. (2009). Work stressors, role-based performance, and the moderating influence of organizational support. *Journal of Applied Psychology, 94*, 254–262.
14. Frazier, P., Tennen, H., Gavian, M., Park, C., Tomich, P., & Tashiro, T. (2009). Does self-reported growth reflect genuine positive change? *Psychological Science, 20*, 912–919.
15. Folkman, S. (2008). The case for positive emotions in the stress process. *Anxiety, Stress, & Coping, 21*, 3–14.
16. Castro, C. A., & Adler, A. B. (2011). Reconceptualizing combat-related posttraumatic stress disorder as an occupational hazard. In A. B Adler, P. D. Bliese, & C. A. Castro (Eds.), *Deployment Psychology: Evidence-Based Strategies to Promote Mental*

Health in the Military (pp. 217–242). Washington, DC: American Psychological Association.

17. Britt, T. W., Adler, A. B., & Bartone, P. T. (2001). Deriving benefits from stressful events: The role of engagement in meaningful work and hardiness. *Journal of Occupational Health Psychology, 6*, 53–63.

18. Wood, M. D., Britt, T. W., Wright, K. M., Thomas, J. L., & Bliese, P. D. (2012). Benefit finding at war: A matter of time. *Journal of Traumatic Stress, 25*, 307–314.

19. Britt, T. W., Herleman, H. A., Odle-Dusseau, H. N., Moore, D., Castro, C. A., Cox, A., & Hoge, C. W. (2013, May). When work demands result in positive outcomes. In *When Positive Work Experiences and Organizational Stressors Collide*, Symposium presented at the Bi-Annual American Psychological Association/ NIOSH Work & Stress Conference, Los Angeles, CA.

20. Deacon, M., Warne, T., & McAndrew, S. (2006). Closeness, chaos, and crisis: The attractions of working in acute mental health care. *Journal of Psychiatric and Mental Health Nursing, 13*, 750–757.

21. Driskell, J. E., Johnston, J. H., & Salas, E. (2001). Does stress training generalize to novel settings? *Human Factors, 43*, 99–110.

22. Cann, A., Calhoun, L. G., Tedeschi, R. G., Taku, K., Vishnevsky, T. . . . et al. (2010). A short form of the Posttraumatic Growth Inventory. *Anxiety, Stress, & Coping, 23*, 127–137.

7

Personal Energy as a Critical Resource for Thriving at Work

When most of us think about the most important factor in accomplishing all the tasks we need to at work, the first thing that typically pops to mind is the amount of time that we have to get things done. However, recent research has shown that personal energy is the critical resource that allows employees to thrive under stress and turn demands into challenges that can be mastered. This chapter addresses why personal energy is so important, those factors associated with higher versus lower levels of energy, and suggestions for increasing and maintaining high levels of personal energy.

It is likely that we all have an intuitive understanding of personal energy and can easily recall times when we felt energized, or conversely when even the simplest action took a tremendous amount of effort. We will see that although different researchers have defined and measured personal energy in different ways, in virtually all studies higher levels of energy are associated with higher levels of motivation, more creative work performance, and an enhanced ability to respond well under difficult conditions. In fact, higher levels of energy can lead employees to seek challenging assignments in order to improve their skills and overall level of performance.

In the present chapter, we first define personal energy and briefly discuss why it is such an important resource. We then discuss energy expenditure and replenishment at work; this will help to illustrate how stressful work conditions can so quickly sap our energy, and conversely how maintaining high levels of energy can offset the negative effects of these same conditions. Within this section, we also provide recommendations for maintaining energy levels throughout the workday. We conclude the chapter with a discussion of what employees *say* they do in order to sustain their energy at work, and how these strategies do not map onto what research has shown is helpful in sustaining energy. In the next chapter, we address the importance of activities individuals can engage in outside work to ensure that their energy levels remain high while at work.

WHAT IS PERSONAL ENERGY, AND HOW DO WE MEASURE IT?

Researchers have defined personal energy in many ways, with some equating high levels of energy with feelings of "vitality," "vigor," and "enthusiasm." Recently, Ryan Quinn and his colleagues have argued for a distinction between *physical energy* and *energetic activation*.[1] They refer to *physical energy* as the energy we possess at a given time that can be used in order to get things done; it is a function of "the chemical bonds that make up glucose or adenosine triphosphate (ATP)" (p. 341). Physical energy is used whenever we engage in some form of action in order to accomplish goals in our work life, whether these goals involve physical actions such as moving equipment, mental actions such as trying to solve a complex problem, or emotional actions related to dealing with an irate customer.

Given the difficulty of measuring and quantifying the actual amount of physical energy we have stored in our bodies at any point in time, Quinn and colleagues point out that most researchers attempt to assess personal energy through our individual perceptions of how energized we feel at any given moment, which they refer to as measures of *energetic activation*. In the present chapter, we use the term *personal energy* to describe an employee's subjective appraisal of his or her energy level. When we are gauging how much energy we have at any given time, we usually think about how much excitement and enthusiasm we have for doing the tasks facing us. As we discussed in the last chapter, high levels of energy are associated with a host of positive outcomes at work. Therefore, it is important to understand those factors that influence the amount of energy we have to deal with demanding conditions we face at work.

In addition to measures of personal energy focused on ratings of vitality, vigor, and enthusiasm, a research team led by the first author of this book has developed a measure of personal energy focused on the perceived resources individuals feel they have available to accomplish different types of tasks.[2] Application Exercise 7.1 contains this measure. Take a minute and complete this measure, which requires you to report how much energy you have to do different tasks at the present moment. This measure was designed to allow individuals to assess where they stand regarding the energy they have to do physical tasks (e.g., exercise, lifting objects), mental tasks (e.g., writing a report, making a complex decision), and emotional tasks (e.g., supporting a coworker,

CALCULATING YOUR ENERGY LEVELS

We are interested in the perceived energy you have to do different types of tasks. We divide tasks into:

- **physical** tasks (e.g., running or lifting weights),
- **mental** tasks (e.g., analyzing information, writing a report),
- **emotional** tasks (e.g., listening to others' problems, managing your own emotions)

The amount of energy you have to engage in different tasks can fluctuate from day to day or throughout the day. For example, you may feel you would get tired quickly doing a mental task (have a very small amount of energy for mental tasks), or you may feel you could perform mental tasks for a long time without getting tired (have a very large amount of energy for mental tasks). Below are a number of items that refer to the energy you have to do different types of tasks. Please write in the number that best describes the amount of energy you have to do these tasks **RIGHT NOW**.

Very small amount of energy		Moderate amount of energy			Very large amount of energy
0	1	2	3	4	5	6

Physical Tasks
1. _____ Athletic activities
2. _____ Physical labor (i.e., moving or lifting objects, sweeping, laundry)
3. _____ Sustained intense activity (i.e., running, jogging, swimming)

Mental Tasks
4. _____ Work on demanding projects
5. _____ Write a report/paper
6. _____ Conduct research in preparation for writing
7. _____ Analyze complex information
8. _____ Read for comprehension
9. _____ Engage in critical thinking tasks

Emotional Tasks
10. _____ Listen to a friend talk about his/her problems
11. _____ Support a coworker through a time of need (e.g. a death in the family)

12. _____ Give relationship advice to someone who has asked for help
13. _____ Discuss problems with a friend
14. _____ Talk about your feelings
15. _____ Show empathy for someone
16. _____ Take care of others

Having responded to the above items, think about the energy you have to do **physical, mental, and emotional** tasks as stored in tanks. We would like you to estimate how full your energy tanks are **RIGHT NOW**.

- For example, if your physical energy tank is currently *very full* you have a lot of energy for doing tasks that require physical effort, but if your tank is currently *near empty* you have little energy for doing physical tasks.

Below is an example of a physical energy tank that is half full:

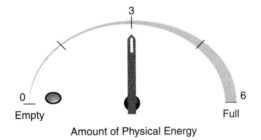

Amount of Physical Energy

My energy tank is completely empty.	My energy tank is close to empty.	My energy tank is a quarter full.	My energy tank is half full.	My energy tank is three-quarters full.	My energy tank is close to full.	My energy tank is completely full.
0	1	2	3	4	5	6

Please write in the number that best describes how full each of your energy tanks is **RIGHT NOW**.

1. _____ Physical energy tank
2. _____ Mental energy tank
3. _____ Emotional energy tank

managing one's own emotions). Although the measure assesses the amount of energy you have to accomplish tasks at the present moment, it can be easily modified to assess the average amount of energy you have had during the past week, or even month, at work.

Most researchers believe that we draw on a single pool of physical energy to accomplish the various tasks we perform at work. However, the perceived resources we have to devote to one type of activity might be lower than the perceived resources we have to devote to a different type of activity, depending on how much of a certain activity we have performed. For example, if we have been unloading supplies at work all day, the perceived energy we have to do additional physical tasks might be low, whereas the perceived energy we have to do mental tasks might still be relatively high. This is because we are likely experiencing fatigue from engaging in a strenuous physical activity, and therefore are experiencing a reduced ability for our muscles to use our available energy resources to perform other physical tasks. However, if our brain has been taking a break while we have performed relatively simple physical tasks, we would still have energy to perform mental tasks. Likewise, we might feel "mentally tired" if we just spent four hours making complex decisions regarding purchases to make for our organization, but we might still have the energy to perform physical tasks such as running or moving supplies. Considering the energy for emotional tasks, one's "emotional energy tank" might be low following a confrontation with a coworker regarding negative behavior, but we might still have energy to solve a work-related problem or engage in physical tasks at work. You can determine the overall amount of available energy you have by summing your scores across the three categories of physical, mental, and emotional tasks.

We believe it is useful to think about one's overall energy level as a reservoir that can range from being empty to full. Our subjective assessment of the energy we have is similar to a fuel gauge. If we sense our energy levels are getting low, it is important to take action to replenish this important resource needed to tackle stressful working conditions. As we will see in this chapter, energy levels can be restored by such activities as taking a quick break, engaging in brief exercise, consuming a snack, reflecting on the significance of your work, or having a meaningful exchange with a coworker.

Despite the different ways in which energy has been assessed, most researchers view the energy that employees possess at a given time period as a key resource that is available to accomplish necessary tasks and to cope with work demands.[1,3,4] Resources are basically anything we have available that allows us to deal with current demands we are facing; resources include tangible things such as money, materials, and supplies, as well as intangible things such as social support, the belief that we can accomplish a given task, and of course personal energy. As discussed earlier, Steven Hobfoll's influential conservation of resources theory emphasizes that people strive to build their pool of different types of resources (including personal energy), and that they experience stress if they lose valuable resources without rebuilding them.[5]

One primary proposition of this model is that people are motivated to build their pool of resources over time, and the actual or threatened loss of resources creates stress for individuals. For example, consider an employee who has worked to establish the support of his or her supervisor for embarking on a new direction for the company. The perceived support of the supervisor is a resource that the employee can use when implementing a new course of action. However, if the employee instead senses a lack of support from the supervisor, this resource is threatened, therefore creating a potentially stressful situation for the employee.

A second component of the model is that people experience more intense negative emotional reactions when resources are *lost*, compared to positive reactions when resources are *gained*. Individuals are especially attuned to negative or threatening stimuli, as opposed to positive or appealing stimuli, probably because an orientation to danger was adaptive in allowing our ancestors to survive long ago. This principle helps explain why the experience of different work stressors can at times have rather immediate effects on employees, whereas positive events at work can remain in the background. This principle also echoes a point made earlier in the book regarding the importance of interpreting work demands as challenges whenever possible. Interpreting work demands in a threatening manner will highlight the potential for resource loss, which has the potential to create a downward spiral for employees. Of course, interpreting work demands in a positive manner requires conscious effort and energy itself, and therefore it is important to engage in strategies to restore energy levels, especially when initially learning how to change the appraisal of a work demand from a threat to a challenge.

Recently, Mina Westman and her colleagues applied Hobfoll's model to the effects of stressors at work.[6] These authors noted that employees are likely to experience burnout when they go through continuous cycles of losing resources without being able to replenish them through rest or adapting better to the demands they are facing. In the context of personal energy as a resource, we can likely all remember a time when our energy levels were sapped, and we did not have the opportunity to replenish our energy reserves because of the continued need to work (or because of having to handle additional family responsibilities after getting home from work). If we repeatedly fail to resupply our energy reserves, we will continue to lose resources we have acquired at work, resulting in a cycle that will not only prevent us from performing optimally under stress, but will also cause us to experience burnout.

Finally, Hobfoll's model states that people must invest resources during the course of meeting the demands of their daily lives in order to prevent the loss of resources and to rebound from the losses that will inevitably occur.[5] This allows employees to develop *resource caravans*, which means that one resource can help an employee acquire additional resources. For example, employees who develop an ability to master the tasks of their primary job (thereby building the resource of self-confidence in being able to do their work) will be in a better position to contribute to the organization's mission, which leads to a better likelihood that their supervisor will support them when they take on more challenging tasks. Supervisor support is an important resource that can then lead to additional resources, such as a possible raise or promotion. Maintaining high levels of personal energy at work will help employees to not only avoid cycles where they continuously lose important resources, but also will put them in a better position to gain the resources they need in order to perform well under stressful working conditions.

PERSONAL ENERGY AS A FINITE RESOURCE

Most researchers believe that the amount of energy we are able to devote to different tasks is limited, and needs replenishment after sustained action at work. Roy Baumeister and his colleagues developed the ego-depletion model to emphasize that individuals have a limited amount of "psychic energy" at any one point in time, and this resource becomes depleted when individuals have to exercise control over their impulses in order to accomplish some goal.[7] Tasks involving self-control require us to refrain from doing something we would rather do, or change the way we are used to doing something (e.g., not eating sweets when we are trying to lose weight, trying out a new approach to work). In a large number of experiments, Baumeister and his colleagues first have individuals perform a task requiring self-control, such as watching a sad movie while trying not to experience any emotions or refraining from eating a chocolate chip cookie when hungry. When individuals perform such tasks, they then perform worse on a different second task requiring self-control (e.g., persistence at solving difficult anagrams, ability to maintain a level of tension on a handgrip). The explanation given for the reduced performance on the second task is that the first task requiring self-control has "used up" energy we have for engaging in those types of activities.

If we apply this to the workplace, most of the activities that employees engage in at work require some degree of self-control, in that employees must try to stay focused on work tasks instead of letting their attention wonder to other matters. However, some tasks at work require more self-control than others. Consider an employee who has an abusive supervisor, and has to continuously refrain from speaking up about the mistreatment. Under these conditions, employees must demonstrate self-control on a daily basis, which continuously uses up energy that could be devoted more productively to their primary job.

What accounts for the negative effects of engaging in self-control tasks on future performance? Matthew Gailliot and his colleagues found that performing a task requiring self-control uses up glucose in our bloodstream, thereby literally sapping the physical energy we have to perform other tasks.[8] These authors not only documented a reduction in blood glucose following the completion of tasks requiring self-control, but also have shown that consuming a glucose drink after engaging in an act of self-control can eliminate the effects of the task on future performance. Therefore, if you have to resist the temptation to take a break while writing a report that requires your sustained attention, it might not be a bad idea to get a small amount of glucose (e.g., a cookie or packet of honey) in your system before turning to your next important project.

In addition to consuming glucose, Mark Muraven has also found that we can build up our energy capacity by practicing tasks that require self-control.[9] For example, individuals who practice such tasks as maintaining control over their posture, monitoring their eating habits, or avoiding cursing experience less of a disruption in performance when having to engage in a task that requires self-control. These authors argue that "self-control strength" is a muscle that can be strengthened through practice.

Interestingly, the types of tasks for building self-control strength may also have an impact on our brain. Lawrence Katz has argued that engaging in tasks that exercise our brain may produce growth factors (neurotrophins) that sharpen mental functioning. Examples of these exercises can be found at http://keepyourbrainalive.com/exercise.html, and include brushing your teeth with your non-dominant hand, closing your eyes while taking a shower, and varying the route you use to go to work. All of these tasks require you to break from well-worn habits, and therefore force you to exert self-control over daily activities. Performing these activities should also increase self-control strength, thereby providing employees with a greater ability to complete tasks at work that require some degree of self-control. Building up your self-control muscle may be especially important for employees engaging in frequent self-control at work (e.g., customer service representatives, teachers).

In addition to employees recognizing the finite nature of their energy supply, managers also need to be aware of how long their employees have been working, and that those employees need to be given the opportunity to take

What This Means for Managers 7.1

BEING ALERT TO EMPLOYEE ENERGY LEVELS

Managers need to be aware of the importance of energy resources for their employees to perform optimally under demanding conditions. Part of getting to know your employees involves recognizing signs that their energy level is getting low, and ensuring that employees take actions during the day to replenish their energy reserves.

- If you have managed multiple employees, you have probably noticed that people differ in how quickly the energy they have to work gets used up. Recognizing this aspect of employees may be helpful in the nature of tasks that are assigned, and recommendations for the length and frequency of breaks a given employee takes.
- Employees who use up their energy reserves quickly may need more frequent breaks of a shorter duration. In contrast, employees who are seemingly able to function at a high level for extended periods of time may need less frequent breaks. However, it is important to check in with these employees to make sure they are not becoming depleted as a function of performing at a high level for an extended amount of time, and encouraging them to take a break if you see signs of strain in the employee.

breaks in order to resupply their energy reserves. In *What This Means for Managers 7.1* we discuss how managers need to be aware that an employee's energy supply is limited, and possible signs that the manager needs to step in and encourage the employee to take a break in order to recover from a sustained high workload.

THE IMPORTANCE OF SLEEP, NUTRITION, AND EXERCISE FOR PERSONAL ENERGY AT WORK

The Centers for Disease Control and Prevention launched an initiative referred to as "Total Worker Health" in 2011, highlighting the importance of physical exercise and nutrition for optimizing employee health and well-being (http://www.cdc.gov/niosh/programs/totalworkerhealth/). In this section of the chapter we discuss evidence for how these healthy behaviors are also critical for sustaining personal energy at work.

Sleep and Energy

So far, we have been considering the importance of prior tasks as contributors to an employee's current state of personal energy. However, employees need to be aware of a number of other ways they can increase the amount of energy in their reservoir. One of the most important predictors of personal energy at work is the amount of quality sleep employees get, with quality sleep being defined as sustained periods of restful sleep. It may seem like we are stating the obvious, but research has shown that lack of quality sleep contributes to reduced feelings of vigor and increased feelings of fatigue, and is associated with poor work performance.[10–12] Recently, researchers have hypothesized that one of the functions of quality sleep is to allow individuals to replenish their reduced energy stores, so they are better able to perform effortful tasks without experiencing a drop in performance on future tasks.[13]

Christopher Barnes and his colleagues have examined the importance of sleep for two very different kinds of outcomes at work: (1) organizational citizenship behaviors (OCBs) such as helping out coworkers, working extra hours when needed, and (2) engaging in unethical conduct.[14,15] In the first study, these authors examined employees who had been in a sleep clinic and then went back to work the next day. Amount of sleep was objectively recorded in the sleep clinic by an electroencephalogram (EEG), and employees then completed a measure of the extent to which they had performed OCBs the next day. The authors found that a higher quantity of sleep was associated with a greater tendency for employees to report engaging in behaviors that benefited the organization. These researchers speculated that a larger quantity of sleep likely provided employees with the energy to not only carry out their primary work tasks, but also tasks that helped the organization more broadly.

In the second study, employees from a number of different organizations responded to questions regarding the average hours of sleep per night they had received during the past three months. The supervisors of these employees then reported on the extent to which the employee had engaged in unethical behavior at work (e.g., claiming credit for someone else's work) during that same three-month time period. The authors found that even after controlling for the overall quality of sleep, employees who reported sleeping fewer hours were judged by their supervisors as engaging in more unethical conduct. Presumably, a lack of sleep results in a reduced amount of self-control strength, which contributes to a greater likelihood that we will fail to inhibit impulses we may have to cut corners or excel unfairly at work. Of course, we should note that it is also possible that those employees who engage in unethical behavior are worried about the consequences, and as a result lose sleep over it.

Another good example of how sleep is important for having the energy to perform optimally at work comes from a recent study among military personnel.[16] Researchers examined US Army helicopter pilots who were attending a leadership training course. The authors had the pilots wear "actigraphs" throughout the training course. Actigraphs are devices worn on the wrist that measure the muscle activity of individuals. Actigraphs are capable of reliably measuring sleep by calculating the amount of time an individual is not showing muscle activity beyond what would normally be expected during a night of sleep. The researchers examined the amount of sleep on the day before a leadership test as a predictor of the pilot's performance on that test, and found a relatively strong relationship. Those aviators who slept less the night before the test performed worse on the leadership test than those who slept longer. The effect of lack of sleep on performance was likely a function of the lack of energy the aviators had for taking the test, as a result of not getting enough sleep.

Therefore, a good starting point for increasing the energy you have to deal with demanding work conditions is to make getting the necessary sleep you need a priority. The National Sleep Foundation (http://www.sleepfoundation.org/) recommends between seven and nine hours of sleep for adults. However, the foundation notes that individuals will differ in the optimum number of hours needed for maximum performance and energy, and therefore employees should experiment with different hours of sleep to find their optimal number. The foundation website also contains a number of good recommendations for getting a good night's sleep, including trying to maintain a regular sleep schedule, not eating two to three hours before bedtime, and avoiding alcohol, caffeine, and smoking shortly before bedtime. We also recommend that if you have periods of chronic poor quality sleep you should see a doctor about it. You may have some medical condition, such as sleep apnea, that can be treated.

Nutrition, Exercise, and Energy

In addition to quality sleep, researchers have also shown that proper nutrition contributes to enhanced feelings of energy during the workday. Jim Loehr and Tony Schwartz provide a detailed discussion of how the food we eat can influence our energy levels at work.[17] These authors note the importance of not only eating the right amount of food (not undereating or overeating), but also the types of food consumed. This includes eating breakfast in order to have energy for the workday, and eating foods that have a low glycemic index (e.g., almonds, apples, turkey) to promote energy throughout the day. Although the authors argue that high glycemic foods and drinks (e.g., soda, candy) can lead to a drop in energy over the long run, remember the study showing that a glucose drink can help offset the effects of engaging in an activity that requires a high level of self-control. Therefore, a small sugar snack may not be a bad idea following a frustrating meeting where you have felt yourself having to restrain the urge to get up and leave.

Another contributor to personal energy at work is exercise. Thirty years ago, Robert Thayer, a pioneer in the study of energy, conducted experiments examining the effects of exercise on individuals' reports of positive energy.[18] Thayer found that walking at a brisk pace for 10 minutes was associated with increased ratings of energy for up to two hours after the activity. More recently, Loehr and Schwartz discussed a number of benefits of engaging in regular exercise (20 to 30 minutes five times a week) for employee energy levels, productivity, and ability to make complex decisions.[17] These authors also note the benefits of engaging in shorter bursts of more intense aerobic activity followed by recovery for maintaining cardiovascular fitness and dealing with the demands of difficult work conditions.

Given the research support for the performance and health consequences of exercise, a number of large businesses now offer employee fitness programs. These organizations recognize that employees who exercise help the bottom financial line in multiple ways, including reduced healthcare costs and increased productivity. Even if your company does not offer a fitness program, you should try incorporating exercise into your daily routine. It's not necessary to join an expensive gym or become some sort of exercise addict. Just taking the time to do 30 minutes of exercise a day and making other modifications to your daily habits (e.g., taking the stairs instead of the elevator at work, parking farther away from the office building) can result in some benefits. Of course, we encourage you to consult your doctor before beginning any exercise program.

MEANINGFUL WORK AND RELATIONSHIPS AS CONTRIBUTORS TO ENERGY AT WORK

In addition to the non-work factors of sleep, nutrition, and exercise, the experiences an employee has at work can also affect his or her level of energy. Richard Ryan and Edward Deci developed their self-determination theory to highlight the benefits of engaging in behavior that flows from the individual versus being controlled by the environment.[18] These authors point out that all individuals have needs for autonomy, competence, and relatedness. That is, people want to feel ownership over their behavior, to be able to demonstrate effectiveness in different life domains, and to feel securely included in interpersonal relationships. A number of researchers have demonstrated that motivation, performance, and well-being are greatest when individuals meet these three needs. In fact, Richard Ryan and his colleagues have argued that subjective vitality (possessing a sense of enthusiasm and aliveness, or positive energy) is greatest when individuals feel autonomous, competent, and connected to others.

Although the workplace has the potential to satisfy these three primary needs and to increase the vitality of employees, this depends a lot on the atmosphere of a given work environment. Employees are most capable of demonstrating competence in the workplace through performing their job. On the other hand, Ryan and his colleagues have shown that individuals tend to experience less vitality at work than in other life domains, and hypothesize that individuals are less capable of having their needs of autonomy and relatedness satisfied in the workplace.[19] Employees who do not have much control over the work they do will have a difficult time feeling autonomous at work, and many work environments may encourage competition between individuals, which decreases the likelihood of quality, trusting, relationships.

However, employees and managers can take steps to create conditions that support employee needs for autonomy and relatedness. Recall that in the previous chapter we discussed the importance of employees trying to craft their jobs to allow greater autonomy and meaning, and we emphasized the role of leadership in creating trusting work environments between employees. One benefit of being involved in meaningful work is that the more you are doing your job out of an inherent interest in a given task, the less energy you use in completing a given assignment. On the other hand, if you feel external pressure to do your work (for example, out of a sense or obligation or purely for an external reward), the tasks you perform will be a greater drain on your overall level of energy.

Recall that earlier in the chapter we discussed how engaging in one task requiring self-control harms performance on a second task requiring self-control. Well, researchers have shown that this performance decrement is much less likely to occur if individuals feel they are autonomously choosing to engage in the initial task, rather than being told to perform the task by others.[20,21] Therefore, one benefit of increasing the autonomy you feel in your job is an ability to do your work in a way that consumes less overall energy.

In addition to how you approach your work, the interactions you have with coworkers can also influence your level of energy. Jane Dutton has argued that when employees interact with each other in respectful ways, they experience increased energy from their interactions.[22] In addition, participating in workgroups characterized by a climate of trust and respect helps to fulfill the need for relatedness that we all have. In addition to the climate of groups to which we belong at work, individual coworkers can also influence our energy levels.

We have all encountered people in the workplace who seem to either energize us or take away our energy. You can probably think of coworkers who are easy to work with, and who want you to succeed; meeting with them seems to rejuvenate you to take on the rest of the day. On the other hand, you can probably also think of coworkers who sap your energy by constantly demanding things from you and expecting you to help them solve problems that they should address themselves.

Adam Grant has noted that people characterized as *givers* and *takers* exist in all organizations.[23] *Givers* are those employees who help others and provide support and advice without expecting anything in return, whereas *takers* are those employees who constantly get people to help them with their work while not reaching out to benefit others. Grant discusses the importance of organizations cultivating givers within an organization, despite the pressures that many employees face to look out for their own self-interests. In addition to givers being better for the organization, giving to others also creates a greater sense of meaning at work that will contribute to your energy reservoir. We would argue that one of the effects of takers within a workgroup or organization is the energy drain they put on the rest of the employees. Not surprisingly, Rob Cross and his colleagues have found that we are drawn to coworkers who contribute to our energy levels, and tend to avoid interacting with people who sap our energy.[24]

Importantly, other people can provide us with energy to fuel our performance, even when our interactions with them are not positive. A good deal of research shows that the mere presence of other people serves to energize our performance. In 1897, Norman Triplett conducted one of the first psychological experiments examining how the presence of other people could facilitate performance on well-learned tasks. Triplett had noticed that cyclists tended to ride faster in the presence of other cyclists than when alone. He then conducted an experiment showing that children reeled in a fishing line much faster when in the presence of another child than when alone.[25]

Several decades after that early experiment, Robert Zajonc coined the term social *facilitation* to refer to the drive created by the presence of other people.[26] However, Zajonc pointed out that although this drive would improve performance on well-learned tasks, it would impair performance on complex tasks that an individual was still trying to master. Therefore, the presence of other people increases physiological arousal, which can be good or bad, depending on what you are doing at work. The major lesson from this line of research is that you should initially learn your primary work tasks alone, and once you become proficient at them, carry out these tasks in the presence of coworkers.

In addition to the mere presence of other people increasing drive, researchers have also examined how our rivals can serve to provide energy that can lead to improved performance. We can probably all remember a time when we were competing with someone who had similar skills, whether at work or in some type of sport. Galvin Kilduff and his colleagues argue that we develop rivalries with those individuals who are close to us in proximity, share similar levels of skill on key attributes, and with whom we have had prior competitive exchanges.[27] The presence of rivals can increase our energy for performing at an optimal level. These authors showed that rivalry among NCAA men's basketball teams predicted indices of defensive performance among team members, a reflection of the effort exerted by team members. Although it is important to avoid rivalries that create a negative workplace atmosphere, a healthy sense of competition, characterized by mutual admiration and respect, with similar coworkers may serve to energize your performance at work.

STRATEGIES FOR MANAGING ENERGY DURING THE WORKDAY

Given the recognition of energy as a critical resource for an employee's ability to perform optimally under difficult work conditions, researchers are beginning to pay more attention to the strategies employees use to manage energy levels during the workday. In the remainder of this chapter, we will discuss a number of strategies for restoring energy, including taking breaks, taking brief naps, and connecting with colleagues who energize you. We devote the entire next chapter to examining how the transition from work to home influences an employee's ability to recover from the workday in order to have the necessary energy to face the challenges that lie ahead the next day.

Recent studies have examined a particular strategy for sustaining energy in detail: taking breaks. Given the findings that personal energy decreases following repeated tasks, it is reasonable to assume that taking breaks from continuous work should serve to allow employees to replenish their energy reserves in order to continue working at a good pace. A number of researchers have shown that taking structured breaks during the workday can have positive effects on employee well-being and health, as well as reducing the likelihood of accidents.[28]

John Trougakos and his colleagues have recently taken a closer look at the nature of breaks employees take during the workday.[29] These authors conceptualized the benefits of workday breaks using Baumeister's ego-depletion model described earlier, examining how the activities engaged in during breaks influence employee energy levels and subsequent performance. The authors make a major distinction between breaks characterized as *respite* and *chores*. Respite breaks occur when an individual stops working as well as thinking about work, and include activities resulting in relaxation or pleasant experiences. During a respite, you are not thinking about work, but take the time to relax or do something you find enjoyable, such as taking a brief walk, listening to music, or surfing the Web. As discussed earlier, most tasks at work involve exercising at least some level of self-control, and therefore in order for a break to be useful, employees need to stop working during the break.

In contrast, chores represent breaks in which employees stop the work they are doing, but turn attention toward another work-related responsibility. For example, employees may decide to take a break by checking e-mail or making a "to-do" list for the rest of the week. In these cases, activities involving mental effort continue to take place during the break, thereby preventing the restoration of energy levels. The researchers conducted a study in which they examined the breaks taken by instructors at a cheerleading camp. Each of the instructors carried a Palm Pilot personal computer, and was beeped randomly throughout the day. Whenever the instructor was beeped, he or she responded to questions on the Palm Pilot regarding any breaks taken since the last session. The authors coded breaks as respites if they involved "napping," "relaxing," or "socializing." They coded breaks as chores if they involved such activities as "running errands," "practicing material," or "preparing for upcoming sessions." Note that the respite breaks represent activities that should help employees rebuild their energy reservoirs, whereas the chore breaks consist of a continuation of activities requiring effort.

The researchers videotaped instructors performing their jobs, and raters judged the extent to which the instructors appeared energetic, enthusiastic, alert, and sincere (i.e., demonstrated positive emotional displays). The results showed that taking breaks characterized as respites was associated with higher ratings of positive emotional displays, whereas taking breaks characterized as chores was not related to the instructor's performance. In addition, instructors reported more positive emotions when taking respite breaks, but reported more negative emotions when taking chore breaks. This study shows that not all breaks are created equal, and supports the idea that only breaks characterized by detachment from primary work tasks will aid in the restoration of energy levels needed for performance.

Given these findings, Charlotte Fritz and her colleagues were interested in examining what employees say they do in order to manage their energy levels at work.[30] The authors examined physical, relational, mental, and spiritual strategies that employees use to sustain energy. Examples of physical strategies include exercising and snacking. Examples of relational strategies include having a positive interaction with a coworker or helping someone out. Examples of mental strategies included planning for either work or non-work activities in the future. Finally, spiritual strategies involved thinking about the meaning of work or the greater significance of one's work for the organization.

The authors further distinguished between strategies that involve taking a break from work for a short period of time ("micro-breaks") versus strategies employees used while doing their work ("work-related strategies"). Examples of micro-breaks include surfing the Web, daydreaming, or having a snack. Examples of work-related strategies include checking e-mail, setting a new goal, or making a phone call. The complete list of strategies is provided in Table 7-1. Take a few minutes and think about which types of breaks you take the most,

Table 7-1. DIFFERENT TYPES OF BREAKS DURING THE WORKDAY

Micro-Breaks

Rank	Strategy	Mean	Relationship with Subjective Vitality	Relationship with Fatigue
1	Drink water	3.54		
2	Have a snack	3.01		+
3	Go to the bathroom	2.92		+
4	Drink a caffeinated beverage	2.90	–	+
5	Do some form of physical activity, including walks or stretching	2.84		
6	Talk to someone about common interests (like sports or hobbies)	2.58	–	+
7	Check in with a friend or family member	2.53		
8	Listen to music	2.53	–	+
9	Surf the Web	2.48	–	+
10	Show compassion to someone who needs help	2.44		
11	Go outside for some fresh air	2.37		
12	Check and send personal e-mails and text messages	2.20	–	+
13	Make plans for the evening or weekend	2.09	–	+
14	Look out the window	2.08		
15	Do an errand	1.93		
16	Read something for fun	1.87		
17	Daydream	1.78	–	+
18	Shop	1.48	–	+
19	Meditate	1.42	+	
20	Nap	1.17		
21	Write in my journal	1.15		
22	Smoke	1.08		+

+/– indicates the direction of the relationship between the strategy and outcome.

(continued)

Table 7-1. (CONTINUED)

Work-Related Strategies

Rank	Strategy	Mean	Relationship with Subjective Vitality	Relationship with Fatigue
1	Check e-mail	3.68		
2	Switch to another task	3.52		
3	Make a to-do list	3.44		
4	Offer help to someone at work	3.24		
5	Talk to a coworker/supervisor	3.23		
6	Learn something new	3.14	+	
7	Focus on what gives me joy at work	2.95	+	
8	Set a new goal	2.90	+	
9	Do something that will make a colleague happy	2.79	+	
10	Make time to show gratitude to someone I work with	2.70	+	
11	Check and update schedule	2.60		
12	Seek feedback	2.52	+	
13	Vent about a problem	2.50	–	+
14	Shut out interruptions	2.38		
15	Reflect on how I make a difference at work	2.34	+	
16	Get out of the office for a meeting	2.34		
17	Find ways to delegate	2.32		
18	Reflect on the meaning of my work	2.24	+	
19	Make a phone call	2.09		
20	Clean the office	1.98		

+/– indicates the direction of the relationship between the strategy and outcome.

Source: Fritz, Lam, & Spreitzer (2011).[30]

and then note the strategies receiving the highest ratings of use for managing personal energy at work. Employees from a number of different occupations completed the measure, along with measures of subjective energy and aliveness (subjective vitality), as well as ratings of fatigue (the lack of energy).

The authors examined the overall use of the different strategies, as well as the extent to which the use of the different strategies predicted subjective vitality and fatigue. The top three work-related strategies endorsed for managing energy were checking e-mail, switching to another work task, and making a to-do list. The top three micro-breaks were drinking water, having a snack, and going to the bathroom. In terms of which strategies were related to vitality and fatigue, the last two columns in Table 7-1 indicate whether the strategy was positively (+) or negatively (–) related to vitality and fatigue. An empty cell indicates that there was no relationship between the strategy and vitality and/ or fatigue. The energy management strategies most predictive of enhanced subjective vitality were learning something new, focusing on what contributes to the experience of joy at work, setting a new goal, and doing something that will make a colleague happy. Note that all of these activities were mentioned earlier in the chapter and in the chapter on thriving under stressful work. Interestingly, endorsement of most of the other micro-break activities was predictive of increased fatigue and/or reduced perceptions of vitality, which indicates that these activities were not effective at sustaining personal energy. The lone exception was meditating, which was predictive of increased vitality.

One possible explanation for these findings is that employees who are under a lot of pressure at work (and are therefore fatigued and not experiencing vitality) may be the ones taking the micro-breaks, which explains why the micro-breaks were associated with increased fatigue and reduced vitality. Research is needed in which the strategies are measured at one point in time, and energy and fatigue levels are assessed at a later point in time. Still, this research shows that some of the most frequently endorsed strategies for managing energy at work are not associated with increased ratings of vitality or reduced ratings of fatigue.

In addition to the importance of taking breaks to restore energy at work, employees should also consider the strategic use of naps to recover during the day. Researchers have found that naps can result in improved energy and performance for employees,[31,32] and may be especially important following long periods of continuous work or during non-standard work schedules (e.g., working the night shift). In one of the few studies examining the benefits of self-selected napping during a night shift, Jonathan Davy and Matthias Göbel had healthy adults participate in a simulated night shift over the course of three nights.[33] The primary tasks during the night shift simulation were making necklaces and bracelets out of beads (which they did 80% of the time), and packing envelopes with paper (which they did 20% of the time).

The researchers randomly assigned the adults to two different conditions. In one condition, the participants received a total of one hour of breaks scheduled throughout the night shift based upon best practices for breaks on a night shift. In the second condition, participants were allowed to take a nap for no longer than one hour, starting no earlier than midnight and beginning no later than 3:00 a.m. The researchers measured how many beads the participants used in their bracelets and necklaces. In addition, the researchers assessed how fast participants responded to different stimuli (e.g., how long did it take to click a mouse when seeing a large yellow circle on the computer screen), how well they recalled words they were asked to remember, physiological measures such as heart rate and heart rate variability, and ratings of subjective measures of sleepiness.

In support of the ability of naps to improve performance and well-being, those participants in the nap condition threaded more beads per hour than participants in the traditional break condition, and this performance improvement grew larger across the three nights of work. In addition, both the reaction time of participants and heart rate were faster in the nap condition, indicating that participants who could take a nap were more alert and demonstrated a higher level of arousal in comparison to participants taking a traditional break. Finally, participants in the nap condition reported being less sleepy throughout the three-night study. Interestingly, participants' reports of how long they napped decreased over the three nights, averaging 36 minutes on Day 1, 29 minutes on Day 2, and 18 minutes on Day 3. These results support a growing body of work suggesting that a nap can be an effective way to recover from work demands in order to have the necessary energy to sustain high levels of motivation and performance.

Of course, actually taking a nap in the middle of the workday may be easier in some jobs than in others. Taking naps is not supported in the organizational cultures of many businesses, therefore preventing the use of this effective recovery tool. In *What This Means for Managers 7.2* we discuss how managers can support the use of different recovery strategies within the workday. One possibility for promoting taking short naps is to allow employees to use part of their lunch hour to take a nap.

What This Means for Managers 7.2

SUSTAINING ENERGY IN YOUR EMPLOYEES

Given that the energy available to employees to accomplish work tasks is limited, managers need to be aware of activities that employees can engage in to replenish energy and to encourage employees to strategically replenish their energy resources through the use of breaks and task management. Below we highlight the manager's role in key recovery activities.

- As discussed in this chapter, employees will have more energy when they see the meaning and importance of their work, and therefore approach their job with more autonomous motivation. Therefore, if you provide employees with the freedom to do their work without constant supervision, they will require less energy to perform their job tasks.

- Employees should be encouraged to take breaks following prolonged periods of work in order to restore their energy reserves. Employees will be hesitant to take breaks if they are not encouraged to do so, and therefore managers should highlight the importance of breaks in staff meetings and policies. In certain cases when an employee works for an extended period of time without taking a break, a manager may need to directly tell the employee it is time to take a break so he or she can return to the task with a higher level of energy.
- Research suggests that naps can be an effective way of restoring energy and enhancing the performance of employees. In many organizations the use of naps is frowned upon. However, naps might be offered as recovery opportunities if managers set parameters on when naps can be taken and the allowed duration of naps.

Our final suggestion for recovery during the workday is to interact with fellow employees who energize you. As we discussed earlier in the chapter, talking with coworkers who share advice, make you laugh, or listen to what you have been going through at work can increase the energy you have for tackling difficult tasks at work. Of course, employees differ in their personalities, and those employees who are more introverted will undoubtedly be less likely to seek out other people at work for meetings and discussion. However, given that interacting with supportive coworkers can provide employees with the additional energy needed to perform well under difficult conditions, we recommend cultivating relationships at work that can restore energy.

Take a minute and complete Application Exercise 7.2, which encourages you to consider how often you interact with fellow employees in your workplace, and the typical outcomes of those interactions. After thinking about it, you can probably identify other employees who both contribute to and detract from your overall energy level. To the extent possible, try to limit interactions (or the duration of those interactions) with the de-energizing coworkers, and increase the frequency of interactions with fellow employees who re-energize you. We believe that employees often fail to appreciate the beneficial impact of coworkers on having the energy necessary to excel in difficult conditions. It is important to remember that in addition to being a potential stressor, fellow employees can also facilitate your ability to thrive under difficult work conditions.

Application Exercise 7.2

Increasing Energy Through Interacting with Others

Many employees may fail to recognize the effects that other people can have on their energy levels at work. In this exercise, you will be encouraged to identify fellow employees at work who energize you, and to consider ways to increase interactions with these energizers. It goes without saying that you should not seek out people who take energy away from you when you are already are feeling drained from work.

Energizers in your Work Environment. Think about your interactions with other employees when you come away feeling better than before the interaction. In the space below, we want you to write the initials of each employee and then provide a brief description of how you could increase the frequency of interactions with the individual. For example, you could make a plan to take a break from work and check in to see how the employee is doing, or you could schedule a short meeting with the employee to discuss current work projects.

Initials of Energizer #1: _____

Strategy for increasing the frequency of interactions with Energizer #1: _____

_____

_____

Initials of Energizer #2: _____

Strategy for increasing the frequency of interactions with Energizer #2: _____

_____

_____

Initials of Energizer #3: _____

Strategy for increasing the frequency of interactions with Energizer #3: _____

_____

_____

Initials of Energizer #4: _____

Strategy for increasing the frequency of interactions with Energizer #4: _____

_____

_____

In addition to these individuals, we encourage you to reach out to other employees in your work environment who are potential energizers. Getting to know these individuals may not only identify an additional energizer, but also contribute to you gaining a better understanding of what other people are doing for the organization.

SUMMARY

In this chapter, we have discussed the critical importance of energy for the ability to thrive under stressful work conditions. Our energy levels can become depleted if we work for a long period of time without recovering from the different work demands we encounter. Seeing the meaning in your work and interacting with employees who are givers rather than takers are ways to sustain your energy levels at work. In addition, we discussed the importance of exercise, nutrition, and adequate sleep to building an energy reservoir that will allow you to face work demands as challenges that have the potential to contribute to your development. Finally, we highlighted the importance of taking breaks and even naps during the workday in order to sustain your energy levels. In the next chapter, we address the importance of recovering from demands when the workday is over.

REFERENCES

1. Quinn, R. W., Spreitzer, G. M., Lam, C. F. (2012). Building a sustainable model of human energy in organizations: Exploring the critical role of resources. *The Academy of Management Annals, 6*, 337–396.
2. McFadden, A.C., Jennings, K.S., Cheung, J.H., Kelley, C., McKibben, E.S. (2015). It's more than a feeling: Assessing subjective energy as the perceived resources to accomplish physical, mental, and emotional Tasks. *Manuscript Under Review.*
3. Hobfoll, S. E. (2002). Social and psychological resources and adaptation. *Review of General Psychology, 6*, 307–324.
4. Shirom, A. (2010). Feeling energetic at work: On vigor's antecedents. In A. B. Bakker & M. P. Leiter (Eds.) *Work Engagement: Recent Developments in Theory and Research* (pp. 69–84). New York: Psychology Press.
5. Hobfoll, S. E. (1998). *Stress, Culture, and Community: The Psychology and Physiology of Stress.* New York: Plenum.
6. Westman, M., Hobfoll, S. E., Chen, S., Davidson, O. B., & Laski, S. (2005). Organizational stress through the lens of Conservation of Resources (COR) Theory. In P. Perrewe & D. C. Ganster (Eds.), *Research in Occupational Stress and Well-Being: Exploring Interpersonal Dynamics* (pp. 167–194). Amsterdam: Elsevier Science/JAI Press.
7. Baumeister, R. F., Bratslavsky, E., Muraven, M., & Tice, D. M. (1998). Ego-depletion: Is the active self a limited resource? *Journal of Personality and Social Psychology, 74*, 1252–1265.
8. Gailliot, M. T., Baumeister, R. F., DeWall, C. N., Maner, J. K., Plant, E. A., Tice, D. M., et al. (2007). Self-control relies on glucose as a limited energy source: Willpower is more than a metaphor. *Journal of Personality and Social Psychology, 92*, 325–336.

9. Muraven, M. (2010). Building self-control strength: Practicing self-control leads to improved self-control performance. *Journal of Experimental Social Psychology*, *46*, 465-468.

10. Pilcher, J. J., & Huffcutt, A. I. (1996). Effects of sleep deprivation on performance: a meta-analysis. *Sleep*, *19*, 318–326.

11. Scott, B. A., & Judge, T. A. (2006). Insomnia, emotions, and job satisfaction: A multilevel study. *Journal of Management*, *32*, 622–645.

12. Sonnentag, S., Binnewies, C., & Mojza, E. J. (2008). "Did you have a nice evening?" A day-level study on recovery experiences, sleep, and affect. *Journal of Applied Psychology*, *93*, 674–684.

13. Åkerstedt, T., Nilsson, P. M., & Kecklund, G. (2009). Sleep and recovery. In S. Sonnentag, P. L. Perrewé, D. Ganster, & C. Daniel (Eds.), *Research in Occupational Stress and Well-Being*, Vol. 7: *Current Perspectives on Job-Stress Recovery* (pp. 205–247). Bingley, UK: JAI Press/Emerald Group Publishing.

14. Barnes, C. M. (2011). "I'll sleep when I'm dead": Managing those too busy to sleep. *Organizational Dynamics*, *40*(1), 18–26.

15. Barnes, C. M., Ghumman, S., & Scott, B. A. (2013). Sleep and organizational citizenship behavior: The mediating role of job satisfaction. *Journal of Occupational Health Psychology*, *18*, 16–26.

16. Killgore, W. D., Estrada, A., Rouse, T., Wildzunas, R. M., & Balkin, T. J. (2009). Sleep and performance measures in soldiers undergoing military relevant training. *US Army Aeromedical Research Laboratory Report No. 2009-13*. Fort Rucker, AL.

17. Loehr, J., & Schwartz, T. (2003). *The Power of Full Engagement: Managing Energy, Not Time, Is the Key to High Performance and Renewal*. New York: Free Press.

18. Thayer, R. E. (1987). Energy, tiredness, and tension effects of a sugar snack versus moderate exercise. *Journal of Personality and Social Psychology*, *52*, 119–125.

18. Ryan, R. M., & Deci, E. L. (2000). Self-determination theory and the facilitation of intrinsic motivation, social development, and well-being. *American Psychologist*, *55*, 68–78.

19. Ryan, R. M., Bernstein, J. H., Brown, K. W. (2010). Weekends, work, and well-being: Psychological need satisfactions and day of the week effects on mood, vitality, and physical symptoms. *Journal of Social and Clinical Psychology*, *29*, 95–122.

20. Moller, A. C., Deci, E. L., & Ryan, R. M. (2006). Choice and ego-depletion: The moderating role of autonomy. *Personality and Social Psychology Bulletin*, *32*, 1024–1036.

21. Muraven, M., Gagné, M., & Rosman, H. (2008). Helpful self-control: Autonomy support, vitality, and depletion. *Journal of Experimental Social Psychology*, *44*, 573–585.

22. Dutton, J. E. (2003). *Energize Your Workplace: How to Build and Sustain High-Quality Connections at Work*. San Francisco: Jossey-Bass Publishers.

23. Grant, A. (2013). In the company of givers and takers. *Harvard Business Review*, April, 90–97.

24. Cross, R., Baker, W. E., & Parker, A. (2003). What creates energy in organizations? *Sloan Management Review*, *44*, 51–57.

25. Triplett, N. (1898). The dynamogenic factors in pacemaking and competition. *American Journal of Psychology, 9,* 507–533.

26. Zajonc, R. B. 1965. Social facilitation. *Science, 149,* 269–274.

27. Kilduff, G. J., Elfenbein, H. A., & Staw, B. W. (2010). The psychology of rivalry: A relationally dependent analysis of competition. *Academy of Management Journal, 53,* 943–969.

28. Trougakos, J. P., & Hideg, I. (2009). Momentary work recovery: The role of within-day work breaks. In S. Sonnentag, P. L. Perrewe, & D. C. Ganster (Eds.), *Research in Occupational Stress and Well-Being* (pp. 37–84). Bingley, UK: Emerald Group Publishing.

29. Trougakos, J. P., Beal, D. J., Green, S. G., & Weiss, H. M. (2008). Making the break count: An episodic examination of recovery activities, emotional experiences, and positive affective displays. *Academy of Management Journal, 51,* 131–146.

30. Fritz, C., Lam, C. F., Spreitzer, G. M. (2011). It's the little things that matter: An examination of knowledge workers' energy management. *Academy of Management Perspectives,* August, 28–39.

31. Purnell, M. T., Feyer, A. M., & Herbison, G. P. (2002). The impact of a nap opportunity during the night shift on the performance and alertness of 12-h shift workers. *Journal of Sleep Research, 11,* 219–227.

32. Takahashi, M., Nakata, A., Haratani, T, Ogawa, Y., & Arito, H. (2004). Post-lunch nap as a worksite intervention to promote alertness on the job. *Ergonomics, 47,* 1003–1013.

33. Davey, J., & Göbel, M. (2013). The effects of a self-selected nap opportunity on the psychophysiological, performance and subjective measures during a simulated industrial night shift regimen. *Ergonomics, 56,* 220–234.

8

How Detaching from Work Restores Personal Energy

Given the importance of personal energy for being able to thrive under stress, it is critical for employees to properly recover from the demands of work in order to replenish this crucial resource. Many people make the erroneous assumption that being able to perform successfully under stressful conditions simply requires working harder and longer—sometimes even bringing work home in order to meet one's work demands. Despite this widespread assumption, and communication technology that allows people to be constantly tethered to the workplace, there is a growing body of research suggesting just the opposite. Specifically, researchers are beginning to find that it is not enough to simply be physically away from the workplace in order to recover; rather, it is just as important that people are able to *psychologically detach* from the demands of work in order to recover and ultimately learn to thrive in the face of a demanding and stressful work environment.

In this chapter, we explore the concept of detachment in detail. As we will show, people often find it very hard to detach from work due to a number of factors, including a sense of duty to their work, preoccupation with work, and advanced communication technology that often keeps one constantly connected to the workplace. Despite the difficulty of detachment, there is a good deal of recent research documenting its value and the various ways that people can potentially detach from work—we review that research in some depth. We also discuss the primary ways that detachment benefits people, and ultimately makes them more capable of thriving under stressful working conditions. We then discuss three ways that people can facilitate detachment, and conclude the chapter by discussing strategies for managing the boundaries between work and other aspects of people's lives.

WHAT IS DETACHMENT AND WHY IS IT HARD TO ACHIEVE?

If you heard someone describe a person she knew, and she used the word "detached," what would your opinion of that person be? Chances are, not very good. That is because we typically associate being detached with not caring. Recent research in occupational health psychology, however, has found that detachment is a key factor in a person's ability to deal successfully with their demands at work. Dalia Etzion, Dov Eden, and Yael Lapidot[1] defined detachment as an "individual's sense of being away from the work situation" (p. 579). This implies that when individuals are detached they are not working at home, or thinking about work during their non-work hours. In essence, detachment means that one psychologically and physically "switches off" and temporarily leaves the workplace behind.

Note from the above definition what detachment *is* and what it is *not*. When a person detaches, this does not mean that he or she does not care about work— a person who is in a state of detachment would certainly react if something bad happened at their workplace. Rather, it simply means that she temporarily gets away from it in both a physical and a psychological sense. Detachment also does not mean that a person is completely inflexible about being away from work—a physician who is away from work and in a state of temporary detachment is not going to ignore a phone call asking her to come to the hospital to help deal with the aftermath of a mass casualty accident.

Given the definition of detachment that we have put forth, why is it hard for many people to detach from work when they leave? One obvious reason is technology. Even in the past five years, extraordinary advances have been made in computing and telecommunications. While these advances help us in many ways, and make our lives more convenient, they also make it very easy to blur the boundaries between different aspects of our lives. We are able to keep up with the latest developments at work, often via e-mail and text messaging, at any time of the day, regardless of our location. Furthermore, being able to do this makes us feel as though we're more productive, efficient, and loyal to our employers. These positive feelings, however, do come at a cost because we are essentially "on call" 24 hours a day. This cost often extends to those around us, who may often find that we're preoccupied with work-related issues, and not "fully present" when we are with them.

A second reason that people often have a hard time detaching, which is related to the first, is that organizations often expect their employees to be perpetually available. In many organizations, one of the first things people receive when they are promoted into higher levels of management is an iPhone or some other sophisticated piece of communication technology. OK, so you've begun your new executive position and have received your new iPhone provided by the company free of change. That's really generous of them, right? Well, maybe and maybe not. Obviously having the free use of an iPhone is a nice perk, but is it really *free*? Most likely the reason that you are being given this "perk" is that you are expected to use it for work purposes. There may be an implicit expectation for you to keep up with your voice and e-mail messages during non-work hours, and that you are generally available most of the time in case some work-related crisis should occur.

Even if an organization does not provide you with a communication device, it still may expect you to be available during non-work hours. Since both of the authors are professors, we can attest to the fact that many students e-mail us with questions during evenings and weekends—and expect responses to those questions. When this is the case, employees are put in a very difficult bind. If you answer e-mails from students during non-work hours, you are conveying the message that you are always available and students come to expect as much. On the other hand, if you don't respond, you may not be seen as "student centered," and students may even complain about your lack of availability to a department chair or other university administrator. Given decreasing enrollments, as well as the increasing costs of higher education, universities can ill-afford to lose disgruntled students and parents; thus, faculty being highly available might be seen as a major source of competitive advantage.

A third reason that many people have difficulty detaching is related to the nature of the job that they hold. For some jobs, it is much easier to leave things at work than it is for others. For example, the work performed by a construction worker is largely physical in nature and it is confined to a certain setting—the construction site. Therefore, when a construction worker leaves his or her job late in the afternoon and goes home, it is unlikely there is much this person can do that's work-related. Contrast this to the work performed by a tax accountant. Tax accounting is a very mentally complex activity, so it is very possible that a person could think about it a great deal during non-work hours. In addition, it would be much easier for a tax accountant to take his or her work home compared to the construction worker. Thus, it would appear more difficult for the tax accountant in this example to detach than it would be for the construction worker.

Another aspect of people's jobs that may influence whether or not they are able to detach during non-work hours is the emotional demands of the work. Some jobs are very emotionally taxing, while others may be much less so. Think of a nurse working in a hospital pediatric oncology unit. Whether readers have children or not, it is hard to imagine anything more emotionally difficult then caring for children who are critically ill and, perhaps even worse, dealing with the parents of these children. Regardless of one's level of experience, or his or her ability to project a professional persona, this has to be very emotionally difficult work, and it's unlikely that a person in this type of job would easily be able to detach.

Contrast this with a person waiting tables at a restaurant. The interactions that such a person would likely have with customers and other restaurant employees are typically pretty cordial, and not likely to be very emotionally charged. Even if a customer is difficult or demanding, the amount of time that the customer occupies the employee's time is still rather small. Therefore, in this type of job, we would argue that it would be much easier for a person to detach.

A final factor that influences whether or not individuals are willing or able to detach from work is the extent to which they enjoy their job. Sometimes people fail to detach simply because they *don't want to detach*. As an example, let's say someone is a teacher and is highly invested in his role as a teacher. For this type of individual, teaching is a major part of their psychological identity and something they find quite enjoyable. As a result, when they leave school and go home, they may take work home with them and think about teaching, so it is unlikely that they will detach from work.

So what's wrong with a person who thoroughly enjoys what they do living and breathing their work 24 hours a day? On the surface, nothing. However, consider the implications of never detaching from work. If a person has a family, it is pretty likely that they will detach from them if they never detach from work.[2] Since people do not have an unlimited amount of physical and psychological energy, it is impossible to devote all of our attention and energy to one aspect of our lives without ignoring other aspects.

Also, based on recent research on detachment, there is evidence that people who fail to detach run the risk of burning themselves out.[3] Furthermore, the risk of burnout is highest when people perform jobs that are highly demanding and stressful.[4] Although we will discuss the specific mechanisms by which this occurs in the following section, consider the following example. Let's say a person derives a great deal of enjoyment from physical exercise. Furthermore, because of this high level of enjoyment, this person exercises five or six times per day, seven days a week. On the surface, one would assume that this person is going to derive five or six times more of the benefits of exercise compared to another person who exercises at a more typical frequencies (e.g., once a day/ three to four times a week).

Although this is certainly possible, and there may very well be some individuals who benefit from this level of exercise, it is not likely. One of the main components of any effective physical exercise program is recovery; that is, people make gains because of the combination of stressing the body and recovering from that stress. In addition, from a psychological perspective, exercising that much is likely to be draining and ultimately may even put a strain on a person's relationships. So even if a person thoroughly enjoys a particular activity, be it exercise or work, it is still important to have at least some time when one is physically and psychologically detached from it. We would also note that for some people, regularly detaching from an activity they greatly enjoy is a tremendous challenge, and we will have suggestions later in this chapter about how to meet this challenge. It is also important to keep in mind that recovery is still a relatively new area of research, so it is quite possible that new insights will emerge over the years as more research is conducted.

Although it is important for individuals to recognize the need for detachment, it is just as important for those who have the responsibility for managing others to recognize this need as well. In *What This Means for Managers 8.1*

What This Means for Managers 8.1

Encouraging Employees to Detach from Work

Every so often you'll see a person at work who is looking tired and worn out and somebody says to them, "You could use a vacation!" This suggests that sometimes other people may recognize that we have a need to detach before we do ourselves. In organizational settings, managers are often in a unique position to make this type of assessment, because they assign work to their employees and often see the effects of that work on their employees. So how does a manager know that an employee might benefit from some temporary detachment from work?

We offer a couple of suggestions below.

- The most obvious scenario is simply when an employee has to work a lot over a sustained period of time. Perhaps there's an important project that has to be completed, or bidding on an important project and the bid has to be completed by a certain date. Employees who go through periods like this often feel some level of satisfaction from completing the work, but also typically need to detach from it at least temporarily.
- Sometimes it's not the *amount* of work one has to perform, but the nature of the work that drains people. Think of people in occupations such as firefighting, emergency medical services, and nursing. Even people in jobs involving customer service sometimes have to deal with intense, emotionally charged situations. Managers should try to understand the nature of their employees' work, and if they have to deal with intense situations, make sure that there are ample opportunities for recovery and detachment.

---

we discuss this issue in more depth. More specifically, we describe some of the signs that managers should look for which may indicate that an employee needs to detach more from work.

WHAT DOES DETACHMENT DO FOR US?

In order to understand the benefits of detachment, it is first useful to consider the theoretical mechanism by which these benefits are typically explained: the conservation of resources (COR) theory, which was developed by Stevan Hobfoll.[5] As discussed in detail in Chapter 7, the basic premise of COR theory is that the daily demands and stressors that we face in the workplace force us to expend psychological and physical "resources" in order cope with them. Recall that COR theory also proposes that people may also engage in activities that are *resource enhancing*, which is really anything that helps us to "recharge." This can be something as simple as taking time out during the day for a short break and friendly conversation with a coworker, to something more elaborate like a week-long vacation from work.

Now that we have established that detachment is a key component of "resource enhancement," it is important to dig a bit deeper and explore *specifically* how detachment enhances our resources. Based on recent research on how people recover from work during their non-work hours, there are three primary pathways by which detachment enhances one's resources: (1) enhancement of mental energy or *engagement*, (2) enhancement of physical energy or *vigor*, and (3) enhancement of sleep quality. Each of these will be described below.

We discussed engagement at work briefly in Chapter 5. In this context, probably the best way to define engagement in general life activities is to equate it with a person's level of *interest* and *enthusiasm*. Think of the last time that you engaged in an activity where you experienced both of these psychological states. This could certainly have occurred during a work-related activity, but may also have occurred during an important sporting event (e.g., Super Bowl, World Series, NCAA Basketball Final Four), a family activity, or even while watching a favorite movie. Regardless of where it occurred, there are likely some common elements to your experience. For example, the level of attention you are allocating to this activity is so high that you are probably not able to pay attention to anything else around you. It is also likely that if anything important or exciting happens during the course of this activity, you have a very enthusiastic response.

Another way that researchers have characterized psychological engagement in an activity is the extent to which people become *absorbed* in the activity. In fact, the term that had been coined to refer to total absorption in an activity is *flow*, discussed briefly in Chapter 5.[6] To really understand total absorption or flow, think of a time that you were working on something that you were both good at and totally enjoyed—perhaps gardening, playing a piece of music, working on a car, running a long distance, or reading a good book. Often when people work on tasks like this, they become so absorbed that they lose track of time, or even forget they have to be somewhere at a certain time. Flow experiences like this are probably less likely in the workplace, but there is evidence that they can and do occur.[7] Furthermore, when people have these experiences, their overall enjoyment of their work is enhanced, which allows them to cope better with the demands of their work.

So what does detachment have to do with psychological engagement in one's work? Going back to COR theory, the basic idea is that we have a finite amount of psychological resources that we can apply to activities that we engage in. Detachment allows us to psychologically "fill the tank," so to speak. As positive as psychological engagement is, we cannot remain engaged in one activity indefinitely or we will eventually burn out. Thus, periodic detachment or "downtime" allows us to be in a position to become engaged with our work—or any other activity, for that matter.

The second pathway by which detachment is resource enhancing is through the enhancement of physical energy, or *vigor*. As discussed in detail in Chapter 5, people who are enthused about what they're doing typically behave differently from those who are less enthused—they put more time into the activity, and generally move more quickly. In everyday terms, we might say that people who are engaged exhibit more *hustle* than people who are less engaged in what they're doing. The reason for this is tied to the previous discussion of psychological engagement. When people are really engaged in what they're doing, they tend not to notice physical fatigue. Again, think of a time when you were completely absorbed in an activity. Not only did you lose track of time and become psychologically oblivious to what was going on around you, you were also probably able to ignore physical fatigue and exhaustion.

Detachment thus also allows us to store up the *physical* resources that we need to enjoy our work and become absorbed in it. When people are able to detach from work, this often has the effect of building up their physical energy, which makes it much easier for people to approach their work with enthusiasm and a sense of vigor. That is likely the reason that researchers have consistently found that long hours of work are negatively related to the physical health of employees.[8]

The third and final pathway by which detachment leads to resource enhancement is by improving sleep quality. We discussed the importance of sleep for energy levels in Chapter 7. A great deal of research over the years has established the negative effects of sleep deprivation,[9] and conversely has shown that both quantity and quality of sleep facilitate mental and physical health. Why? Although many different theories have been developed to explain the value of sleep, most converge on the idea that sleep serves a *restorative* function for both the body and brain. Stated differently, sleep allows the body and brain to repair and fine-tune many of its functions. Therefore, when we are getting the proper amount of sleep we generally feel better and can think more clearly.

Despite the indisputable value of sleep, many people today are sleep deprived. Due to long work hours, media saturation, and a fondness for caffeinated beverages, many people today try to get by on much less sleep then they actually need.[10] Furthermore, sleep deprivation is often cited as the cause of accidents, poor decision-making at work, and general irritability.[11]

When people are unable to detach from work, it is often difficult for them to get to sleep and to maintain a high quality of sleep throughout the night. As a result, people do not feel rested when they wake up in the morning, and then must rely on coffee or energy drinks to get through their day. This ultimately makes it more difficult to get to sleep that night, and this cycle may repeat itself over and over again.

On the other hand, when people are able to detach from work, they are able to "wind down" at night and are ultimately able to get to sleep in a reasonable amount of time, and are able to sustain their sleep over longer periods of time.[12] As a result, these individuals are more likely to wake up feeling energized to begin their day, and as a result approach their day with a sense of vitality and positive energy. This type of approach is likely to be met with more positive reactions from others, and ultimately to result in a more positive experience at work overall. Given these generally positive experiences at work, people may be more likely to leave work feeling more positive, and this type of positive spiral will continue to repeat itself over and over again.

LEARNING TO DETACH: FROM WHY TO HOW

Up to this point, we have defined detachment, and explained how it can facilitate well-being. Some readers may now be thinking, "OK, this is great. But *how* do I make myself detach from work?" This is certainly a fair question. Despite the many benefits to be found from detaching from work, it is hard for many people to actually do it. In the first part of this chapter, we discussed some of the factors that often prevent people from detaching from work. In addition to those factors we discussed previously, some people are simply more likely than others to worry and ruminate over problems and issues at work—for those people, detachment often seems next to impossible.

Despite the difficulty of detaching from work, we believe that *it is possible for people to do it if they want to.* Note that we're not saying it's easy—but that it is *possible.* In this section we discuss three primary strategies that can be used to help develop a healthy level of detachment from work. These strategies, which are based on research conducted by Sabine Sonnentag and Charlotte Fritz, include (1) *relaxation*, (2) *mastery*, and (3) *control*. Each of these is discussed below.

Relaxation

Just like detachment, we tend to have a somewhat negative view of relaxation in our "24/7," always available, world of work. That is, we often equate relaxation with laziness or a lack of motivation. Despite this potentially negative view, we know that relaxation is often an important precondition to detachment.

Despite the potential value of relaxation, many people either feel they do not have time to relax or simply don't know how to relax. So how does a person learn to relax? Based on recent research on recovery from work demands,[13] one key step is simply for people to *discover things that they find relaxing.* Since everyone is different, this is going to be different for everyone. For example, some people find it relaxing to read, while others find it relaxing to watch a movie on TV. For others, simply taking a long walk puts them in a relaxed frame of mind. The point is for people to find things that tend to put them in a *mentally* and *physically* relaxed state.

The second key to relaxation, and this may be the most challenging part, is making the time to engage in these relaxing activities. Again, we tend to live in a world where we feel like we need to be "on" and available all of the time, so for many people making time for relaxation may seem to be frivolous or selfish. Nevertheless, as we have stated above, it is an important precursor to detachment. So, then, how do you find the time to engage in relaxing activities? Obviously, there is no "one size fits all" solution to this general dilemma. However, we feel that a major step toward increasing one's level of relaxation is simply *making it a priority.* In other words, to the extent that people have discretion over their time, actually *scheduling* relaxation or leisure activities is often helpful. If we fail to provide time for relaxation, we will often be completely driven by the demands of our jobs or other people in our lives.

Mastery

The basic idea of mastery is that we can detach from work by becoming more involved and absorbed in our non-work lives. Typically, mastery experiences involve learning new things (e.g., a new language), seeking out intellectual challenges (e.g., playing chess), doing things to challenge ourselves (e.g., competing in triathlons), or simply doing things to broaden our horizons (e.g., taking a class in a field different from our job). Mastery experiences help us in two major ways. First, they force us to devote our mental and intellectual resources to something other than work, and doing so enables us to achieve some level of detachment from it.

Second, mastery experiences can be highly reinforcing, so they allow us to feel a sense of achievement and accomplishment. Why is this important? For many people, the only instances in which they feel a sense of achievement and accomplishment have to do with work. Thus, to the extent that people can experience these emotional states from things they do outside the workplace, it allows them to psychologically detach. That is, they are able to detach from work psychologically because they can experience these positive and powerful emotions from something other than work.

Control

Control is relatively self-explanatory, and is really tied to the other two strategies. When employees are at work, they often do not have complete control over how they are going to spend their time. However, when employees leave work, they typically can exercise control in terms of how they schedule their non-work time. Although there are certainly cases when how we spend our non-work time is out of our control (e.g., anyone who has been the parent of an infant knows how little control they have over such basic factors as sleep), the fact is that we do have some discretion over our non-work time if we choose to use it. For example, a person might decide that she finds it relaxing to go for a 45-minute walk every night after dinner, so she "schedules" the walk into her evening. Being able to do these sorts of activities leads to relaxation, and this ultimately makes it easier to achieve some level of detachment from work.

One thing we know about control, though, is that it's not always easy. Even though exerting control over our time may simply be a matter of saying "no," this may not always be easy to do. Many times, we are afraid to say "no" out of the fear of alienating others, or appearing rigid or inflexible. Obviously, there may be instances where we have to deviate from things that we had planned to do, but at the same time, there is a danger in having our time completely driven by circumstances or other people. More to the point, it is unlikely that we can relax and ultimately detach if we have little or no control over how we spend our time.

Having described the strategies that can be used for detachment, it's now time to see how much you use them. Table 8-1 contains items measuring each of these three strategies. Take a moment and complete this measure, paying

Table 8-1. A Measure of Strategies for Detachment

Think about what you typically do when you are away from work. Based on that, indicate the extent to which you agree with the items below on a scale from 1 (*I do not agree at all*) to 5 (*I fully agree*). In order to calculate your score for each dimension, just sum up your responses and divide by the number of items. This will give you a sense of what you currently do in order to recover from the workday.

Relaxation

1. _____ I kick back and relax.
2. _____ I do relaxing things.
3. _____ I use the time to relax.
4. _____ I take time for leisure.

Mastery

1. _____ I learn new things.
2. _____ I seek out intellectual challenges.
3. _____ I do things that challenge me.
4. _____ I do something to broaden my horizons.

Control

1. _____ I feel like I can decide for myself what to do.
2. _____ I decide my own schedule.
3. _____ I determine for myself how I will spend my time.
4. _____ I take care of things the way I want them done.

Source: Sonnentag & Fritz (2007).[13]

particular attention to the differences in the three scores. Having considered these strategies, we would like you to complete Application Exercise 8.1. This exercise encourages you to think of ways you can better recover from the work demands you are facing so that you can start the day with the energy needed to thrive under these demands.

MANAGING BOUNDARIES BETWEEN WORK AND OTHER AREAS OF LIFE

In addition to the three strategies that we discussed above, another key to detachment is how we manage the boundaries between work and other areas of our lives (e.g., family, leisure time, community involvement, etc.). We treat this as separate from the other three strategies discussed above because it is much broader and encompasses a number of sub-strategies. To begin to understand boundary management, consider the role of transitions that we make during a typical day. For example, when we leave for work in the morning we may make the transition from the role of spouse and parent to employee. Throughout the

Application Exercise 8.1

BETTER RECOVERING FROM WORK DEMANDS

As we have discussed in this chapter and in Chapter 7, it is critical to recover from the demands you encounter at work by detaching from your job and engaging in non-work activities. Table 8-1 provides a number of different strategies for recovering from work demands in a way that will restore energy levels for work the next day. In this brief exercise, we encourage readers to think about how they can use these strategies to recover from the demands of work. Below we want you to describe **THREE** strategies you can implement to better recover from your work demands. In addition, identify whether these strategies fall under relaxation, mastery, or control.

Recovery Strategy #1: _____

_____

Type of Strategy (circle one): Relaxation Mastery Control

Recovery Strategy #2: _____

_____

Type of Strategy (circle one): Relaxation Mastery Control

Recovery Strategy #3: _____

_____

Type of Strategy (circle one): Relaxation Mastery Control

day, however, we often make what are called *micro-transitions* between different roles. We might be at work and receive a call that our child is ill, and at that moment, we may have to immediately make the transition to the parental role. We might be at home with our spouse and children and receive a call that our elderly parent has fallen and needs medical assistance; thus, we may have to instantly make the transition to the role of son/daughter.

Given the inherent unpredictability of life, there are many instances where we are forced to make very quick role transitions, and therefore the boundaries between different life domains become blurred. It is also true, however, that there are inherent differences in the *permeability* of the boundaries in the different areas of life. Generally speaking, the boundary that keeps work from spilling over into family is more permeable than the boundary that prevents family from spilling over into work. In other words, most people make adjustments in their family life based on their work demands, rather than the reverse.

Despite the differences in *boundary permeability*, and the notion that it is acceptable for work to spill over into multiple aspects of people's lives, people do have *some* control over managing this boundary. Unfortunately, people often choose not to exercise the control that they do have. Think of the last time that you checked work-related e-mail at home. Did you really *have* to check your e-mail during your time at home, or was checking your e-mail at home just a means of getting ahead with work? If it was a means of getting ahead, how much did it *really* get you ahead?

Continuing with this same example, when you checked your e-mail did you come across an e-mail that made you angry or worried about something happening at work? Did the fact that you knew about this prior to the next day help you deal with this issue *more effectively*, or did it just cause you to ruin your evening worrying? If the answer to the first question is "yes" and the second question is "no," then we would argue that you didn't accomplish much by allowing work to spill over into your non-work time; you also didn't allow yourself to detach from work.

The point we are trying to make here is not that work should *never* spill over into one's non-work life—that is simply unrealistic. What we are suggesting, though, is that people can purposefully and strategically manage their boundaries in a way that allows for some level of detachment from work. How do we do this? Glen Kreiner, Elaine Hollensbe, and Mathew Sheep[14] conducted a number of qualitative interviews with Episcopal parish priests on how they managed boundaries between work and other aspects of their lives, and based on those interviews, they proposed a number of boundary management strategies that are summarized in Table 8-2.

As can be seen, *behavioral tactics* represent specific behavioral strategies that can be used to segment work from one's non-work life. This category includes using other people, leveraging technology, and invoking triage. *Using other people* is self-explanatory. For example, a person may have his or her spouse screen work-related calls at home to determine whether they require immediate attention. This could also include using other employees in the workplace to determine whether something requires immediate attention.

The sub-category *leveraging technology* includes the use of technologies such as caller ID, voice mail, or e-mail. With caller ID, a person may be able to discern whether a call is work-related, and if it is, use of voice mail can be used to determine whether it needs to be taken care of immediately. We mentioned e-mail earlier, largely in the context of people's failure to disengage from work. In some cases, however, e-mail can also be used to facilitate disengagement. Sometimes a question can be answered, or problem solved, by the

Table 8-2. SUMMARY OF BOUNDARY MANAGEMENT TECHNIQUES

General Category	Sub-Categories
Behavioral Tactics	Using other people
	Leveraging technology
	Invoking triage
	Allowing differential permeability
Temporal Tactics	Controlling work time
	Finding respite
Physical Tactics	Adapting physical boundaries
	Manipulating physical space
	Managing physical artifacts
Communicative Tactics	Setting expectations
	Confronting violators

Source: Kreiner, Hollensbe, & Sheep (2009).[14]

use of e-mail. This can enhance the ability to disengage because it may save a person a trip into work or a lengthy work-related phone conversation.

The third behavioral sub-category, *invoking triage,* may seem a bit confusing at first. Essentially, what the authors are getting at here is *prioritization,* that is, determining what has to be done versus what can be done or what would be desirable to do. Consider the following example. Let's say a student calls a professor at home in the evening (yes, that does happen sometimes) to ask about an item that may potentially be on an exam later that week. The student leaves his number and asks the professor to call him back that night. Should the professor call the student back right away? Although it may make the student happy if the professor does call him back, and in fact this may make the professor somewhat of a hero among his or her peers, there is really no reason that student can't wait for his answer the next day when the professor holds his or her office hours.

Contrast that example with the following one. A physician is not on call and is spending time at home with her family. She receives a phone message that there has been a mass casualty accident with many serious injuries, and the hospital is in need of any physicians who will be able to help in the overloaded emergency room. Should this physical interrupt her family time and help out in this emergency? Although this physician is undoubtedly enjoying the time she is spending with her family, ignoring this situation would be inconsistent with the professional oath that she took when she became a physician. In other words, this would be a situation in which one's professional obligations would take priority over family time.

The behavioral sub-category *allowing differential permeability* really has to do with the decisions people make about what they do and do not bring home from work. As we stated earlier, for most people it is simply unrealistic to think that work can be kept *completely* separate from other areas of one's life, and vice versa. It is possible, however, to make decisions concerning which aspects of work one allows to spill over into his or her non-work life. For example, a person may decide not to talk about negative things that go on at work such as office politics, conflict with coworkers, or negative workplace rumors. He may also decide not to deal with any work-related issues on Sundays. On the other hand, that same person might spend 30 minutes alone on a Saturday afternoon planning what he has to do the next week, or may spend 15 minutes each night going over his work-related text messages in order to plan for the next day.

Notice that in both cases a person is making a conscious choice to allow or not to allow work to spill over into non-work time. This raises the interesting question of whether there is a *correct* amount of permeability that people should allow between the work and non-work aspects of their lives. We do not believe there is, because people do differ in the degree to which they want to segment different parts of their lives.[15] That is, some people enjoy blending work and non-work activities together, while other people prefer to keep work completely separate from the other areas of their lives.

If we look at this issue from a detachment perspective, however, making a conscious decision *not* to allow work to spill over into other areas of one's life at certain times is important. If we always allow work to spill over into other areas of life, it is very difficult, if not impossible, to achieve some level of detachment from work and ultimately achieve some level of recovery for the next day.

The second general category, *temporal tactics*, represents things that people can do to enhance the control that they have over their time. The first sub-category under this general category, *controlling work time*, represents a variety of strategies that can be used in order to help individuals gain greater control over the time they spend in the workplace. For example, many professors block of segments of time for tasks such as writing or grading exams. This strategy can also involve trading time in different domains; for example, if one works on a work-related project for three hours on a Thursday night, he or she may take Friday afternoon off and engage in some leisure activity. Note, though, that there is a great deal of variability in the level of flexibility that people may have in implementing this strategy. An employee who works in an hourly job may not be able to exert a great amount of control over his or her time.

The second temporal tactic, *finding respite*, involves temporarily removing oneself from work or home demands for a significant amount of time. The most common method of finding respite from work-related demands is to take a vacation, which typically lasts from a couple of days to a week or more. Researchers have studied the impact of vacations on employee well-being,[16] and they can be beneficial. However, in order for vacations to provide some benefit, two conditions must be present. First, the vacation itself must provide some opportunity for relaxation and recovery.[16] Many readers have probably heard the expression "I need a vacation from my vacation" to describe the experiences of those who do not have relaxing experiences during a vacation, and the evidence suggests that such individuals do not receive a great deal of benefit from vacations.

The second condition, and this is quite relevant to the present discussion, is that people must be able to detach from work during the time they are away. As many readers undoubtedly know, it is very easy to stay tied to work during a vacation due to the availability of computers at hotels, as well as other technology (e.g., iPhones). Furthermore, even if one does not really want to stay connected to work during a vacation, there is still some incentive to do so— you don't want to end up with 8,000 e-mails in your inbox when you return! Nevertheless, research on vacations has clearly shown that people who are able to detach from work during vacation time derive much greater benefit than those who are either unable or unwilling to do so.

The third general category, *physical tactics*, represents a variety of strategies that involve the physical environment. The two most common strategies within this category, *adapting physical boundaries* and *manipulating physical space*, essentially involve managing the physical distance between work and other areas of one's life. Some people, for example, choose to live some distance from work so they can separate the work and home domains. Conversely, in other cases people choose to live very close to work so it's very easy for them to integrate the two.

The final sub-category, *managing physical artifacts*, involves the use of tangible items in order to separate or blend work with other aspects of one's life. If individuals want to keep their work and home lives separate, they might use separate calendars to keep track of their work and family activities. We also know, however, that many people also use this strategy to integrate work with other areas of their lives. Many people, for example, decorate their workspace with pictures of family, and many handle work-related matters with their personal e-mail accounts. This strategy of managing role transitions again highlights the differences among people in their preferences for managing work and non-work transitions.

The final general category, *communicative techniques*, really has to with communicating boundary-related expectations to others. The first sub-category, *setting expectations*, involves letting people know up front what the boundaries are. A manager, for example, may let her employees know what is and what is not an acceptable reason to call her about a work-related matter at home—presumably to preserve her private time with her family. It is also possible to create expectations of a high level of availability; for example, a college professor may put his cell phone number on the course syllabus and tell his students that it's acceptable to call him after work hours if they have a course-related question.

The other sub-category, *confronting violators*, has to do with the actions taken against those who violate the boundaries people have set up between work and other areas of their lives. These actions can occur when the actual violation occurs, or a person may have no choice but to allow the violation to occur and then deal with it at a later time. Consider the following example. Let's say a physician is at a restaurant having dinner with her family and a patient decides to come up to her table and ask a question about the medication the she has recently prescribed for this patient. Let's further assume that this patient's condition is not serious or life-threatening, so this patient could obviously wait until the next day and contact the physician through her office staff.

Unless this physician has created the expectation in her patients that it's OK for them to interrupt time with her family, this clearly represents a boundary violation on the part of this patient. What can the physician do in this case? One strategy would be to politely tell the patient that she is having dinner with her family, and that she would be happy to answer any questions if the patient calls her office the next day. On the other hand, she could excuse herself from the table and briefly talk with the patient in another area of the restaurant in order to answer the patient's questions. The next time this patient has an appointment, she could gently remind the patient that it's not appropriate to expect the physician to provide medical advice during a family meal.

Of all the strategies that people may use to manage the boundaries between work and other areas of their lives, this can be a very difficult one to implement. Generally speaking, most of us like to please other people, and it's uncomfortable to have to tell people that you can't give them what they want at that particular moment, or at a later time tell them that they have engaged in what you consider to be inappropriate behavior. It may also be very uncomfortable when the violator is one's immediate supervisor, or someone else within the organization who holds a higher-level position.

This strategy may also be difficult to implement for those working in occupations where there is a focus on service to others (e.g., teaching, clergy, social work, etc.). Since most people who choose to go into these professions do so because of a genuine desire to serve others, confronting those who violate work/non-work boundaries may make the individuals feel like they are being inconsiderate or callous. However, in the long run, failing to establish any boundaries between work and other areas of one's life may cause service providers to resent those they are trying to help, and ultimately cause them to leave their profession.[17]

As was shown in this section, there are a variety of strategies that people can use to balance the demands of work and other aspects of our lives. Furthermore, the choice of *specific* strategies is going to depend largely on the nature of the demands one is facing, and to a certain degree individual preferences. The important point is that regardless of the strategies used, successfully balancing these demands provides us with the opportunity for recovery and makes us better able to meet the demands that we may face in the future. In order to help you think about how you might be able to use these strategies to better manage your work/non-work interface, please complete Application Exercise 8.2.

Although the strategies discussed in this section are directed at individual employees, managers also play a key role in helping employees balance the demands of work and other aspects of their lives. In *What This Means for Managers 8.2* we discuss how managers can help their employees to achieve better balance in their lives, which ultimately will help them to be more productive in the workplace.

Application Exercise 8.2

MANAGING WORK/NON-WORK BOUNDARIES

A major point that we make toward the end of this chapter is that managing the boundaries between work and other aspect of one's life is one of the major keys to detachment. We also describe in some detail strategies that can be used to manage these boundaries (see Table 8-2). In this brief exercise, we encourage readers to think about how they can use these strategies to manage the boundaries in the own lives.

Step 1. Thinking about the past week, recall TWO instances where you needed to manage boundaries between work and other aspects of your life. This may be instances where work has intruded into your non-work life, or perhaps where areas of your non-work life have intruded into work. Write each of these down.

Step 2. Looking at Table 8.2, indicate whether you used any of the strategies in managing your work and non-work lives during the TWO occasions you identified in Step 1. Note that you may have used *multiple* strategies in each case, and if that's true, write them down.

Step 3. Provide your thoughts on how successful each strategy was in managing the boundaries between work and other aspects of your life.

_____

_____

Step 4. Think about the *upcoming* week, and consider TWO strategies in Table 8-2 that you think will better allow you to manage the interface between your work and non-work lives. Write down each strategy, and then indicate how you are going to implement the strategy:

_____

_____

_____

_____

What This Means for Managers 8.2

FACILITATING WORK/NON-WORK BOUNDARIES

As is evident in this chapter, considerable research has been on balancing the demands of work with aspects of people's lives, and the reason for this is pretty simple—the boundaries between work and other aspects of our lives are "fuzzier" than ever before. Although we believe that individuals are ultimately responsible for balancing the demands of different aspects of their lives, in organizations managers play a key role in this process.

Given this importance, we offer the following suggestions to managers to help employees balance all of these demands.

- Recognize that people differ in the priority they place on different aspects of their lives. For example, a manager may be highly focused on work and devote a great deal of time and energy to it. Other people, however, may have different priorities yet still are able to get their work done effectively.
- Intrude on people's personal lives only as a *last* resort. People value their non-work time, so managers should try not to ask people to work late or bring work home unless it's absolutely necessary. Obviously, there may be times when this is necessary, but again we believe that it should only be done if other options are exhausted.
- We believe that managers should be good role models as far as balancing work and other aspects of their lives. There is no "correct" balance between work and other aspects of a person's life, but the weight of the evidence suggests that people are much happier and fulfilled when they have a balanced life.

SUMMARY

In this chapter, we have discussed the important concept of detachment. We began the chapter by focusing on the challenges people face when they attempt to detach from work, and then described the various ways that detachment leads to decreased strain and enhanced employee well-being. We then described the various ways that people can detach from work, and offered a number of practical suggestions on how to do so.

Since detachment often involves managing the boundaries between work and other aspects our lives, we described a number of strategies that can be used to manage these boundaries. These strategies tend to involve making choices about how one's time is spent, actively managing the physical boundaries surrounding work, communicating expectations to others about boundaries, and confronting those who violate the work/non-work boundaries they have set up. Setting up and maintaining a boundary is important, because without boundaries people are never able to fully detach from work and gain the benefits from doing so.

REFERENCES

1. Etzion, D., Eden, D., & Lapidot, Y. (1998). Relief from job stressors and burnout: Respite service as respite. *Journal of Applied Psychology, 83*, 577–583.
2. Sonnentag, S., Binnewies, C., Mojza, E. J. (2008). "Did you have a nice evening?" A day-level study on recovery experiences, sleep, and affect. *Journal of Applied Psychology, 93*, 674–684.
3. Etzion, D. (2003). Annualized vacation: Duration of relief from job stressors and burnout. *Anxiety, Stress, & Coping, 16*, 213–226.
4. Fritz, C., & Sonnentag, S. (2005). Recovery, health, and job performance: Effects of weekend experiences. *Journal of Applied Psychology, 10*, 187–199.
5. Hobfell, S. E. (1989). Conservation of resources: A new attempt at conceptualizing stress. *American Psychologist, 44*, 513–524.
6. Csikszentmihalyi, M. (1990). *Flow: The Psychology of Optimal Experience.* New York: Harper & Row.
7. Eisenberger, R., Jones, J. R., Stinglhamber, Shanock, L., & Randall, A. T. (2005). Flow experiences at work: For high achievers along? *Journal of Organizational Behavior, 26*, 755–775.
8. Sparks, K., Cooper, C. L., Fried, Y., & Shirom, A. (1997). The effects of hours of work on health: A meta-analytic review. *Journal of Occupational and Organizational Psychology, 70*, 391–408.
9. Burns, C. M. (2012). Working in our sleep: Sleep and self-regulation in organizations. *Organizational Psychology Review, 2*, 234–257.

10. Swanson, L. M., Arnedt, J. T., Rosekind, M. R., Belenky, G., Balkin, T. J., & Drake, C. (2011). Sleep disorders and work performance: Findings from the 2008 National Sleep Foundation Sleep in America poll. *Journal of Sleep Research, 20,* 487–494.

11. Barnes, C. M., & Hollenbeck, J. R. (2009). Sleep deprivation and decision-making in teams: Burning the midnight oil or playing with fire. *Academy of Management Review, 34,* 56–66.

12. Ten Brummelhuis, L. L., & Bakker, A. B. (2012). Staying engaged during the week: The effect of off-job activities on next day work engagement. *Journal of Occupational Health Psychology, 17,* 445–455.

13. Sonnentag, S., & Fritz, C. (2007). The Recovery Experience Questionnaire: Development and validation of a measure for assessing recuperation and unwinding from work. *Journal of Occupational Health Psychology, 12,* 204–221.

14. Kreiner, G. E., Hollensbe, E. C., & Sheep, M. L. (2009). Balancing borders and bridges: Negotiating the work-home interface via boundary work tactics. *Academy of Management Journal, 52,* 704–730.

15. Ashforth, B. E., Kriener, G. E., & Fugate, M. (2000). All in a day's work: Boundaries and micro role transitions. *Academy of Management Review, 25,* 472–491.

16. Eden, D. (1990). Acute and chronic stress, strain, and vacation relief. *Organizational Behavior and Human Decision Processes, 45,* 175–193.

17. Taylor, B., & Barling, J. (2004). Identifying sources and effects of career fatigue and burnout for mental health nurses: A qualitative approach. *International Journal of Mental Health Nursing, 13,* 117–125.

9

Failure to Thrive at Work

Although the recommendations included in this book will help employees to use stressful work conditions for their benefit, there are some instances when an employee may try to thrive under difficult working conditions but may not be able to do so. In the present chapter, we focus on the experience of failing to thrive at work, and distinguish this experience from burnout.[1]

We argue that the failure to thrive at work results from two primary factors. The first factor is a fundamental lack of fit between employees and their job and/or their organization, resulting in a lack of meaning, significance, and the experience of inauthenticity at work. Individuals who feel a high level of person-environment fit at work see a good match between their skills, abilities, and personality and their job and the organization for which they work. Individuals perceiving a low person-environment fit feel out of sync with their job, organization, and/or vocation, not seeing the connection between important parts of who they are and the work they are performing. The second factor is the chronic experience of boredom, which prevents employees from experiencing meaning in their work and the challenge necessary in order to thrive.

Importantly, leaders within an organization also play a critical role in the failure of employees to thrive. Leaders who dismiss the recommendations provided throughout this book are likely to create environments that prevent thriving. We highlight the role of managers in employees' failure to thrive in the *What This Means for Managers* boxes of the chapter. In the present chapter, we first discuss why the failure to thrive at work is different from burnout. We then address the importance of person-environment misfit as a contributor to failure to thrive, followed by an examination of boredom at work. We conclude the chapter with a discussion of why taking action to address failing to thrive at work is just as important as taking action to decrease burnout.

THE DIFFERENCE BETWEEN FAILURE TO THRIVE AND BURNOUT

As we will show in this chapter, failure to thrive at work results from the lack of meaningful and challenging activity caused by either a lack of fit between the employee and his or her job, or the failure of organizational leaders to provide a work environment that facilitates thriving. In contrast, burnout is a syndrome caused by the experience of chronic interpersonal stressors encountered on the job.[1,2] As we have discussed at different points in this book, it is useful to think about burnout and thriving as not being on opposite ends of a single continuum, but rather as two separate experiences that can exist independently of one another.

Most important, employees may experience a failure to thrive in the absence of burnout. That is, employees may encounter a sustained period of a lack of thriving-related experiences in the absence of the interpersonal stressors that produce burnout. We have all encountered employees at work who do not appear to experience strain caused by high levels of work demands, but who also do not appear to be experiencing thriving-related states of personal engagement, vigor, and developing along an upward trajectory. All of us will occasionally fail to experience a sense of thriving at work. However, a prolonged inability to be personally engaged in work and to approach our work tasks with a sense of enthusiasm and vigor, despite attempts at making one's job more challenging and meaningful and to recover from work demands, is indicative of a failure to thrive. Failing to thrive at work could easily occur in the absence of the experience of burnout. Of course, if an employee experiences a prolonged lack of thriving-related experiences at work in the presence of sustained interpersonal stressors on the job, he or she may be likely to experience both a failure to thrive and burnout.

PERSON-ENVIRONMENT FIT AND THE FAILURE TO THRIVE

A long history exists within the field of organizational psychology examining how the fit between an employee and his or her job and organization can affect the employee's motivation, health, and performance. Broadly speaking, person-environment fit refers to the compatibility between qualities of the person (e.g., the person's knowledge, interests, abilities, attitudes, personality, and values) and the person's vocation, job, or organization.[3] Most of the time, researchers measure the *perceived* fit between the person and some aspect of his or her environment, although researchers occasionally assess the individual and environment separately and calculate the degree of fit more objectively based upon the demonstrated compatibility between the employee and environment.[4] For example, a researcher might ask employees to rate the extent to which they value such things as creativity, order, and teamwork, and then assess the extent to which the employee's organization also values those attributes. Either way, a lack of fit between the employee and his or her environment has been associated not only with a lack of commitment to the job and/or organization and poor performance, but also with a lack of meaning and dissatisfaction with one's job.[4]

In the present section we address the most common types of person-environment fit, those between employees and their vocation or career choice (person-vocation fit), their job (person-job fit), and their organization (person-organization fit). Employees who experience a lack of fit with their vocation, job, or organization for an extended period are at risk for experiencing a lack of meaning and significance at work. We argue that these factors will lead employees to experience a consistent state of inauthenticity at work, which contributes to a failure to thrive.

At the broadest level, *person-vocation* fit refers to whether there is compatibility between the skills and abilities of the individual and those required by a particular career.[4] People typically decide to pursue a particular career because they believe the career is consistent with their interests and abilities. Career counselors administer tests to assess the skills, interests, and personality of the individual and attempt to match those aspects of the individual with an appropriate vocation or career. In many cases, poor person-vocation fit is usually detected early, as individuals typically choose a career that they think is already consistent with their interests and abilities.

Once in a particular career, employees typically quickly learn whether they have the skills and abilities to succeed in a particular vocation. For example, an individual who dislikes interacting with others is probably not going to be happy in a career as a customer service representative. On the other hand, a more extraverted individual who tends to derive energy from other people is ideally suited for this type of position.

In the context of the failure to thrive at work, it will be very difficult for individuals to respond well to challenges at work and to find significance in what they are doing when there is an incompatibility between aspects of the individual and those required by a particular occupation. Therefore, if you find yourself in a constant state of being unable to experience enthusiasm for what you are doing, one of your first questions should be whether you have chosen a career that is consistent with key aspects of who you are. Of course, changing careers is a big deal. If you find yourself questioning whether you should switch careers, we recommend finding a career counselor to determine your compatibility with your current career and to help identify which careers might be more of a match with your skills, abilities, and values. You can also visit the website http://www.self-directed-search.com/, where for a fee you can assess which careers are most compatible with key aspects of your personality, including your skills, abilities, interests, and traits. The tests included on the website are based on the work of John Holland, who pioneered the study of career assessment.[5] A good book that discusses how to choose the right career is *What Color Is Your Parachute? A Practical Guide for Job Hunters and Career Changers*, written by Robert Bolles.[6]

Assuming that you are in a career that is compatible with your skills, abilities, and interests, a second form of person-environment fit to consider is *person-job* fit. A particular job is narrower than an overall career, and individuals typically have multiple choices for jobs at a given point in time. Jobs have unique requirements that may or may not be compatible with the individual. For example, an employee may be in a job where he is expected to work on the weekend, but does not want to be away from his family during that time. As another example, you may feel that working with others is a strength of yours, but you may be in a job where you do not get to do many group projects. Many of us have had experiences where we started a job, only to realize that the requirements of the job were different from what we expected.

A popular measure of person-job fit is provided in Table 9-1.[7] Take a minute and think about how you would complete this measure regarding your current job. If you find yourself not agreeing with items such as "my abilities, skills, and talents are the right type for this job," you probably are not in a job that fits well with key aspects of your personality and abilities. Often employees begin a job thinking it will be a great fit based upon the job description provided by the employer, only to find that the job is completely different once they start it. One way for organizations to decrease the likelihood of person-job misfit is to be sure to provide realistic job previews to prospective employees. A large amount of research shows that realistic job previews are associated with higher levels of job satisfaction among employees, and a lesser likelihood of employees leaving the organization.[8]

Although the job you are in is likely to be relatively stable over time, it is worth assessing your person-job fit from time to time to see whether your lack of job fit is consistent over time. A chronic pattern of low person-job fit might not only be stressful, but will also prevent the establishment of meaning at work that will contribute to your ability to thrive under difficult work stressors. Researchers have examined how the measure contained in Table 9-1 predicts a number of different outcomes.[7] Person-job fit was most strongly related to the meaning employees assigned to their work, indicating that those employees reporting a low person-job fit were less likely to find their work meaningful in comparison to employees reporting a higher person-job fit. These results

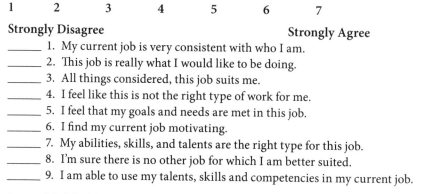

Table 9-1. A MEASURE OF PERSON-JOB FIT

Respond to the following items regarding your current job on the scale below.

1	2	3	4	5	6	7

Strongly Disagree   **Strongly Agree**

_____ 1. My current job is very consistent with who I am.

_____ 2. This job is really what I would like to be doing.

_____ 3. All things considered, this job suits me.

_____ 4. I feel like this is not the right type of work for me.

_____ 5. I feel that my goals and needs are met in this job.

_____ 6. I find my current job motivating.

_____ 7. My abilities, skills, and talents are the right type for this job.

_____ 8. I'm sure there is no other job for which I am better suited.

_____ 9. I am able to use my talents, skills and competencies in my current job.

Source: Modified from Brkich et al. (2002).[7]

were obtained from employees at a single point in time. A prolonged period of person-job misfit would likely have a cumulative draining effect on the meaning that employees derive from their work, which would contribute to a failure for employees to thrive in their current job.

While person-vocation and person-job fit refer to the compatibility between employees and their careers and the jobs within their careers, *person-organization fit* refers to the extent to which employees are compatible with the organizations in which they work.[9] Recently organizational scholars have devoted a lot of attention to understanding the differences between organizations in both their culture and climate. Organizational culture addresses the broad-level values and ways of doing things that characterize a particular organization, and the unquestioned assumptions that people have in organizations. In contrast, organizational climate refers to shared perceptions among employees within an organization regarding targeted issues like the use of safety equipment, importance of customer service, the tendency to be innovative versus risk-averse, and so on. Both organizational culture and climate characterize the "psychological" and interpersonal environment in which employees spend their working lives, and have the potential to shape the motivation and behavior of employees.[10,11]

Whereas person-vocation and person-job fit highlight the skills, abilities, and personality of the employee, *person-organization fit* highlights the values possessed by the employee and the values espoused by the organization. In fact, Jennifer Chatman originally defined person-organization fit as "the congruence between the norms and values of organizations and the values of persons" (p. 339).[12] Examples of the types of values examined by researchers include creativity, equality, fairness, stability and continuity, innovativeness, dependability, and teamwork. When there is a correspondence between the values of the employee and the organization, the employee becomes committed to the organization and is willing to go beyond his or her job requirements to help further the goals of the organization. In contrast, when individuals perceive a lack of fit between their own values and those of the organization, they consider leaving the organization, and are less likely to work hard on behalf of the organization. Consider an engineer who believes that it is very important to protect the environment and avoid unnecessary pollution and waste. This engineer is going to experience low person-organization fit if her organization emphasizes profits over any damage that might be done to the environment. This example highlights that person-organization fit can be especially affected by congruence on values that are centrally important to the individual employee.

As with other forms of fit, researchers have examined both employees' *perception* of fit between their values and those of the organization, as well as the degree of actual fit between employee values and an independent assessment of the values espoused by the organization. One popular measure of perceived person-organization fit simply asks employees to respond to the following statements, using a scale ranging from 1 (*strongly disagree*) to 7 (*strongly agree*):[9]

1. The things that I value in life are very similar to the things my organization values.
2. My personal values match my organization's values and culture.
3. My organization's values and culture provide a good fit with the things that I value in life.

Take a minute and think about how you would respond to these items with regard to the organization for which you currently work. If you are likely to agree or strongly agree with these statements, you generally perceive a good fit between your own values and those of the organization. However, if you tend to disagree with these items, you sense a disconnect between what your organization values and what you value.

As with person-job fit, employee perceptions of person-organization fit are likely to be stable over time. However, if your organization goes through a substantial change (e.g., gets a new CEO, makes a conscious attempt to change its culture), it may be worth responding to the above questions at different points in time. If your perception of person-organization fit remains low, you may find yourself thinking about leaving the organization in order to work for an organization that shares your values, especially if there is lack of agreement on values that are very important to you.

Considering the three types of person-environment fit together, it becomes easy to see how a chronic lack of fit with your career, job, and/or organization could affect the meaning and significance of the work you do, and your ability to approach demands you encounter at work as challenges to master. Remember that thriving-related experiences include vigor, engagement, and learning, and we argue that the chronic perception of lack of fit is likely to sap the energy you need to perform well under different conditions. Furthermore, a poor person-environment fit almost by definition signifies that employees are not developing along an upward trajectory of learning new skills within their job and organization.

We argue that one critical experience linking person-environment misfit and failure to thrive is employees feeling a lack of authenticity at work. Psychologists have discussed the importance of authenticity for decades, beginning with the humanistic psychologist Carl Rogers. In Chapter 7, we discussed Edward Deci and Richard Ryan's self-determination theory, which highlights the importance of individuals behaving autonomously. Authenticity refers to the experience of one's behavior in a given setting as a representation of his or her "true self."[13] The experience of inauthenticity results when individuals behave in ways inconsistent with key aspects of their identity (e.g., their values, attitudes, or personality).[14]

We can probably all recall times when the situation we were in required us to act differently than we normally would. For example, an introverted sales manager might have to act extraverted when meeting with a group of potential buyers, or an employee who values getting along with others might have to confront a coworker regarding poor performance on a team project. During our work lives there will be times when we need to act in ways that may not represent our "true selves." Modifying our behavior based on the requirements of a situation at work is an interpersonal skill that is required in today's workforce. However, employees who believe they are constantly acting in ways inconsistent with who they are will eventually experience a sense a lack of authenticity at work, which we argue will be associated with a failure to thrive.

A recent measure of authenticity at work is provided in Table 9-2. Take a few minutes and think about how you would respond to these items regarding how you typically feel in your current job. If you tend to agree with the items, you feel like you can be yourself at work and determine what you do. If you tend to disagree with the items, you do not feel like yourself at work, and perhaps even have the feeling that you are an imposter in your work environment. Recent studies have found that higher scores on this measure are associated with greater satisfaction at work and higher scores on overall well-being.[15] We argue that low scores on this measure, particularly over an extended period, are likely a function of a lack of person-environment fit in an employee's career,

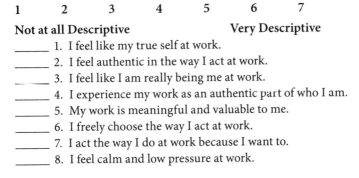

Table 9-2. THE EXPERIENCE OF AUTHENTICITY AT WORK

Using the scale below, please indicate the extent to which each of the following statements describes how you currently feel at work.

1	2	3	4	5	6	7
Not at all Descriptive				**Very Descriptive**		

_____ 1. I feel like my true self at work.

_____ 2. I feel authentic in the way I act at work.

_____ 3. I feel like I am really being me at work.

_____ 4. I experience my work as an authentic part of who I am.

_____ 5. My work is meaningful and valuable to me.

_____ 6. I freely choose the way I act at work.

_____ 7. I act the way I do at work because I want to.

_____ 8. I feel calm and low pressure at work.

Source: Modified from Kifer et al. (2013).[15]

job, and/or organization. Furthermore, the consistent experience of inauthenticity at work will likely be associated with a failure to thrive.

In addition to individuals varying in the extent to which they experience
authenticity in their work environment, researchers have recently highlighted
that work groups can also differ in their climate of authenticity. Alicia Grandey
and her colleagues studied healthcare providers and assessed whether a climate
of authenticity existed within the different units.[16] A climate of authenticity
means that providers in a given unit feel they can express their true emotions
to colleagues within the unit, instead of having to act a certain way they might
not be feeling. The authors found that providers who were part of a unit that
possessed a climate of authenticity were better able to cope with work demands
such as mistreatment from patients, in comparison to providers who were part
of a unit that did not have a climate of authenticity. This study highlights the
role of managers in creating a climate where employees feel safe being themselves, which we address in more detail in *What This Means for Managers 9.1.*

Employees who are experiencing a failure to thrive as a function of inauthenticity caused by a lack of person-environment fit should consider changing their job or organization, especially if they have tried the strategies for
thriving under stressful conditions discussed in the book. Of course, we are
aware that leaving a job can be a scary prospect, and especially in today's econ-
omy employees may be happy to have any job, even if that job does not permit
them to thrive at work. When external constraints prevent moving to a job
that is a better fit with the employee, we recommend trying to make the best of
the situation by making slow progress toward creating the best work environment possible given the constraints that are present.

What This Means for Managers 9.1

AVERTING THE FAILURE TO THRIVE

As we have discussed throughout this book, managers are in a unique position to create climates that can either facilitate thriving or result in employees being unable to thrive. Some years ago, William Kahn[25] discussed the importance of psychological safety in employees being truly engaged in their work. Kahn noted that disengaged employees do not feel safe to be themselves at work, or to recommend changes that may better the organization. Managers who create a climate of authenticity in their workgroup support employees being themselves and "playing to their strengths," as well as having a voice in making suggestions regarding how to enhance the unit. Specific suggestions for managers regarding how to create a climate of authenticity include the following:

- Get to know your employees, including their strengths and interests. When managing unit projects, consider unique employee strengths and interests when assigning tasks to employees in order to accomplish unit objectives.
- Encourage your employees to voice recommendations they have for how to accomplish unit objectives, and to feel free to express themselves when dealing with stressful aspects of their work.
- Be on the lookout for employees who appear to belittle fellow employees for expressing how they feel or doing their job in their own way. Emphasize that employees need to support one another in dealing with the demands that come up on the job.

CHRONIC BOREDOM AND FAILURE TO THRIVE AT WORK

In addition to a lack of person-environment fit, we view chronic boredom as a key indicator of a failure to thrive at work. Of course, chronic boredom can result from a lack of fit between the employee and the requirements of a given job, but we believe the experience of boredom at work is worth highlighting as an additional indicator of failure to thrive. John Eastwood and his colleagues recently defined boredom as "the aversive experience of wanting, but being unable, to engage in satisfying activity" (p. 482).[17] This definition highlights that we experience boredom as a negative emotion that is not simply the result of performing mundane tasks, but being unhappy with the fact that we are performing tasks that are not satisfying to us.

Given the importance of chronic boredom to an employee's failure to thrive, it is worth considering the experience of boredom in more detail. Researchers have pointed out that boredom is a relatively recent emotional experience in human history.[18] It was not until after the Industrial Revolution that human beings had extra time on their hands to be bored. Before that, we spent all of our time foraging for food and protecting ourselves from the elements and other predators.

Contrary to the belief that boredom is associated primarily with such low arousal states as lethargy and dullness, recently researchers have emphasized that boredom can also be associated with high arousal experiences such as irritation and agitation.[17] Within a work context, an employee may go through a period of being lethargic at work, barely mustering up the energy to do the minimal amount that is required. If an employee continues to be lethargic, she may become worried and anxious regarding the low motivation, which further impairs her ability to focus on work.

Similar to the study of boredom more generally, organizational scholars have argued that boredom is the opposite of enthusiasm at work, and reflects not only a lack of interest in work, but also the experience of distress because of this lack of interest.[18] All of us have experienced times at work when we could simply not pay attention to our current activity, and found our thoughts wandering to what we were going to have for lunch or what we were going to do that evening. Being bored at work is something that happens to all employees, at least from time to time. However, a constant state of boredom is a cause for concern.

Most scholars believe that the primary cause of chronic boredom is the lack of meaning at work, driven by the continued failure to be involved in tasks that are significant in some way to the individual.[18] As we discussed in Chapter 5, being involved in personally significant work is critical in order for an individual to thrive under demanding conditions. Boredom results from an employee being dissatisfied or worried about the lack of meaning and significance of her work, which is why we believe the experience of continued boredom is a good indicator of the failure to thrive.

In addition to the lack of significant work contributing to boredom, researchers have also argued that a lack of challenge is a critical component of the experience of boredom. Researchers from the University of Limerick in Ireland had individuals write in detail about a recent experience when they were bored or experienced a different type of negative emotion (sadness, anger, or frustration).[19] The individuals then rated their experience on a number of different dimensions. Those who wrote about a boring experience were much more likely to endorse items reflecting restlessness and lack of challenge in comparison to the other emotion categories. These researchers also conducted another study where they manipulated the experience of boredom by changing how long participants worked on a boring task. Participants were randomly assigned to copy down either 10 different academic references (high boredom) or two different references (low boredom). Individuals were more likely to endorse items reflecting lack of challenge (along with restlessness and lack of purpose) in the high boredom condition relative to the low boredom condition.

This research suggests that lack of challenge and lack of meaning are two primary characteristics of the boredom experience. Throughout this book, we have highlighted the importance of both challenge and meaning for employees to be able to thrive under stressful working conditions. Completely eliminating stressors at work will result in a lack of challenge, which should have the effect of increasing boredom, which eventually will contribute to the failure of employees to thrive in the workplace. Employees are unlikely to experience boredom when they are challenged to accept greater responsibilities at work or to find creative solutions to demands that come up. Although employees could potentially construe these situations as stressors, these demands have the potential to develop the skills and abilities of employees, and to reduce the negative effects of boredom.

In order to gain a better understanding of how workplace boredom differs from other experiences, it may be helpful to consider the unique experience of three hypothetical employees (Mary, Joe, and John) who manage the account records of a large firm. Mary sees the significance in her work and enjoys the challenge of producing reports that are satisfying to company leadership. Mary is likely to experience a sense of thriving at work, and will be in a good position to respond to the demands she encounters as she carries out her job. Joe, however, does not see the significance of what he does for the company, and finds himself occasionally disengaged from the work he is doing. Still, Joe recognizes that he is lucky to have a good paying job, which enables him to do enough at work to meet deadlines and keep his position. Although one would not characterize Joe as thriving, and he might be negatively affected by unexpected job demands, he is not particularly anxious or worried about the lack of meaning in his work.

In contrast, John also does not see the significance of what he is doing for the company, and begins to reflect on the lack of purpose on a daily basis. Although John is initially able to refocus on work tasks with a high degree of effort, he eventually finds it difficult to do his job consistently without quickly losing interest and reflecting on how he is spending 50 hours a week in a job that appears to lack any significance. The lack of significance worries John, and he finds himself unable to break out of the pattern of quickly losing interest in his work and reflecting on his dissatisfaction. John is experiencing chronic boredom at work, and for him boredom itself is becoming a stressor that ends up harming his health and performance.

Not surprisingly, the experience of boredom at work is associated with a host of negative consequences for the employee's well-being and job performance, as well as for the organization.[18] Employees who experience chronic boredom are more likely to make mistakes at work and take longer to notice errors, as well as fail to show up at work at all. Boredom is also associated with employees engaging in behaviors that may harm the organization itself and fellow employees in the organization, including damaging organizational property, verbally abusing others, and failing to work at full effort. Employees who are chronically bored are also more likely to develop mental health problems such as depression, and are more likely to engage in maladaptive behaviors such as smoking, drinking, illicit drug use, and gambling.[18]

One popular measure of boredom at work is included in Table 9-3. Take a minute and think about how you would respond to this measure concerning your current job. We would recommend considering your responses to this measure from time to time in order to get a more stable estimate of your experience of boredom at work. If you find yourself frequently endorsing these items over repeated assessments, you should definitely take actions discussed in Chapter 5 to increase your experience of thriving at work, which should result in a simultaneous decrease in your boredom levels. If these actions fail to relieve the negative experience of boredom at work, the next

Table 9-3. LEE's (1986)[24] JOB BOREDOM SCALE

Please respond to the following items regarding how you have felt about your work in the past **TWO WEEKS.**

1. Do you often get bored with your work?	Yes	No
2. Is your work monotonous?	Yes	No
3. Would you like to change from your type of work to another from time to time (if the pay were the same)?	Yes	No
4. Do you dislike the work you do?	Yes	No
5. Do you often get tired on the job?	Yes	No
6. Do you find the job dull?	Yes	No
7. Does the job go by slowly?	Yes	No
8. Do you become irritable on the job?	Yes	No
9. Do you get apathetic on the job?	Yes	No
10. Do you get mentally sluggish during the day?	Yes	No
11. Do you get drowsy on the job?	Yes	No
12. Does the time seem to go by slowly?	Yes	No
13. Are there long periods of boredom on the job?	Yes	No
14. Does the job seem repetitive?	Yes	No
15. During the day, do you think about doing another task?	Yes	No
16. Does monotony describe your job?	Yes	No
17. Is your work pretty much the same day after day?	Yes	No

step you should consider is whether you are recovering from work demands in healthy ways (Chapters 7 and 8). If you continue to experience boredom at work despite efforts to replenish your energy reserves, you should consider whether the lack of enthusiasm you experience at work reflects a more fundamental lack of fit between you and your work environment discussed earlier in this chapter.

It is worth noting that some people are more prone to boredom no matter what they are doing. People high on boredom proneness are generally less vigilant, more distractible, and experience negative emotional states such as loneliness.[20] Not surprisingly, employees scoring high on general boredom proneness are also likely to report being bored at work, and experience lower satisfaction with their work, colleagues, and supervisor.[21] Therefore, if you are the type of person who becomes bored generally doing any activity, you may need to pay extra attention to doing things like setting challenges for yourself at work and trying to be engaged in significant projects.

WHY ADDRESSING THE FAILURE TO THRIVE IS JUST AS IMPORTANT AS ADDRESSING BURNOUT

In the final section of this chapter we want to discuss why it just as important to be alert to the failure to thrive as it is to be alert to the experience of burnout. As discussed earlier in this book, a large amount of research has been devoted to understanding the experience of burnout, and attempting to address the causes of the syndrome. In fact, a recent review estimated that "6,000 books, chapters, dissertations, and journal articles have been published on burnout" (p. 204).[2] We are not arguing that the attention devoted to burnout is unwarranted. There is no doubt that employees and their families suffer when they are emotionally exhausted, have a cynical attitude toward their work, and lack a sense of accomplishment. In addition, if an employee is experiencing burnout from chronic workplace stressors, he or she needs to take action in order to "stop the bleeding" and escape or change the stressful environment.

However, we suspect that an even greater number of employees do not experience a level of thriving that allows them to excel and develop at work, thereby positively contributing to their overall well-being. Researchers recognized long ago that positive psychological health is not simply the absence of distress. In 1948, the World Health Organization (WHO) offered the following definition of health: "Health is a state of complete physical, mental and social well-being and not merely the absence of disease or infirmity" (p. 100). The

WHO's website makes the point that this definition has not been amended since it was offered 65 years ago. Psychologist Carol Ryff echoed this sentiment when she argued that well-being was characterized by multiple factors, including having a purpose in life, a sense of personal growth, autonomy and mastery, and quality relationships with others.[22]

When employees are failing to have thriving-related experiences at work, they not only are less likely to respond productively to work demands; they are also less likely to have their work life contribute to their overall level of purpose and growth in life. We recognize that people differ in the importance they assign to their job and the extent to which their job provides meaning to their life in comparison to other life domains, such as one's family or favorite hobby. However, most people spend a significant amount of their lives at work, and the failure to experience positive states such as enthusiasm, engagement, and learning can take a toll on the employee's overall well-being, especially given the definition of well-being as being more than the absence of disease.

Most stress management books train employees to help cope with the stressors in their work environment in order to reduce the likelihood that they will experience burnout and other maladaptive symptoms. The focus of this book has been on doing what it takes to thrive under demanding work conditions that may provide you with the ability to grow and develop. In prior chapters we discussed ways to approach and even change your work and work environment in order to put you in a better position to thrive, and highlighted the importance of recovery to replenish the resources necessary to thrive. The present chapter has been devoted to better understanding what happens when you have taken steps to increase thriving at work, but continue to be unable to experience thriving-related states.

If you are experiencing a failure to thrive as a function of a lack of person-environment fit, the chronic experience of boredom, or exposure to a work environment that fails to provide the support necessary to thrive, we encourage you to be as concerned about rectifying the inability to thrive as you would be to address being burned out. If you are unable to experience thriving at work despite your best attempts, it may be worth considering leaving your current organization for one with an environment more conducive toward creating employees who are personally engaged in their work. If the inability to thrive is a function of the fundamental incompatibility between the person you are and the requirements of your career, you may need to think about switching careers.

We recognize that changing organizations and/or careers is an enormous decision, not to be taken lightly. However, just as employees may leave organizations or change careers to prevent the experience of burnout and other negative symptoms, they may need to leave organizations and careers in which they are unable to thrive. A few years ago the first author wrote a piece for the *Harvard Business Review* discussing how those employees who are the most personally engaged in their work are those who may be most affected by constraints in the work environment that prevent them from performing their best.[23] Employees who are highly engaged and care about the outcomes of their performance may choose to leave organizations that do not position them to excel. If an organization is characterized by a lack of emphasis on those factors that create thriving-related experiences in their employees, the ones who remain working for the organization may be those who are the least committed. In *What This Means for Managers 9.2* we emphasize that managers need to be as concerned with creating a work environment supportive of thriving as they are about creating a work environment that reduces the likelihood of burnout.

What This Means for Managers 9.2

It's More Than Just Avoiding Burnout

Throughout this chapter we have echoed many of the suggestions made for managers in Chapter 5, where we talked about the important role of managers in creating conditions necessary for employees to thrive at work, including promoting autonomy, communicating to employees why their work is significant, and creating a positive interpersonal climate among employees. Not engaging in these recommendations contributes to employees being unable to thrive. In this segment we encourage managers to be as concerned about employees failing to thrive as they are about employees being burned out.

Specific suggestions for managers include the following:

- Managers should not be content with only creating a work environment that reflects the absence of stress-related symptoms among employees. They should also work to prevent boredom and monotony in the work environment. Taking an example from the sports world, Joe Maddon, the manager of the Tampa Bay Rays, does things to liven up the clubhouse like having live bands, theme days, and so on. Managers who do things to break up the monotony at work will not only decrease the experience of boredom, but will provide opportunities for employees to take breaks in order to restore their energy reserves for completing tasks. Getting employees together in informal settings will also allow a greater opportunity for interpersonal exchanges between employees that can facilitate thriving at work.

- Be on the lookout for employees who do not seem to be personally engaged in their work. These employees may show up late for work, and when they are at work, may not appear to be giving their full effort on the job. If you encounter employees showing a chronic lack of engagement or energy in their work tasks, consider strategies for increasing their level of engagement through the strategies recommended in Chapter 5.
- Employees who are more personally engaged in their work may be especially sensitive to work contents that inhibit their ability to thrive, and may leave your organization in order to find a work environment more conducive to peak performance. Be sure to provide your highly engaged employees with the autonomy they desire to do their work, and also ensure that they have the resources they need to channel their motivation into high levels of performance.

CONCLUSION

In the present chapter we have focused on the experience of failing to thrive, and highlighted how that experience is different from burnout. We made the case that failing to thrive at work despite attempts at recovery could be due to a fundamental misfit between the person and his or her environment, the experience of chronic boredom brought on by a lack of challenge and job significance, or employees being in a work environment that does not facilitate personal engagement and enthusiasm. We concluded the chapter by highlighting the importance of doing something about failing to thrive at work, given the importance of thriving at work for an employee's overall well-being. In the next chapter we review the principles covered throughout the book, and encourage employees to develop an action plan for increasing their ability to thrive under stressful conditions.

REFERENCES

1. Maslach, C., Schaufeli, W. B., & Leiter, M. P. (2001). Job burnout. *Annual Review of Psychology, 52*, 397–422.
2. Schaufeli, W. B., Leiter, M. P., & Maslach, C. (2009). Burnout: 35 years of research and practice. *Career Development International, 14*, 204–220.
3. Kristof, A. L. (1996). Person-organization fit: An integrative review of its conceptualizations, measurement, and implications. *Personnel Psychology, 49*(1), 1–49.

4. Jansen, K. J., & Kristof-Brown, A. (2006). Toward a multidimensional theory of person-environment fit. *Journal of Managerial Issues, 18*, 193–212.

5. Holland, J. L. 1985. *Making Vocational Choices: A Theory of Careers* (2nd ed.). Englewood Cliffs, NJ: Prentice-Hall.

6. Bolles, R. N. (2013). *What Color Is Your Parachute? A Practical Guide for Job Hunters and Career Changers.* New York: Random House.

7. Brkich, M., Jeffs, D., & Carless, S. A. (2002). A global self-report measure of person-job fit. *European Journal of Psychological Assessment, 18*, 43–51.

8. Earnest, D. A., Allen, D. G., & Landis, R. S. (2011). Mechanisms linking realistic job previews with turnover: A meta-analytic path analysis. *Personnel Psychology, 64*, 865–897.

9. Cable, D. M., & DeRue, D. S. (2002). The convergent and discriminant validity of subjective fit perceptions. *Journal of Applied Psychology, 87*, 875–884.

10. Ostroff, C., Kinicki, A. J., & Muhammad, R. S. (2013). Organizational culture and climate. In N. W. Scmitt, S. Highhouse, & I. B. Weiner (Eds.), *Handbook of Psychology*, Vol. 12: *Industrial and Organizational Psychology* (2nd ed.). Hoboken, NJ: John Wiley & Sons.

11. Schein, E. H. (1990). Organizational culture. *American Psychologist, 45*, 109–119.

12. Chatman, J. (1989). Improving interactional organizational research: A model of person-organization fit. *Academy of Management Review, 14*, 333–349.

13. Sheldon, K. M., Ryan, R. M., Rawsthorne, L. J., & Ilardi, B. (1997). Trait self and true self: Cross-role variation in the Big-Five personality traits and its relations with psychological authenticity and subjective well-being. *Journal of Personality and Social Psychology, 73*, 1380–1393.

14. Wood, A. M., Linley, P. A., Maltby, J., Baliousis, M., & Joseph, S. (2008). The authentic personality: A theoretical and empirical conceptualization and the development of the Authenticity Scale. *Journal of Counseling Psychology, 55*, 385–399.

15. Kifer, Y., Heller, D., Perunovic, W. E., & Galinsky, A. D. (2013). The good life of the powerful: The experience of power and authenticity enhances subjective well-being. *Psychological Science, 24*, 280–288.

16. Grandey, A., Foo, S. C, Groth, M., & Goodwin, R. E. (2012). Free to be you and me: A climate of authenticity alleviates burnout from emotional labor. *Journal of Occupational Health Psychology, 17*, 1–14.

17. Eastwood, J. D., Frischen, A., Fenske, M. J., & Smilek, D. (2013). The unengaged mind: Defining boredom in terms of attention. *Perspectives on Psychological Science, 7*, 482–495.

18. Mael, F., & Jex, S.M. (in press). Workplace boredom: An integrative model of traditional and contemporary approaches. *Group & Organization Management.*

19. Van Tilburg, W. A. P., & Igou, E. R. (2012). On boredom: Lack of challenge and meaning as distinct boredom experiences. *Motivation and Emotion, 36*, 181–194.

20. Farmer, R., & Sundberg, N. D. (1986). Boredom proneness—the development and correlates of a new scale. *Journal of Personality Assessment, 50*, 4–17.

21. Kass, S. J., Vodanovich, S. J., & Callender, A. (2001). State-trait boredom: relationship to absenteeism, tenure, and job satisfaction. *Journal of Business and Psychology, 16*, 317–327.

22. Ryff, C. D. (1989). Happiness is everything, or is it? Explorations on the meaning of psychological well-being. *Journal of Personality and Social Psychology, 57,* 1069–1081.

23. Britt, T. W. (2003). Black Hawk Down at work: When your most motivated employees can't do their job, get ready for an exodus. *Harvard Business Review, 81,* 16–17.

24. Lee, T. W. (1986). Toward the development and validation of a measure of job boredom. *Manhattan College Journal of Business, 15,* 22–28.

25. Kahn, W. A. (1990). Psychological conditions of personal engagement and disengagement at work. *Academy of Management Journal, 33,* 692–724.

10

Epilogue

Your Next Steps Forward

We recognize that many readers may have chosen to read this book because they are stuck in a stressful situation at work, and they want to respond to work-related difficulties in a way that produces positive outcomes. We structured the book the way we did so that readers would gain a better understanding of the demands they are likely to face at work, the potential negative and positive consequences of these demands, and ways in which individuals can approach and recover from demands in order to increase the probability that they will thrive under difficult circumstances.

Throughout the book we have provided practical exercises to facilitate a better response to difficult work conditions, with many of these exercises encouraging employees to consider how they are currently approaching a difficult situation at work, and how they might change the way they approach the situation in order to produce better outcomes. Practical exercises in the book also encourage employees to consider aspects of their work that are personally meaningful and/or meaningful to other people, and to take measures to ensure that they adequately recover from the demands they face at work, both during the workday and at home.

In addition, most of the measures we have included in the book are designed to highlight where you currently stand on how you are responding to the difficulties you face at work, as well as your strategies for responding in a more positive way. Finally, we have emphasized that employees are not solely responsible for being able to respond positively to stressors at work. The *What This Means for Managers* boxes in each chapter highlight the important role played by managers and organizational leaders in creating a work environment that supports employees thriving under challenging conditions. Many readers of this book likely have managerial/supervisory responsibilities, and are therefore in position to create thriving-supportive work environments.

We have two primary goals in the epilogue to the book. Our first goal is to highlight a point we mentioned in the Introduction: that each employee is unique, and the strategies that allow one employee to thrive under difficult work conditions may not be the same as those that allow another employee to thrive. Our second goal is to encourage readers to prioritize the changes they need to make in order to respond better to difficult work conditions, and to form specific goals regarding actions they are going to take in order to respond more positively to work demands.

THE IMPORTANCE OF EMPLOYEES DETERMINING WHAT WORKS FOR THEM

Throughout this book we have made a number of suggestions for dealing more effectively with the demands you face at work, and how to frame demands so that they can be viewed as challenges that drive you to perform better and develop new skills and strengths. The research supporting these suggestions typically shows that employees who interpret work demands as challenges and who proactively address the difficulties they face will perform and feel better than employees who do not respond in these ways. However, we recognize that not all of the suggestions made in the book will work equally well for all people. Some may find it easier to approach work demands as challenges than others, and some may find it difficult to reflect on the significance of what they are doing for the organization or for customers of the organization, or to use this source of motivation to perform well under stressful conditions.

Given that many of the recommendations made throughout the book will work better for some employees than others, we encourage readers to think about the proposed strategies as tools in a toolbox, and to experiment with which tools best allow you to respond better under difficult work conditions. Take the example of the importance of scheduling breaks within the workday, discussed in Chapter 7: although we could provide specific guidelines for taking breaks during the workday (e.g., "take a 10-minute break for every hour worked"), we recognize that employees differ greatly in how long they can work before they start to feel fatigued, and that even the same employee may need to take breaks more or less frequently depending on the nature of the particular activities he or she is performing on a given day. For example, an employee doing a particularly demanding mental or physical activity may need to take breaks more frequently than when doing work tasks that require less effort. The more important point to take away is that breaks are necessary to conserve energy, and you need to experiment with the frequency and duration of breaks necessary to allow you to recover from demanding work tasks.

We encourage you to experiment with the different strategies provided in all the chapters to see which ones allow you to appraise and cope with the demands of work in more adaptive ways. One advantage of experimenting with the strategies proposed in the present book is that trying out different ways of approaching and doing your work will help you recognize that there are things you can control in your work environment that can change how you respond to the demands you face.[1,2] One point emphasized throughout this book is that employees often have more control over how they do their work, and certainly how they approach their work, than they recognize.[1] The field of organizational stress has had a tendency to treat employees as passive victims of the demands they encounter;[3] we believe, however, that employees can actively alter the way they perceive, approach, and recover from the stressors they encounter at work. Furthermore, finding out which strategies are the most successful, and then integrating these strategies into your work and home life, will facilitate your ability to thrive under difficult work conditions.

DEVELOPING A COMPREHENSIVE PLAN TO RESPOND BETTER TO WORK DEMANDS

Our goal in the present book has been to discuss both the negative and positive responses that employees can have to stressful work conditions. We certainly recognize that thriving under difficult work conditions is not easy, and that gaining the ability to experience positive responses to challenges at work may involve a number of steps, depending on how you currently respond to stressors at work. For example, if you are currently experiencing many of the symptoms described in Chapter 2 as a result of prolonged exposure to the work stressors identified in Chapter 1, it is unlikely that you are going to increase your thriving-related experiences at work by thinking about the personal significance of what you are doing. Instead, you may be better served by trying to change the way you appraise the stressors in your work environment, and/or cope with the demands that are present. In addition, you may want to consider the recovery strategies you are utilizing, both during the workday (Chapter 7) and when at home (Chapter 8).

On the other hand, you may be in a position where you are not experiencing many of the negative symptoms described in Chapter 2, and therefore you do not feel a high level of strain from your job. Instead, your main concern is a lack of thriving-related experiences, such as being personally engaged in your job, having high levels of energy and vitality at work, and feeling like you are developing along an upward trajectory. In this case, you may be ready to implement the suggestions made in Chapters 5 and 6 of the book, which involve considering the significance of the work you do for yourself, the organization, and/or other people affected by your work, or increasing the challenges you have at work in order to develop new skills and competencies. You may also benefit from considering how you are recovering from the work you are doing, both during the day and when at home.

In this final chapter of the book, we want you to consider your responses to the application exercises included in the different chapters in order to come up with a comprehensive strategy for moving forward in your attempt to respond more positively to the conditions you face at work. The goal is to consider where you currently are in terms of your ability to respond positively to the work stressors you are experiencing, to develop a plan for enhancing your ability to respond better to these demands, and then to set specific goals for your next steps forward.

Part A of Application Exercise 10.1 provides a space for you to write about how successful you have been at implementing these practical exercises throughout the book. We would first like you to consider your responses to Application Exercise 2.1, which assessed the negative outcomes you perceived coming from your top three job stressors. Next, consider whether your responses to Application Exercises 3.1 (focusing on appraising demands as challenges) and 4.1 (focusing on selecting the best coping strategy to address the demand) helped you to reduce the negative outcomes of those job stressors. If not, we encourage you to reconsider how you are approaching your top work demands.

Moving from the absence of negative outcomes in the face of work demands to thriving-related experiences, consider your responses to Application Exercises 5.2 and 6.1. These exercises encouraged you to consider the significance and impact of your work and to think about positive outcomes that may have resulted from dealing with demanding work conditions. Consider whether your responses to these exercises have resulted in higher levels of personal engagement, vigor, enthusiasm, and personal development at work. If not, think of additional responses to these exercises that might increase these experiences.

Application Exercises 7.2, 8.1, and 8.2 addressed maintaining energy levels at work, and recovering from work when you are at home. Consider whether you were able to interact with fellow employees who energized you versus those who took your energy away, and whether the strategies you identified to recover from work and manage work/non-work boundaries were helpful. Being better able to manage energy and recover from work will not only reduce the negative outcomes identified in Application Exercise 2.1, but also increase the thriving-related experiences identified in Application Exercise 5.1 and the positive outcomes identified in Application Exercise 6.1.

Application Exercise 10.1

Reflections on Earlier Exercises and Specific Goals for the Future

Part A
Below you will find brief descriptions of key exercises in each of the chapters, followed by a space for you to describe how you responded to those exercises, and whether your responses to the exercise were successful. Completing this exercise should highlight those strategies that have been successful and those that need to require modification.

1. Exercise 2.1 asked you to describe negative effects of these demands on your well-being, physical health, or performance. Briefly describe any negative effects of these demands.

   _____

   _____

2. Exercise 3.1 asked you to consider how you were appraising the identified demands, and to consider whether the demand could be appraised as more of a challenge and less of a threat.
   First, briefly describe how you planned to develop more of a challenge appraisal for at least one demand. Then, consider how successful you have been in viewing the given demand as more of a challenge and less of a threat.

   _____

   _____

3. Exercise 4.1 asked you to consider how you were coping with the identified demands, and whether you could develop better coping strategies for addressing the demands.
   First, briefly describe how you planned to develop positive coping strategies for dealing with at least one demand. Then, address whether these coping strategies have been successful.

   _____

   _____

   _____

4. Exercise 5.2 asked you to consider how your job benefited yourself, your organization, and other people.
   First, briefly describe how you responded to the questions regarding the importance and impact of your job. Then indicate whether these strategies

enabled you to better understand the meaning and significance of your work, which should have increased your thriving-related experiences.

_____

_____

_____

5. Exercise 5.1 asked you to describe when you were thriving at work, and to consider what determined your experience of thriving.

6. Exercise 6.1 asked you to consider possible positive effects of the demands that you encounter at work.

   Were you able to identify possible positive effects of these work demands? If so, describe how these positive effects changed the way you appraised the demands.

_____

_____

_____

7. In Application Exercise 7.2 you identified fellow employees who were energizers (giving you energy following interactions), and you intended to interact with these individuals more.

   First, briefly describe whether you increased the frequency of interactions with these individuals. Next, indicate whether these interactions have increased your energy levels.

_____

_____

_____

_____

8. Application Exercise 8.1 and 8.2 asked you to indicate your current strategies for recovering from work demands after the workday is over, and to consider better ways to manage your work/non-work interface.

   First, briefly describe the strategies that you thought would more effectively allow you to recover from work demands and better manage your work/non-work interface. Then, indicate whether these strategies were effective in allowing you to recover from the workday so you would have more energy at the start of the next workday.

_____

_____

_____

_____

Part B

Based on your responses to the practical exercises above, please identify three specific goals you have for responding more positively to the demands you encounter at work. You will also indicate when and where you are going to begin implementing each goal.

Specific Goal #1: _____

_____

Specific date/time and location where this goal will be implemented: _____

_____

Specific Goal #2: _____

_____

Specific date/time and location where this goal will be implemented: _____

_____

Specific Goal #3: _____

_____

Specific date/time and location where this goal will be implemented: _____

_____

_____

The goal of going back through the exercises is to judge the progress you have made, to attempt to implement the strategies that work on a routine basis, and to reconsider strategies that have not been successful. As mentioned in Chapter 9, if you have done all you can to change the way you respond to work demands in a more positive manner, and are still unable to have experiences of thriving at work, you may need to consider changing organizations, jobs, or even your career. If you have not yet completed or implemented the strategies included in these practical exercises, we encourage you to respond to the exercises and identify plans for better responding to the demands in your work environment. Then test out the different strategies to see which ones help you the most. Again, trying out different ways of approaching and responding to the demands you face at work will have the added benefit of illustrating the control you have regarding how you think about and potentially do your job.

As a final step in moving forward, we want you to identify three specific goals you have for responding better to the demands you face at work by completing Part B of Application Exercise 10.1. Even those employees who already experience thriving at work in the face of a difficult job can benefit from thinking about things they can do to better approach their work demands. Your specific goals may involve any of the areas discussed in this book, such as appraising demands at work, coping with those demands, considering the importance of your work, changing the way you do work, attempting to form more interpersonal connections at work, and changing the way you recover during and after work.

As can be seen in Part B of Application Exercise 10.1, we want you to state a specific goal, and then indicate exactly when, where, and how you are going to start implementing the goal. Prior research has shown that we are much more likely to follow through on the goals we set when we form specific "implementation intentions" regarding when and where we are going to start the goal.[4] Carrying out these specific goals will be a good beginning toward enhancing your ability to thrive under stressful work.

Although our focus in this final chapter has been on employees developing a plan for better responding to demands at work, a point we have highlighted throughout this book is that managers are also responsible for creating the conditions that will allow employees to thrive under difficult work conditions. We encourage managers and leaders reading this book to revisit the *What This Means for Managers* boxes contained in all the chapters, and to consider whether they are following the recommendations provided. Ultimately, thriving in a stressful work environment is most likely when employees and managers are both doing their part to approach demands in adaptive ways.

REFERENCES

1. Wrzesniewski, A., Berg, J. M., & Dutton, J. E. (2010). Turn the job you have into the job you want. *Harvard Business Review*, June, 114–117.
2. Parker, S. K., Bindl, U. K., & Strauss, K. (2010). Making things happen: A model of proactive motivation. *Journal of Management, 36*, 827–856.
3. Tims, M., Bakker, A. B., & Derks, D. (2013). The impact of job crafting on job demands, job resources, and well-being. *Journal of Occupational Health Psychology, 18*, 230–240.
4. Gollwitzer, P. M. (1999). Implementation intentions: Strong effects of simple plans. *American Psychologist, 54*, 493–503.

Page numbers followed by an f *or a* t *indicate figures and tables respectively.*